THE LYONS PRESS
HORSEMAN'S DICTIONARY

Steven D. Price and Jessie Shiers
With forewords by William Steinkraus
and Don Burt

The
Lyons Press
Horseman's
Dictionary

FULL EXPLANATIONS OF MORE THAN 2,000 TERMS
AND PHRASES USED BY HORSEMEN

THE LYONS PRESS

GUILFORD, CONNECTICUT

AN IMPRINT OF THE GLOBE PEQUOT PRESS

Revised edition © 2007 by Steven D. Price and Jessie C. Shiers
First Lyons Press edition © 2000 by Steven D. Price
First Lyons Press paperback edition © 2003 by Steven D. Price

Photography and illustrations in this book
are copyrighted under the names appearing next to each image.

The Lyons Press
Attn: Rights and Permissions Department
P.O. Box 480
Guilford, CT 06437

The Lyons Press is an imprint of The Globe Pequot Press.

10 9 8 7 6 5 4 3 2 1

Printed in the United States of America

Designed by Lisa Yee
Typeset by Christopher Woo

ISBN 978-1-59921-036-0

Library of Congress Cataloging-in-Publication Data is available on file.

Foreword
to the Revised Edition

The first edition of **The Horseman's Illustrated Dictionary** started off with an excellent and very comprehensive foreword by Don Burt, which follows, and which I strongly urge you to read. So instead of merely attempting to replicate and paraphrase its insights and good advice to help launch this second revised edition, I have chosen instead to make a few personal comments and to discuss the inevitable general need for such revisions.

It seems quite natural for me to introduce a Horseman's Dictionary, for I am both a certifiable horse nut and a self-admitted word person. I discovered both these things at about the same time, well before I was ten. In fact, I can recognize now that the two passions were and still are closely related and very complementary to each other. As a child, if I were not in school, eating, sleeping, or doing homework, my waking hours were divided about equally between reading about horses, thinking about horses, drawing pictures of horses, and eventually, riding or caring for horses—well, more accurately, ponies. And at night I dreamed mostly about horses. I still give horses a lot of thought and a lot of reading time, and they still show up frequently in my dreams.

My mother was thoroughly complicit in my childhood horse interests. Though not a horse person herself, she was an animal person and a book person, and a parent who believed that children should be permitted or even encouraged to follow their passions wherever they led them. She had also been a teacher and made it plain that the way to cope with words you didn't understand from context should be looked up in the glossary, if any, or a dictionary. (She correctly warned that guessing at meaning based only on context can be dangerous.)

If you have a passion for horses, you will quickly learn that all the different horse activities have languages all their own, using very specialized vocabularies. I started learning a couple of these specialized horse vocabularies pretty early. Some of the terminology of English riding I got from the wonderful English children's books about Exmoor ponies written by "Golden Gorse," and my early exposure to Western riding and cowboy lingo came from the wonderful children's books written by Will James, whose writing and drawings were equally colorful and informative.

As my horse interests deepened and broadened, so did my collection of horse magazines and my modest library of horse books. I was in my teens when War Admiral and Seabiscuit came along, and Battleship became the first American-owned and -bred horse to win the

Aintree Grand National Steeplechase, so my interests quickly expanded to include flat racing and steeplechasing. In the mid-1930s the unforgettable 10-goal polo player Tommy Hitchcock inflamed my interest in that ancient sport, while coverage of the 1936 Berlin Olympic Games got me interested in international equestrianism. Before long I was acquiring books about these activities as well as dressage and three-day eventing, and dictionaries in French and German to help me understand the equestrian terminology that originated in those languages. I also continued to read a lot about foxhunting.

In the early 1940s I went off to college and then into the Army Cavalry, first with horses and later, on foot. When I returned from World War II and went back to my horse books, many things were different, and both fiction and nonfiction (as well as dictionaries) were struggling to keep up with the ways in which the postwar world had changed. In fact, one recognizes that this is and has always been part of the essential nature of the publishing business. Events from the more recent past constantly crowd out and supplant those from more distant times. Rules evolve and terminology changes, based on usage. New ideas, concepts, and techniques are concocted and need constantly to be explained, defined, and added to the literature. A variety of new products is constantly entering the market, and even (perhaps especially) slang is constantly changing. In a way it doesn't make much difference since older books retain considerable historical interest long past the time when their content is totally relevant. Perhaps they can no longer tell you how things are, but they can tell you how things were indefinitely.

The present volume, like most second and subsequent editions, has been enlarged, revised, and corrected in the effort to bring it more nearly up to the present, recognizing that the standard refuses to stay in one place for very long. (Don't worry too much about being totally up-to-date. Bear in mind that from a vantage point of fifty years hence, most current things will appear to be hopelessly outmoded and old-fashioned.) Even so, a book like this still serves the very useful purpose of providing the novice horse enthusiast with the basic terminology for a variety of different disciplines and horse activities, and a good start in knowing what many things look like, as well as describing how various tricky words are pronounced. I hope this will not be the last book you acquire and consult as your interest in horses develops, but I am confident that it will serve a very useful purpose in adding to your present knowledge, no matter what your current level of interest or experience may be. Good riding and good reading!

WILLIAM STEINKRAUS

Foreword
to the First Edition

I believe there is much to learn from the title of a book. Many words mean different things to different people, and there are a lot of phrases among horsemen that can bear likeness to a foreign language, especially to those not "in the know."

This book defines for everyone the horseman's language. If a stranger to the sport of horses should stumble across a group at a show, race, rodeo, or trail ride and not be savvy to their lingo, he could miss the point of the entire conversation. The words and phrases depicted in this illustrated dictionary truly enable everyone to understand what those horsey people are all talking about.

Throughout history, the horse has been man's companion. They have lived together, fought together, worked together, and played together, producing a rich variety of words that have become an intrinsic part of our equine heritage. The horse, once a part of every family before being replaced by machines, is still an essential component of many individuals' lives. Today, there is that same desire to communicate with our horses. We talk to them, listen to them, and even carry on long conversations with them in our daily quest for a relationship.

The pleasure of the horse has taken on new forms, and we now find ourselves in an era of specialization, creating the need for a greater understanding between those of different backgrounds or pursuits. It would be great if every horse enthusiast spoke the same universal language. Horses and those who care about them would find that with a standard vocabulary, communication would be simplified. For the horse, confusion is always present when going from one handler to another; the same applies to the rider who decides to switch from English to Western or vice versa. So, when everyone understands the same words, it makes any transition easier for both, whether two- or four-legged.

Steve Price has put together a book not only for beginners but for specific equine groups to bridge the gap from one horse sport to another. He has compiled a great deal of information that allows newcomers and old-timers to recognize the vocabulary of each other's interest in the horse world. It guarantees that reiners can understand jumper jargon and trail riders will feel right at home visiting with racehorse enthusiasts. Hunter lovers won't be at odds with bull riders and ropers, cowboys can become fluent in dressage, and driving competitors can be privy to what the judges are looking for in Western pleasure.

This publication also gives the reader the opportunity to gain a working knowledge of different breeds of horses, their origins, needs, and training methods, as well as descriptive horsemanship terms created by individual teachers. The reader will be able to readily identify the different tack or equipment used by various breeds or in individual riding styles and training techniques. This book explains the various horse show class titles and their specifications. In a short time one can become conversant with those who have learned the language from everyday use on the range, in the barn, or in the saddle shop or feed store.

If you were in a foreign land and someone gave you an animal that you had never seen or heard of before, one of the first questions you would ask might be, "What does it eat?" This volume furnishes much more detail than just answering your first query and the reading is easy, enjoyable, and very enlightening. Those of us who have been in the horse business all of our lives will find, when studying

this book, that the old adage "What you learn after you know it all is what really counts," is a truism.

The Lyons Press Horseman's Dictionary gives the reader an opportunity to learn several horse languages at once. Becoming proficient in horse-related terminology will improve your understanding in many areas of the horse industry. As every golfer knows, when someone shouts "fore," it's time to duck, and likewise, when a horseman yells "heads up," a wreck is about to happen.

Steve Price has demonstrated his ability to take the complex and reduce it into simple terminology. This book fully illustrates the language of many great horsemen who are basically seat-of-the-pants riders and are far better at showing than telling. Many are not likely to verbalize what it is that they do; they just do it. In the past, the only avenue to learning was to watch. *The Lyons Press Horseman's Dictionary* adds another dimension to the process, and you don't have to read between the lines. This book in reality speaks for the many great horsemen who had trouble putting into words what they did or didn't do, giving the reader the words and meanings for all horse talk.

One of the greatest pleasures extended by working with horses is the opportunity to share knowledge. As you grow in knowledge, you will find yourself helping others to better understand this very unique animal we call the horse; you'll be able to pull up a bale of hay and chat with the best of horsemen, regardless of discipline. Even the slang expressions thrown out by those clever teachers are readily available in this guide. Those who thought a horn was something to blow or honk will learn how important it is to the Western rider. You'll discover that a coop does not necessarily contain chickens, nor a coffin a body, and you'll concur with why some horsemen try to avoid the ominous "grob" (German for grave). Many who make their livelihood in the horse world cannot describe the "airs above the ground." There are some who don't know what a phaeton is, or its origin, or that a piggin' string has nothing to do with pigs. You'll wonder how an alligator could get loose in a horse arena and learn that a fender doesn't have to relate to your car. You will also find out that a ratcatcher is not on the endangered species list and that an elevator goes neither up nor down but fits in a horse's mouth. And, when horsemen talk about the bottom line, don't look for it at the end of your financial statement.

The Lyons Press Horseman's Dictionary contains a wealth of knowledge and should be in the library of anyone remotely interested in this most athletic animal. Learning is a never-ending process, and I'm sure this publication will pique your interest in exploring all the aspects of the world of horses.

DON BURT

Introduction

Even in the seven years since the original edition of this dictionary saw the light of day, the horse world has expanded considerably, and in many directions. More and more people, and of all ages, are riding and driving, while the spectator base of equestrian competitions has grown too.

"Natural horsemanship" is no longer considered the arcane possession of so-called "horse whisperers," but is now an accepted and widely practiced approach.

Veterinary medicine has made great strides, as has horse care, particular in the area of "natural" (there's that word again) alternatives to traditional practices.

The information and technological revolution has brought all-horses-all-the-time television channels in addition to websites and instructional DVDs.

Then, too, there has been a greater cross-pollination between and among disciplines. The sight of a show jumper competing in a hackamore or another once-exclusively Western bit or bridle is no longer rare. Hunter-seat classes at Western breed horse shows have grown in popularity. Dressage riders and trainers use round-pen schooling techniques, while Western trainers have added classical dressage movements to their programs.

Greater interest among equestrian participants and spectators has created

a demand for greater knowledge about all aspects of the sport. Hence, the revision of this dictionary. Every activity has its esoteric vocabulary, and horse sports and the industry that supports the sports are no exception. Some words mean nothing to outsiders (renvers, latigo, chukka). Others might mean one thing to outsiders, but quite another to the horse world (leak, near, hock).

Greatly expanded over its earlier edition, this dictionary still presents words and phrases in the context of how a user would come across them, whether while taking a riding lesson (wrong lead, roached back, crest release), spectating (photo finish, fence work, clear round), overhearing the lingo of experienced horsemen (weedy, rub on, blank covert) or reading books, magazine, tack shop catalogs, and website chat-room entries (Spanish Riding School, Coggins test, full-cheek snaffle).

We continued to include word derivations whenever they were of particular interest. For example, *canter* comes from the gait at which Chaucer's *Canterbury* *Tales* pilgrims traveled along their loquacious way, *phaeton* is named for the son of a Greek god, and *bug boy* refers to the insect-looking asterisk beside the name of an apprentice jockey as listed in the racetrack's program.

Finally, the authors tip our hats to everyone who suggested words, provided definitions, and otherwise sped this project along its way. We are especially grateful to the keen eye of Sue Ducharme and the good humor and encouragement of our editor, Holly Rubino.

STEVEN D. PRICE
JESSIE SHIERS

THE LYONS PRESS
HORSEMAN'S DICTIONARY

above the bit
The position of a horse that is holding his head above the rider's hands, done to evade the effects of the bit.
🐸 *See also* on the bit; behind the bit.

above the ground
🐸 *See* airs above the ground.

abscess
A pus-filled pocket of infection within the body. Hoof abscesses can cause severe lameness. However, they are usually very treatable with prompt veterinary attention. Treatment involves soaking or packing the hoof with a drawing agent, such as Epsom salts or poultice, and possibly a course of antibiotics prescribed by a veterinarian. Tooth abscesses may cause oral pain, bit resistance, and a foul odor from the mouth. They are treated with antibiotics.

account for
In foxhunting, to kill or put a fox to ground.

Acepromazine (Ace)
Brand name of the tranquilizer acetylpromazine, which is used to calm a nervous or panicky horse that may become a danger to itself or to its handlers, such as during veterinary work or shipping.

acey-deucy
In racing, stirrups adjusted so the inside one is lower than the outside one, in order to give the jockey better balance while riding around turns.

across the board
In racing, one wager to win, place, and show (in effect, three bets in one). If the chosen horse finishes first, the ticket holder receives the win, place, and show payoffs. If the horse finishes second, payoff is for place and show; if third, for just show.

acrylic resin
A compound used in farriery to fill cracks or chips in a horse's hoof.

action
The elevation of a horse's legs, especially with regard to knees and

Horse's head above the bit.
© J. SHIERS

feet. The animatedly high action of a Saddlebred or Tennessee Walking Horse contributes to the breed's showiness, while the low, daisy-cutter action of a show hunter's trot is valued for its ability to cover ground at each stride.

acupressure
A form of alternative health care in which a practitioner manually presses on specific points on the horse's body for the purpose of relieving pain and promoting health.

acupuncture
A form of alternative health care in which a practitioner inserts needles into specific points on the horse's body for the purpose of relieving pain.

acute
A word used to describe a severe illness or injury, typically of a short duration, that requires immediate veterinary care.
Compare to chronic.

add a stride
A term meaning to increase by one the number of strides between two jumps, done when the rider shortens the horse's stride.
See also leave out a stride.

added money
In racing, money added to a purse, often by the track or a sponsor, in addition to nominations and entry fees.

Adequan
Brand name of polysulfated glycosaminoglycan, a drug used to treat arthritis by injection directly into the diseased joint (intraarticular) or into the muscle (intramuscular). It reduces inflammation and enhances repair of the cartilage and synovial membrane.

adhesion
A word used to describe an abnormal attachment of two surfaces within the body. In horses, adhesions most often occur in association with colic surgery (intestinal adhesions) or foaling (uterine adhesions in the mare).

Adios
This Standardbred trotter is widely viewed as the greatest sire in harness racing history. He sired eight Little Brown Jug winners, more than any other horse, and his sons Adios Butler and Bret Hanover both became winners of the Triple Crown of Harness Racing for Pacers. Prior to his death in 1965, Adios had sired 589 offspring.

Adult Amateur
A category of horse show classes open to amateur riders over the age of eighteen.
See also Amateur Owner; amateur.

advanced
1 The highest level of national competition in combined training events. This level is intended to prepare horses and riders for the

Three- and Four-Star levels of international competition. The dressage test may include extensions in all three gaits, half pass at the trot and canter, and single flying changes. The cross-country phase includes combinations with multiple elements, such as bounces into water, coffins with short distances or significant slopes, and bending lines or related distances between narrow obstacles. The cross-country course will incorporate 32 to 40 obstacles over a distance of 3,000 to 3,800 meters, to be ridden at 570 meters per minute. Fences may be up to 3 feet 11 inches in height, with spreads of up to 5 feet 11 inches and drops of up to 6 feet 7 inches. The show-jumping course includes 13 to 15 obstacles, with heights up to 4 feet 1 inch and spreads of up to 5 feet 3 inches.

🐎 *See also* beginner novice; novice; training; intermediate. **2** A rider who is capable of riding with a high level of skill (as compared to a beginner or intermediate rider).

Affirmed
The last (as of this writing) Thoroughbred to win the Triple Crown. In 1978, Affirmed defeated his rival Alydar in the Kentucky Derby, Preakness, and Belmont Stakes.

against
Resistant or unresponsive to the rider's aids (e.g., "against the bit").

aged
In racing, a horse that is four years or older. In general terms, a horse that is 15 years old or older.
🐎 *See also* senior.

aging
The process of determining a horse's age from tooth size, shape, and markings. Permanent incisor teeth appear before the age of five; cuplike indentations in the incisors disappear by eight; the tops of incisors change from rectangular to triangular by 15 years, at which time Galvayne's groove appears on the third incisor and extends the length of the tooth by age twenty.

ahead of the motion
🐎 *See* motion.

AI
Artificial insemination.

aid
A command signal from the rider to the horse. The natural aids are leg pressure, rein pressure, the weight of the rider's seat, and the voice. Artificial aids, which reinforce the natural aids, include the spur and the whip.
🐎 *See also* cue.

airs
Certain advanced movements in classical dressage, such as the piaffe, passage, Spanish walk, and the airs above the ground.

airs above the ground
The movements in which two or

FROM TOP TO BOTTOM:
A horse's teeth at five, seven, and twenty years of age.
© CHRISTINA BERUBE

A

An Akhal-Teke stallion.
© LINDA AARON/AKHAL-TEKE
ASSOCIATION OF AMERICA

Alfalfa.
CREDIT: PHOTOS.COM

more of the horse's feet leave the ground, such as the levade, capriole, and courbette. These so-called high school movements (from the French *haute école*) are said to have come from the requirement during the late Middle Ages and Renaissance that a mounted warrior's horse act as both an offensive weapon and a shield. A rearing horse could disable an opponent or his steed, while also stopping a sword or spear thrust directed at the rider.

Akhal-Teke
A breed of Russian sport horse that originated in present-day Turkistan (north of Iran). It has a fine, solid-colored coat with a metallic sheen, stands on relatively long and slender legs, and reaches a height of about 15.2 hands. Possessing great stamina, the Akhal-Teke is used for racing in its native region and for endurance riding: In 1935, Akhal-Tekes were ridden from Turkistan to Moscow, some 2,500 miles (including 600 miles of desert) in 84 days.

Al Barak
In Islamic legend, the milk-white mare that conveyed Mohammad from Earth to heaven. She had the wings of an eagle and a human face. Every one of her strides was equal to the farthest range of human sight.

alfalfa
A nutrient-rich legume widely used for hay, usually mixed with a grass hay such as timothy. Its high protein content makes it too rich for some horses.

all-around champion
In Western horse shows, the contestant who wins the most aggregate points in all events in which he takes part; in rodeos, the winner of the most aggregate money in all such events.

allelomimetic
Describes the behavior of a horse that is imitating the actions of another horse in its herd.

alligator
In cutting, a difficult cow that makes every effort to escape back to the herd.

allowance race
In racing, a race in which eligibility is based on amounts of money won or the number of races won over a specified time.

all-purpose saddle
An English saddle with a forward flap and deep seat to allow a variety of rider positions.

all-rounder
A horse that is suitable for a variety of uses, from trail riding to competition.

alpha
The dominant horse in a herd.

alsike clover
A plant that is highly toxic to horses.

also eligible
In racing, a horse that is officially entered but not permitted to start unless the field is reduced by scratches.

 See also scratch.

also-ran
In racing, a horse that did not finish first, second, or third.

alternative medicine
Any of several types of therapies not traditionally associated with Western veterinary practices, including chiropractic, homeopathy, acupuncture, acupressure, massage therapy, and magnetic therapy.

amateur
One who rides or drives horses without receiving compensation (as distinguished from a professional).

 See also non-pro.

Amateur Owner (A/O)
A horse show class open to horses that are ridden by their adult owners or a close adult relative of the owner.

Amazone
An obsolete term for a female rider or driver.

amble
The slow form of the pace, approximately the speed of a jog or slow trot. Not all horses can amble; the gait is performed naturally by Standardbreds, Tennessee Walking Horses, and several other breeds to whom lateral gaits come naturally. Horses that ambled were especially valued for their comfortable gait in the centuries before riders discovered posting.

American Cream Draft
The only draft breed to originate in the United States, the American Cream Draft is descended from "Old Granny," whose foaling date has been placed between 1900 and 1905. The horses are a medium cream color with white mane and tail, pink skin, and amber eyes; height averages 16.3 hands; weight between 1,600 and 2,000 pounds. The American Cream Draft is used for agricultural work and for showing.

American Horse Council
An equine trade association that is especially active in federal and state legislation involving horses, headquartered in Washington, D.C.

American Horse Shows Association
The older organization that is now known as the United States Equestrian Federation (USEF).

American Quarter Horse
The most populous breed of horses in the world, noted for their quick bursts of speed (the name comes from the ability to run one-quarter of a mile faster than any other breed). The breed originated during the colonial era in America after a Thoroughbred named Janus was bred to native

American Quarter Horse.
© D. R. STOECKLEIN/AMERICAN QUARTER HORSE ASSOCIATION

A

A three-gaited American Saddlebred in the show ring.
© SARGENT/AMERICAN SADDLEBRED HORSE ASSOCIATION

mares; their offspring possessed the ability to cover short distances at great speed. Quarter Horses went west with the settlers, where their speed and agility made them useful for cattle ranching. Many were crossed with descendants of the horses brought over by Spanish settlers in Mexico and the American Southwest and with wild mustangs, all of which added to the hardy stock.

American Quarter Horses ("American" was added to the breed's name in 1940) are characterized by a compact shape, strong hindquarters, and a quiet, sensible temperament. They are now used for ranching, Western and English horse showing, Quarter Horse racing, and pleasure riding.

American Quarter Horse Association (AQHA)

The breed registry for American Quarter Horses. The AQHA also sponsors and sanctions all American Quarter Horse breed shows.

American Saddlebred

A breed of horses used as three- and five-gaited riding horses and for fine harness driving. Created by crossing pacers with Morgans and Thoroughbreds, the breed was popular throughout the southern states in the 19th century as an animated yet comfortable riding horse. With their arched necks and elegant bodies, Saddlebreds are now used primarily as show horses; their high-stepping walk, trot, and

canter (and in the case of five-gaited horses, their slow gait and rack) prompt enthusiastic cheers from spectators.

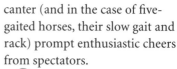 *See also* saddleseat equitation.

American Warmblood

Technically, this term refers to horses registered with the American Warmblood Society (AWS) or the American Warmblood Registry (AWR). In practice, it is often used to refer to horses bred in the United States that have warm blood or draft blood. In particular, crosses between draft breeds and Thoroughbreds are frequently labeled "American Warmbloods," registry status notwithstanding.

analgesic

A drug that relieves pain, such as aspirin or bute.

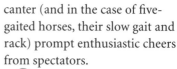 *See also* bute.

Andalusian

The native breed of Spain, created by crossing the Barb and Arab with heavier types. These horses helped create classical horsemanship centuries ago; the first horses at Vienna's Spanish Riding School came from Spain (hence the establishment's name). Standing at about 15.2 hands, the Andalusian has a well-muscled body that lends itself to dressage and trail riding.

anemia

A condition in which the horse has a low red blood cell count.

Andalusian.
© KENTUCKY HORSE PARK

anestrus

The part of the mare's reproductive cycle in which she is not sexually reactive; she is not "in heat."

Anglo-Arab

The term for a crossbred between a Thoroughbred sire and Arabian dam, used for foxhunting, jumping, and pleasure riding.

anhidrosis

A condition in which a horse fails to produce sweat; such a horse may become overheated to the point of death if exercised excessively.

animal communicator

A person who claims to be able to communicate with animals telepathically.

animated

Characterized by lightness, brisk action, and a high head and tail carriage.

ankle boots

Coverings for the hind fetlock joints as protection against brushing.

🐎 *See also* brushing.

anthelmintic

A chemical that kills internal parasitic worms. Known colloquially as "wormer" or "dewormer."

anthropomorphize

To explain or interpret the behavior of animals in human terms.

For example, "My pony thinks he's a racehorse."

anticast roller

A surcingle with a metal prong that presses uncomfortably against the horse's back when the animal rolls. Its purpose is to discourage horses that have a tendency to become cast from lying on their backs.

🐎 *See also* cast.

antigrazing rein (or device)

A strap running from the saddle through the browband and attaching to the bit, to prevent the horse from grazing and, in the process, pulling the rider over his head. Also known as daisy reins.

Appaloosa

A breed developed in the 18th century by the Nez Percé tribe of Native Americans and named for the Palouse River region of Idaho, Oregon, and Washington. The breed is easily recognizable by the spotted "blanket" over its rump (although leopard Appaloosas have spots all over their bodies), which the Nez Percé believed had magical qualities. Appaloosas also have striped hooves and a white sclera around the pupil of the eye. They can be found doing ranch work, competing in Western horse shows, and performing as jumpers and pleasure mounts.

Appendix Registry

The section of the American Quarter Horse Association registry for horses that are American

Ankle boots.
© MILLER HARNESS COMPANY LLC

Antigrazing rein becomes taut when the horse lowers his head.
© MILLER HARNESS COMPANY LLC

Blanket-patterned Appaloosa.
© DON SHUGART/
APPALOOSA HORSE CLUB

A

Quarter Horse-Thoroughbred crossbreds.

appointments

Saddlery and harness when worn by horses and ponies. In a horse show appointments class, the appropriateness and condition of these items are judged.

apprentice

In racing, a jockey who is just beginning his or her career. In handicapped races, apprentices receive weight allowances: until they have won ten races, they carry ten fewer pounds, seven fewer pounds from 11 to 15 wins, and five fewer pounds from the 35th win until one year from the date of the victory. This system provides an incentive for trainers to give unproven jockeys a chance to ride. Apprentice allowances are indicated in racetrack programs by one or more asterisks (*). Because the asterisk resembles an insect, apprentices are known as bug boys.

apron

1 The skirt of a sidesaddle habit. **2** In driving, a protective cloth wrap worn around the driver's waist to keep dirt off his or her clothing.

Arabian

The breed that has been the foundation stock for all light breeds and is itself acknowledged to be the world's oldest breed. The Arab—the breed is the Arabian; a member of the breed is an Arab—

Arabian.
© JOHNNY JOHNSTON/INTERNATIONAL ARABIAN HORSE ASSOCIATION

is characterized by a dish-shaped convex head with a forehead bulge called the *jibbah*, fine body features, and a high tail-carriage. Its skeletal structure is unique among horses: 17 ribs, 5 lumbar bones, and 16 tail vertebrae (as compared with 18, 6, and 18 in other breeds and types).

Beginning in the 17th century, these so-called desert horses were imported from the Middle East and North Africa into Europe and then to America. Their ability to pass along their speed and endurance, as well as their fine looks and docile temperament, led to widespread crossbreeding. Almost every modern breed, most notably the Thoroughbred, Andalusian, and Lipizzaner, can trace a portion of its bloodlines to the Arabian.

The four most prominent strains of Arabians are the Polish, the Egyptian, the Spanish, and the Russian. Supporters of each group carefully maintain the purity of the lines through selective breeding.

Because of the ease with which they can travel long distances over the most rugged terrain, Arabians excel at endurance and competitive trail riding. They are also raced, used as pleasure riding horses, and shown in Western and English classes. Some of the most popular events at an all-Arabian show are Native Costume classes, in which horses and riders wear authentic or fanciful Bedouin tack and attire.

A

Ardennes

A lighter and hardy version of the Belgian draft horse, originating in the Ardennes forest of Belgium and northern France.

arena

An enclosed, level area with special footing, usually sand or crushed stone, for riding or working horses.

arena polo

Another name for indoor polo, which is played in a covered arena. In contrast to the outdoor version, three players constitute a team, six chukkars of seven minutes each comprise a match, a rubber ball is used instead of one made of solid wood, and the goalposts are painted on the sideboards at the ends of the arena.

 See also polo.

Aristides

Winner of the first Kentucky Derby in 1875.

Arkle

Considered by many to be the greatest steeplechase horse of all time, the Irish-bred Arkle won the British Cheltenham Gold Cup three times (1964–1966), as well as many other important races over fences.

artificial aid

The spur or the whip, used to reinforce the natural aids (leg, hands, seat, and voice).

 See also aid.

artificial insemination (AI)

Manually implanting a mare with semen that has been collected from a stallion, as distinguished from a cover, or live, breeding. The purpose may be to prevent injury to the stallion and the mare or to breed two animals that are geographically remote.

arthritis

A degenerative joint disease in which the cartilage and synovial tissues are inflamed and may erode, causing pain and excessive wear on the joint structures.

ascarid (ASS-kar-id)

A parasitic roundworm that, when ingested as eggs during grazing, causes diarrhea, colic, and other internal problems. Ascarids can be both prevented and treated with deworming medication.

ass

An equine species that originated in central Asia and Africa. Characterized by a small (approximately 13-hand), chunky body and longer ears than horses have, the wild ass and its cousin the onager were crossed with horses and ponies. The result was the domesticated ass, of which the donkey is the best-known member of that family. Because domesticated asses do not thrive in severely cold and damp climates, they are most prevalent in Mediterranean and South American regions for use as pack animals and for riding.

A

ASTM/SEI

The acronym for American Society for Testing and Materials, an organization that develops standards for various items, including horseback riding helmets. The SEI, or Safety Equipment Institute, tests helmets with regard to ASTM standards. Most equestrian organizations require that members wear helmets that meet or exceed ASTM standards while competing, and it is highly recommended that riders wear such headgear while mounted at any time.

astringent

A substance applied externally that causes the tissues to contract. Most often used as a liniment to prevent swelling of the lower legs following hard work.

ataxia

Term for lack of muscle coordination, seen in horses with neurologic conditions such as equine protozoal myeloencephalitis (EPM) or wobbler syndrome.

See also EPM; wobbler syndrome.

atlas

The first vertebra of the neck.

atrophy

Term describing muscle wasting. Atrophy may be a visible symptom of chronic pain or a neurological disorder that prevents a certain muscle from being used in a normal way.

Automatic waterer.
CREDIT: J. SHIERS

audit

To observe without participating, as in a clinic or lesson.

aural plaques

Term for white or gray spots on the inside of a horse's ears. The cause is not known, but plaques typically do not cause any adverse effects.

Australian stock saddle

A saddle traditionally used on cattle ranches in Australia, with very long flaps and a deep seat, that may or may not have a horn.

automatic release

See out-of-hand release.

automatic waterer
(or fountain)

A stall or pasture fixture that supplies drinking water and automatically refills the basin whenever the water level drops below a certain point. Because a horse's water intake cannot be monitored when using such a device, many horsemen prefer to use hand-filled buckets.

auxiliary starting gate

In racing, a second starting gate used when the number of horses in a race exceeds the capacity of the main starting gate (which usually holds 12 horses).

away

In foxhunting, a fox and/or pack of hounds that are running are said to be away or have gone away.

azoturia

Severe muscle cramping caused by the buildup of lactic acid in the muscle. The condition is characterized by a stiff, wobbling walk and trot and by dark-colored urine. It is often seen in horses that have eaten protein-rich feed on rest days following exercise. Azoturia is familiarly known as Monday-morning disease because horses that rested following exertion over weekends came down with it. It is rarely seen nowadays, thanks to proper stable management and care. Also known as "tying up."

A

babble

In foxhunting, a hound that is baying at anything other than a good scent is said to be babbling.

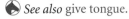 *See also* give tongue.

Babie'ca

The warhorse of the Spanish legendary hero El Cid.

baby pad

A thin, easily washable saddle pad liner used under a thicker pad to protect it from dirt and sweat.

babysitter

A horse that can be trusted to provide a safe ride for even the most inexperienced rider or child.

bachelor band

A wild herd of male horses.

back

1 To cause a horse to step or walk backward, also known as rein-back. **2** To introduce a horse to being ridden. **3** In polo, the player whose primary function is to defend his team's goal.

back at the knee

 See calf-kneed.

back cinch

The rear girth of a Western saddle. The second cinch adds extra security during strenuous activities, such as roping.

back fence

In a cutting competition, the part of the fence directly behind the herd. If the cow being worked is allowed to reach any part of the back fence, the horse will lose points.

backhand

In polo, a stroke that sends the ball behind the player.

backside

The colloquial word for a racetrack's stable area.

backstretch

The far side of an oval racetrack, the side opposite the finish line.

backyard

Describes a horsekeeping situation that is small in scale and not run as a business, generally with only a

Back cinch.
© CHERRY HILL

B

Balanced seat.

A banded mane.
© LESLI GROVES

few horses, all owned by the property owner. Sometimes used in a derogatory sense to imply substandard care or training.

Badminton
A major international horse trial held in the spring on the Gloucestershire, England, estate of the Duke of Beaufort (which also gave its name to the racket sport of badminton). Started in 1949, it ranks with Burleigh, Rolex Kentucky, and the Olympics as one of the world's most demanding three-day events.

Baker blanket
A blanket held in place by straps that cross under the horse's belly. Designed by the late horse show trainer D. Jerry Baker.

balanced seat
Term describing the standard riding position, in which the rider's upright upper body remains over the horse's center of balance at all gaits. By far the most prevalent style of riding, it acquired its name in the early 20th century to distinguish it from the forward seat.

bald
A wide, white facial marking that extends from forehead to nostrils, usually covering one or both eyes.

balding girth
A leather girth with a contoured shape designed to prevent chafing of the skin of the horse's elbow.

bale
Hay or straw that has been cured, compressed, and bound with twine. Square bales are rectangular in shape and segmented into flakes. They range in size from 30 to 100 pounds, depending on dimensions, density, and the moisture content of the hay. Round bales are large, rolled cylinders weighing between 1,000 and 2,000 pounds. They are sometimes wrapped in plastic for protection from precipitation and must be moved by means of heavy equipment.

ball
A large medicinal pill for horses, given orally by means of a balling gun, a syringe-like device that forces the pill down the horse's throat.

ballotade
An air above the ground, this is a variation of the capriole, in which the horse leaps off the ground with the soles of his hind feet visible from the rear.
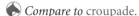 *Compare to* croupade.

band
To divide the horse's mane into small sections held together with rubber bands or tape; commonly seen on Western show horses.

bandage
Term for a cloth strip that is wrapped around the horse's lower leg, either to protect a wound or to provide protection from interference during exercise.

bandage bow

Swelling of the tendons along the back of the lower leg caused by wraps that were applied unevenly or too tightly.

bangtail

A slang expression for a horse whose tail has been made shorter by being cut straight across, usually at hock level.

bank

A jumping obstacle composed of a natural or artificial mound of earth that, depending on the course, the horse jumps onto or off from. In some parts of the world where timber to make fencing was scarce, fields were separated by series of banks and ditches (the earth scooped up to make the ditches became the banks); the banks became the inspiration for such show-ring obstacles.

bar

1 The space between the horse's incisors and lower molar teeth that accommodates the bit. 2 The part of the hoof between the toe and heel.

Barb

A native North African breed similar to the Arabian, although with slightly coarser features and without the dish face. Native to the Barbary States, once a North African confederation, the breed was imported into Europe, where, like the Arabian, it contributed to the formation of the Thoroughbred,

Andalusian, and other breeds.

See also Godolphin Barb.

barbed wire

A type of wire fencing, often used for cattle, that has short, sharp pieces of wire knotted along its length. Barbed wire is unsafe to use for horse fencing due to the high risk of injury.

bareback

Describes riding without a saddle.

bareback bronc riding

A rodeo event in which a bucking horse is outfitted with only a strap around its midsection. The rider may hold the strap while trying to complete an eight-second ride.

bareback pad

A thick pad, often made of fleece, with a surcingle, used to cushion the horse's back while riding without a saddle.

barefoot

A horse that does not wear horseshoes.

barley

A cereal grain used as feed.

barn-sour

Describes a horse that does not willingly leave the area near its stable, such as for a trail ride. The barn-sour horse may object to being ridden away from the stable by rearing, bucking, attempting to bolt back to the stable, or simply fussing and jigging.

Bank obstacle.
© ED CAMELLI

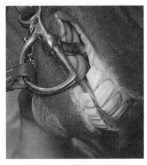

Placement of the bit in the horse's bar.
© MILLER HARNESS COMPANY LLC

Bareback bronc riding.
© LESLI GROVES

B

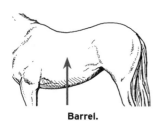

Barrel.

Barrel racing competition.
© AMERICAN QUARTER HORSE
ASSOCIATION

Bar shoe.
© CHERRY HILL

barrel

The midsection of a horse, between the forelegs and the loins.

barrel racing

A timed Western horse show and rodeo event in which riders maneuver horses around three barrels in a cloverleaf pattern at a gallop. It originated strictly as a sport (that is, without any practical ranching antecedents). Although events are open to both men and women, barrel racing is almost exclusively a women's sport.

barren

Term used to describe a mare that is unable to conceive.

barrier

In roping, a cotton or elastic rope, or a photoelectric device, in front of the calf's and the roping horse's starting boxes. The barriers are released to make sure the calf gets a head start; if the horse breaks the barrier before it is released, penalty seconds will be added to the roper's time.

bar shoe

A type of horseshoe that has a strip of metal added across the back between the two heels to support the heel of the horse's hoof. Egg-bar shoes are ovoid in shape, while heart-bar shoes feature a triangular extension that covers the frog of the foot, giving the shoe a somewhat heart-shaped appearance.

bascule

The smooth arc of the horse's body, from poll to croup, over a jump. The word is French, meaning "smooth bend."

base narrow

A conformation fault in which, when viewed from the front, the horse's legs are closer together at the bottom than at the top.

base wide

A conformation fault in which, when viewed from the front, the horse's legs are closer together at the top than at the bottom.

bastard strangles

A form of strangles in which the infection causes abscesses in body parts other than the lymph nodes of the neck and throat.

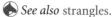 *See also* strangles.

bat

A short crop with a wide tab end, used primarily in racing or jumping.

Baucher, François

An 18th-century French horseman, instructor, and trainer, Baucher spent much of his career applying dressage principles to the training of circus horses and cavalry mounts.

Baucher bit

A snaffle bit with two rings on each cheek, invented by François Baucher. The lower ring is attached to the mouthpiece and the

B

reins, while the upper ring is fixed to the lower ring and is attached to the cheekpiece of the bridle.

bay
A body color ranging from dark to light brown, always with a black mane and tail, and usually black markings on the lower legs.

bean
1 A waxy, gray mass of smegma (a protective secretion) that develops inside the sheath of a male horse and must be removed regularly to prevent it from obstructing urination. 2 The smooth, ovoid center link in a double-jointed bit such as a French link.

bearing rein
A rein aid in which the rein presses against the horse's neck on the side toward the direction of the turn.
  ◐ *Compare to* neck rein, in which the rein presses against the horse's neck on the opposite side from the direction of the turn.
  ◐ *See also* check rein.

beat
The number of footfalls at a gait. The walk is a four-beat gait, the trot has two beats, and the canter or lope has three.

bedding
A cushioning layer of material with which stall and trailer floors are covered for comfort and to absorb moisture. Wood shavings, shredded paper, and straw are popular choices.

beet pulp
A feed for horses, made from the dehydrated fibers of beets and processed into pellets or flakes, that may be used to provide supplemental forage fiber. Because the pellets or flakes must be reconstituted with water before feeding, beet pulp is also used as a means to increase the horse's water intake.

beginner
A rider who is new to riding.

beginner novice
The lowest level of national competition in combined training events. The dressage test includes walk, trot, and canter and 20-meter circles. The cross-country phase may include a bank, a ditch, a water crossing, and a brush fence. The cross-country course will incorporate 14 to 18 obstacles over a distance of 1,400 to 2,000 meters, to be ridden at 300 to 350 meters per minute. Fences may be up to 2 feet 7 inches in height, with drops of up to 3 feet 3 inches and spreads of up to 2 feet 9 inches. The show-jumping course includes 9 to 11 obstacles with heights up to 2 feet 7 inches and spreads of up to 2 feet 9 inches.
  ◐ *See also* novice; training; intermediate; advanced.

behind
A term referring to the hind legs.
  ◐ *See also* in front.

behind the bit
The position of a horse that has

Horse holding his head behind the bit.
© CHERRY HILL

Belgian.
© KENTUCKY HORSE PARK

lowered his head or overflexed his neck or his head in order to evade the effects of the bit. Also called "below the bit."

behind the motion
 See motion.

behind the vertical
A position of the head and neck in which the horse is overflexed at the poll, causing the nose to fall behind an imaginary vertical line dropped from his forehead to the ground. This position may be caused by the horse evading the bit due to weakness, lack of training, incorrect training, or a rider who is too aggressive with the reins.

Belgian
A draft breed that originated in Belgium and is a descendant of the medieval Flemish War Horse (which also contributed to the Clydesdale and Shire draft breeds). Standing approximately 17 hands high and almost always roan or chestnut in color, the Belgian has a deep barrel and strong shoulders and back. Like other draft breeds, it is used for hauling and agricultural work.

Bell boots.
© MILLER HARNESS COMPANY LLC

bell boot
A shaped rubber boot worn on the ankles that covers the bulbs of the heels to protect against overreaching. Bell boots can also help prevent a horse from accidentally pulling off his own shoe by stepping on the edge of the shoe with the opposite hoof.

bell mare
A mare with a bell tied to her neck who leads a string of pack mules. Mules seem to have a special affinity for mares and will follow the bell mare without being tied to her. The bell helps them hear where she is.

Belmont Stakes
The final race of the Triple Crown, a distance of one and a half miles, held at Belmont Park in New York City three weeks after the Preakness.

bench-kneed
A conformation fault characterized by knees that are set to the outside of the cannon bones.

bend
To create a lateral curve of the horse's body. The purpose is to allow the horse to make symmetrical turns, with the hind feet to follow the tracks of the front feet. It is accomplished by the use of the rider's legs and hands; the horse is made to bend its body around the rider's inside leg (the leg closer to the center of the arena).

Bend Or spots
Darker-colored spots or splotches on the coat of a lighter-colored horse, especially a chestnut horse. Named after a Thoroughbred stallion who had them.

bends
Horseshoes whose ends are bent down, usually one-quarter of an

inch (quarter-inch bends), to provide greater traction. Bends are most often found on racehorses.

Bennett, James Gordon

American newspaper publisher and sportsman who introduced polo in the United States. He organized the first match in a New York City riding academy, then helped found the Westchester Polo Club in 1876, the first polo club in America.

benzimidazole

The active ingredient in some dewormers. It is effective against threadworms, pinworms, hookworms, roundworms, and tapeworms.

Bermuda grass

A grass used for hay.

Betadine

Brand name of an iodine solution commonly used for topically disinfecting wounds and surgical sites in horses.

Betathane (Beta)

A material used to make horse tack, consisting of nylon webbing impregnated with synthetic compounds, that looks like leather.

between-the-legs shot

In polo, a stroke in which the player's mallet makes contact with the ball under the pony's belly.

bezoar

🐎 *See* enterolith.

bib martingale

A triangular piece of leather sewn between two forked chest straps. The device, which prevents horses from getting their feet caught in the tack, is used during Thoroughbred racing exercise workouts, show jumping, and the cross-country phase of eventing.

bight

The loose end of a rope or reins.

big lick

Term used in reference to a gaited horse, especially a Tennessee Walking Horse, having unusually expressive and high-stepping gaits. The term has come to refer to a particular type of Tennessee Walking Horse showing, in which the horses are fitted with large, heavy pads on their shoes and chains around their ankles to encourage an unnaturally high-stepping stride.

bike

A light sulky used in Roadster Pony classes. Also, slang for a harness-racing sulky.

Bill Daly, on the

In racing, the tactic of taking a horse to the front at the start and then trying to remain on the lead all the way to the finish. The strategy capitalizes on a particular horse's running style of accelerating quickly and then maintaining that speed and stamina (as distinguished from horses with a come-from-behind ability).

A horse trotting with a bend to the left.
© BARBARA BURN

B

Named after trainer "Father Bill" Daly.

billet
One of the straps on a saddle to which the girth or cinch is buckled. All-purpose and competition saddles have three billet straps, of which two are used; the third is a spare. Dressage saddles have only two because an extra strap would interfere with the contact between the rider's leg and the horse.

biopsy
Surgical removal of a tissue sample for diagnostic analysis.

Biothane
A synthetic material used to make horse tack, similar to Betathane, except its appearance is similar to patent leather.

biotin
A vitamin supplement given to horses to improve hoof and coat condition.

Birdcatcher spots
Small white spots on a horse's coat. Named after a Thoroughbred stallion who had them.

birdsfoot trefoil
A legume grass used for hay.

bishoping
Filing down a horse's teeth to give a false impression that the animal is younger than its real age. The word is said to come from the name of an unscrupulous 18th-century English horse dealer.

bit
The mouthpiece part of a bridle to which the reins are fastened. Bits control the horse's movement and direction by exerting pressure, sometimes in conjunction with other parts of the bridle, on the bars, cheeks, tongue, or roof of the mouth, the jaw, the nose, and the poll. Bits evolved from leather, bone, or bronze mouthpieces of antiquity into the modern era's sophisticated appliances made of metal (now usually stainless steel), rubber, or vulcanite. Bits can be categorized as either snaffle or curb and sometimes as a combination of the two.
See also on the bit; above the bit; behind the bit.

bit burr
A rubber disk with stiff, burrlike projections on it. Inserted between the bit ring and the horse's cheek, the burrs press against the cheek when rein pressure causes the horse to turn, thus reinforcing the rein aid. Used primarily on racehorses.

bit guard
A rubber or plastic disk placed between the horse's cheek and the rings of a loose-ring snaffle, to protect the horse's lips from being pinched between the mouthpiece and the rings of the bit.

bitch pack
In foxhunting, a pack of hounds that consists of only females. The advantage is that they will not be distracted by the presence of male hounds (or vice versa).

bitting rig
A device comprised of a surcingle from which elastic side reins snap onto the rings of the horse's bit. Its purposes are to encourage a horse to accept a bit and to develop flexion at the poll.

black
A body color of true black, without any light areas, except possibly white markings on the face and legs; the mane and tail are also black.

Black Beauty
The title of and central character in Anna Sewell's 1877 novel. Told from the horse's point of view, *Black Beauty* chronicles the animal's life from foal, to becoming a saddle horse, to the cruel demands of pulling a London cab, to a happy retirement in the country. The novel's depiction of cruelty to horses became a major force in the animal welfare movement.

Black Bess
The mare ridden by the notorious 17th-century British outlaw Dick Turpin.

black oil sunflower seeds
A seed sometimes used as a supplemental feed for horses due to its high fat content.

blacksmith
A person who shoes horses; another word for farrier. The word comes from iron's having been considered a "black" metal (as distinguished from such "white" metals as tin).

Black Stallion, The
The first and most popular of the series of 21 novels by Walter Farley. Written by Farley in 1941, it describes how young Alec and an Arabian stallion that he frees during a shipwreck are stranded on a deserted island, where they develop a friendship that lasts a lifetime. When rescued, the boy trains the horse and then rides him to victory in a match race.

black type
1 In racing, bold-faced type used in sale catalogs to distinguish horses that have won or placed in a stakes race. If a horse's name appears in uppercase bold-faced type, it has won at least one stakes race. If the name appears in upper/lowercase bold-faced type, it has placed in at least one stakes race. 2 A method of distinguishing successful show horses in horse show programs, sale catalogs, and so forth.

blank
In foxhunting, failure to find a fox in a covert, as in "draw a blank."

blanket
1 A lined and filled garment that covers the horse from withers

B

to tail, to protect the horse from cold, wind, and precipitation. **2** A marking pattern on an Appaloosa horse in which a large white patch covers the hindquarters of an otherwise dark horse. **3** A Western saddle pad.

Blaze.
CREDIT: PHOTOS.COM

blaze
A broad, white vertical marking extending the length of the face, of a relatively uniform width, narrower than a bald face.

bleeding
Rupturing of capillaries in the nose or throat that often leads to choking. It is caused by excessive strain, most often occurring during a horse race. A horse with this condition is known as a bleeder and is treated with the diuretic furosemide (commonly called Lasix).

blemish
Any permanent physical imperfection, such as a scar, that does not affect a horse's serviceability or soundness.

bling
Tack or riding apparel that is embellished with rhinestones.

blinkers (also, blinders)
A pair of cups or flaps attached to the bridle or a hood, used to keep a horse from becoming distracted by objects to the side or rear. They are routinely used in driving and harness racing and occasionally in flat racing.

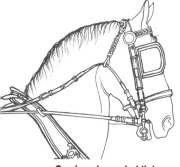

Carriage horse in blinkers.
© CHRISTINA BERUBE

blister
v. To apply an irritant in order to draw blood to the area and relieve muscle or tendon strains. A once-prevalent practice, blistering has been replaced by such techniques as medication and acupuncture, although iodine blistering is still commonly used to treat weak stifles or upward fixation of the patella (UFP).

blister beetle
Often found in alfalfa, the blister beetle's body contains a highly toxic substance that can cause death if ingested; the poison first causes blisters in the horse's mouth and intestines. Prevention begins with examining bales of alfalfa for the insect's presence, then burning any such infected hay.

block
1 A veterinary diagnostic procedure in which the nerve impulses of the legs are temporarily chemically suppressed. If the nerves to a given joint are blocked and a lame horse becomes sound as a result, the vet can identify that joint as the precise source of the lameness. **2** The large, thick pad sometimes applied to the hooves of Tennessee Walking Horses to achieve a more animated gait in the show ring.

blood
1 *n.* A term that describes the amount of Arabian or Thoroughbred in a horse's ancestry. A "blood" or "blooded" horse is all or mostly Arabian or Thoroughbred.

2 *v.* In foxhunting, to dab a bit of the fox's blood onto the cheek of a novice hunter as initiation into foxhunting. Because kills are now rare, many veteran foxhunters have never been blooded.

blood bay
Term describing a bright reddish bay coat color.

bloodstock
Term describing Thoroughbred horses bred or sold for racing.

bloodstock agent
A person who helps prospective owners find and buy horses for racing or for breeding racehorses.

blood work
The general term for the laboratory analysis of a blood sample. Blood work may be used to assess the horse's levels of nutrients, to perform a titer, to look for toxins or drugs, to identify kidney or liver problems, or for many other purposes.

blow
One of the vocalizations of the horse; a loud whistle, similar to a snort but higher in pitch, is made by air being forced through the nostrils. A horse may blow to express excitement, alarm, or nervousness.

blow-out
1 In racing, a fast sprint workout one or two days before a race to sharpen a horse's speed. **2** A

horizontal crack in the hoof wall.

blow up
To violently misbehave under saddle.

blue
The color of the prize ribbon awarded for first place in the United States. (Curiously, red is the color of the first-prize ribbon in Great Britain and Ireland.)

bluegrass
A grass used as hay or roughage.

blue roan
A coat of white and black hairs, with black mane, legs, and tail.

blue stem
Any of several forage grasses grown in the western United States.

board
Accommodations, feed, and care for a horse.
See also full board; rough board.

bob
1 To cut the hair of a horse's tail very short. **2** *See* nod, definition 1.

bobble
To stumble, usually when leaving the starting gate in a race.

bobtail
A horse whose tail has been docked, or cut short, for decorative purposes or to keep mud off

B

it. The term appears in Stephen Foster's "Camptown Races": ". . . bet my money on the bobtail nag / Somebody bet on the bay."

body brush
A grooming tool with relatively long, hard bristles used to remove dirt and loose hair.

Body brush.

body condition score (BCS)
A rating system from 1 (emaciated, near death) to 9 (very obese) that ranks the condition of a horse in terms of body fat. A healthy BCS is between 4 and 6, depending on the horse.

bog spavin
A chronic swelling on the front of a hock due to a collection of fluid. Although the cause is not known, it most frequently occurs in horses with poor hind leg conformation. Since lameness does not occur, a bog spavin is often considered an unsightly blemish. Treatments include draining the affected joint and administering anti-inflammatory medication.

bolt
1 To run away, usually out of control. Bolting usually results from an unexpected sight or sound that frightens the horse to the point of panic. **2** To consume feed very quickly, often without chewing. Bolting may lead to choke.

bombproof
Describes a horse that will not startle or spook at anything; the

Boot hook.
© MILLER HARNESS COMPANY LLC

implication is that even if a bomb exploded, the horse would not spook.

bone
A measurement taken around the leg below the knee or hock as an indication of a horse's projected ability to carry weight without injurious consequences. The phrase "good bone" refers to a large circumference.

bone chip
 See chip, definition 2.

bone scan
 See nuclear scintigraphy.

bone spavin
A degenerative arthritis of the lower hock joint. Most often occurring in older horses, it is most prevalent in horses with poor hind leg conformation or those that have been subjected to hard work that puts stress on the hock (e.g., reining, polo, jumping, and harness racing). Treatment includes corrective shoeing, anti-inflammatory medication, and moderating the amount of work the horse does.

book
1 The group of mares bred to a stallion in a year. **2** *See* stud book.

bookmaker (or "bookie")
A person who accepts bets on horse races. The name comes from the practice of keeping a notebook in which wagers were entered. Bookmakers are licensed in Great

Britain, Ireland, and other foreign countries, but are illegal in the United States.

boot
A protective covering for a horse's lower legs or hooves to prevent injury from interference during work or turnout.

boot hooks
Metal devices rounded at one end and with handles at the other, used to pull on a rider's tall boots.

bootjack
A device into which the heel of a riding boot is inserted, to assist in removing the boot.

boot pulls
Fabric tabs on the inside of tall boots that help the wearer pull the boots on, with or without the use of boot hooks.

borium
A durable metal used as caulks in horseshoes, especially for riding in ice and snow.

bosal (bo-SAL)
A length of braided rawhide that is the part of a hackamore that applies pressure to a horse's nose and chin.

bot knife
A specialized knife designed to remove the eggs of botflies from the horse's coat.

bots (or botflies)
The parasitic larvae of the gaster-

ophilus fly. The eggs appear as tiny yellow dots on a horse's lips and front legs and are ingested into the stomach, where they hatch and can cause colic and weight loss. A deworming program reduces the chance of a horse's being afflicted, as does shaving off any eggs found on the horse's hair. Removing manure, in which the larvae and flies live, is another preventive treatment.

bottom
Term for endurance or stamina, most commonly used in describing a racehorse with staying power. The implication is that a horse with bottom has a great depth of stamina from which to draw.

bottom line
The maternal side of a horse's pedigree, so called because the mare's lineage is listed on a chart below the sire's lineage:

NAME OF SIRE　　NAME OF DAM

NAME OF FOAL

botulism
A toxic condition caused by the horse ingesting *Clostridium botulinum* bacteria, which is found in rotting organic material. One source of botulism toxin in horses is dead field animals accidentally bound up into a bale of hay.

bounce
The familiar term for a combination of two fences set one

Bootjack.
© MILLER HARNESS COMPANY LLC

Bosal with rope fiador and mecate.
© CHERRY HILL

Botfly eggs on a horse's foreleg.
© RICHARD KLIMESH

cantering stride (usually twelve feet) apart. The horse will land over the first and immediately bounce over the second.

bowed tendon

An injury caused by the excessive stretching and tearing of a front leg's flexor tendon sheath. It is usually caused by repeated strain to the tendon, which then loosens from the cannon bone and develops the appearance of a taut archery bow. Initial treatment includes ice, support bandages, and anti-inflammatory medication, followed by prolonged rest until the bow "sets," or heals.

Although a horse with a bowed tendon can return to work, the tendon will never regain its former strength.

 *See also* bandage bow.

bow hocks

A conformation fault in which the hocks are set too far apart and turn outward (the opposite of cow hocks). Also known as bow legs.

box

1 A British term for horse van. **2** In driving, the seat or platform on which the driver sits. **3** In racing, a single bet that combines two or more horses to make multiple combinations. For example, an *exacta box* of horses identified by the numbers 1, 2, and 3 pays out if the order of finish is 1–2, 1–3, 2–1, 2–3, 3–1, or 3–2.

box stall

A square or rectangular compartment in which a horse lives.

 Compare to straight stall.

brace

1 *n.* Liniment used to rub down a horse after exercise. **2** *v.* To resist the bit by leaning against it, often while raising the head and hollowing the back.

braid

To twist together three strands of a horse's mane and/or tail. Usually done for decorative purposes and required for showing, braiding a mane also keeps the hair from flying into the rider's face. Braiding a tail keeps mud from collecting on it in foul weather.

bran

The husk of oats used in feed or in a mash as a laxative.

brand

A permanent marking made on the skin of a horse for the purpose of identification. The brand may indicate the horse's breed (e.g., registered warmboods), owner (e.g., ranch stock), or identity number (e.g., Thoroughbred and Standardbred racehorses). Fire brands are made by cauterizing the skin with a hot iron implement. Freeze brands are made by cauterizing the skin with a frozen iron implement. Freeze brands on the upper lips of racehorses are also known as "tattoos." Acid brands are made by applying

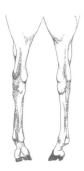

Bow hocks.
© CHRISTINA BERUBE

An illustration from a 19th-century book on horse training, showing a now-outdated breaking method.

acid, such as hydrochloric acid, to the skin.

bray
The vocalization made by a donkey or mule.

break
1 To train a horse to accept tack and then accept a rider or driver. Because of the harsh methods that horsemen once used, such as encouraging a horse to buck and then trying to outlast him, the term now has an unpleasant connotation in this era of kinder and gentler methods. Accordingly, the word "start" is more frequently used in this connection. **2** In racing, to leave the starting gate.

breakaway roping
A timed Western show class for young riders, in which the lariat is attached to the saddle horn by means of a thin cord that breaks when a catch is made.

break down
To suffer an injury severe enough to end the horse's taking part in the race or other competition. In many instances, breaking down can end a horse's entire competitive career.

breaking bit
A bit used in the early training of a green horse.

break off
To move a horse rapidly to one side by the use of the rider's lower leg or spur.

breakover
The point in the horse's stride at which the toe of the hoof is lifted off the ground.

break stride
To change from one gait to another. In harness racing, to go into a gallop instead of maintaining the trot or pace. If the driver does not immediately put the horse back on gait, or if the break occurs at the end of the race, the horse will be disqualified.

breastcollar
A piece of tack that keeps a saddle from slipping back; also known as breastplate.

breeches (BRIT-ches)
English riding pants having legs that extend to the calf. They are worn with tall boots.
Compare to jodhpurs.

breeching
In driving, wide harness bands that fit around the wheel horse's buttocks. The horse braces back against the breeching to assist in slowing down or stopping the vehicle.

breed
1 *n.* Any group of animals capable of passing along distinctive characteristics to their offspring. In the horse world, the word usually refers to any of more than

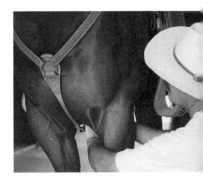
Western breastcollar.
© RICHARD KLIMESH

Breeches.
© MILLER HARNESS COMPANY LLC

Breeching.
© CHRISTINE BERUBE

B

one hundred recognized breeds that have been created and maintained by selective breeding. Pedigree registries are maintained by breed organizations, such as the Jockey Club for Thoroughbreds or the Appaloosa Horse Club, for each breed. In addition to "man-made" breeds are the ones that occur in nature, such as wild mustangs or the wild native ponies of Britain. Although these types of horses are not usually selectively bred, clubs and organizations exist for owners of horses of such breeds. **2** *v.* To mate a horse in order to produce a foal.

breeder
The owner of a dam at the time she is bred (according to the rules of the American Quarter Horse Association), or the owner at the time the dam gives birth (according to the rules of the Jockey Club).

Bridle with snaffle bit.

Breeder's Cup
Thoroughbred racing's year-end championship, first run in 1984, consisting of seven races conducted on one day at a different racetrack each year for million-dollar purses. Winners in each category are widely considered that year's champion in that category: Juvenile (two-year-old colts at one mile); Juvenile Fillies; Spring (three-quarter mile); Mile; Distaff (fillies and mares at a mile and an eighth); Turf (a mile and a half); and Classic (a mile and a quarter). In addition, a Breeder's Cup steeplechase race is held on another day somewhere along the eastern seaboard.

breeze
In racing, a fast, short training gallop, usually timed and often viewed as indicative of a horse's racing condition.

bridged reins
Describes a technique for overlapping both reins across the withers, with each of the rider's hands holding both reins, so that if the horse pulls at the bit, the rider can press the reins into the withers for support. The technique is often used by eventers during the cross-country phase, as well as by riders of racehorses.

bridle
A headpiece consisting of a bit, straps to keep the bit in place, and a set of reins.

bridle hand
The rider's hand that holds the reins.

bridle lameness
A gait abnormality that is only apparent while the horse is being ridden. Also called "rein lameness."

bridle path
1 The clipped area of the mane running several inches behind the poll, where the crownpiece of the bridle lies. Its purpose is to keep the mane from becoming entangled in the bridle. **2** A trail designed for horseback riding.

bridlewise
A relative and highly subjective view of a horse's responsiveness to directions from the reins and/or bit.

bridoon
The narrow snaffle bit used in a double bridle in combination with a curb bit.

brio
n. A desirable character trait of Paso Fino and Peruvian Paso horses; it denotes spirit, boldness, and confidence.

broke
Trained to be ridden. In Western jargon, a horse that is "well broke" or "dead broke" is very well trained, responds easily to the aids, and is generally quiet and complacent.

broken neck
Of a ridden horse, having an abrupt angle in the neck instead of the more desirable smooth curve from withers to poll.

broken wind
Also known as *heaves*, this describes a respiratory condition known as chronic obstructive pulmonary disease (COPD) marked by obstructions of airflow in the lungs. The symptoms are difficulty in breathing and loss of energy. Causes include exposure to dust and allergies, especially when the horse is stabled in poorly ventilated quarters or on dusty bedding, or is fed dusty hay. Most horses with COPD quickly respond to a change of environment that eliminates the source of the problem.

bromegrass (broom-grass)
A variety of hay grass.

bronc (or broncho)
Originally applied to an unbroken feral horse, the term now refers to a bucking horse used in rodeo's saddle bronc and bareback bronc riding, two of the timed events in which the cowboy has to outlast the horse for eight seconds.

broodmare
A mare used for breeding purposes.

broomtail
A slang term for a low-quality horse.

Brougham (BROOM)
In driving, a four-wheeled enclosed carriage with an exposed driver's box; named after a British nobleman.

browband
The part of the bridle that lies across the horse's forehead and holds the cheekpieces.

brown
1 A body color of brown or black with light areas at the muzzle, eyes, flank, and inside upper legs; the mane and tail are black. 2 The color of the prize ribbon awarded for eighth place.

brush
In foxhunting, the fox's tail. In the

B

event of a kill, the brush is awarded as a trophy to a member of the hunt who was close to the hounds when they captured the fox.

brush box
A type of jump made of an open wooden box filled with natural materials such as twigs and sticks.

brushing
Interference caused by one foot rubbing against or into the fetlock or cannons of the opposite leg.

brushing boots
A piece of protective equipment worn on the fetlocks by horses that are prone to brushing. Also called galloping boots or splint boots.

bubble bit
Slang term for an elevator bit with three rings.

Brushing boots, or galloping boots.
CREDIT: JAMES C. WOFFORD

Bucephalus
The favorite horse of Alexander the Great. As a young man, Alexander tamed the high-strung horse; noticing that the horse shied at its shadow on the ground, he faced the horse toward the sun and so calmed the animal. The name is Greek for "ox-headed."

buck
To jump with an arched back, kicking both hind legs up and out, followed by landing on straightened legs.

buckaroo
A colloquial American term for cowboy, from the mispronunciation of the Mexican-Spanish word *vaquero,* meaning cowboy.

buckboard
An open, four-wheeled carriage.

bucked shin
An inflammation of the front of the cannon bone, usually in the front legs. Occurring in young horses, the condition happens when bones that cannot stand up to the stress of training fracture and hemorrhage. Treatment includes ice, rest, and, in the case of severe fractures, surgery.

bucking rolls
On a Western saddle, thick padded attachments to the swells, which help to hold the rider in place if the horse bucks.

bucking strap
1 A snug leather strap placed around a rodeo bucking horse's flank to encourage him to buck; also known as flank strap. **2** A short strip of leather attached at the pommel of an English saddle, which the rider can hold if she becomes unbalanced or anticipates that the horse will buck.

buckskin
A dark yellow- or gold-colored coat with a black mane, lower legs, and tail, without a dorsal stripe.

buckstitching
Decorative white stitching on a Western saddle or bridle.

buddy
A horse with which another horse is stabled or pastured on a regular basis.

buddy sour
 See herdbound.

bug boy
 See apprentice.

buggy
A light, two-wheeled carriage.

build
Conformation.

bulb
One of the two wide areas on the back of the hoof.

bulldogging
The original term for steer wrestling. The word was suggested by the way a bulldog's teeth grip the face or the neck of a bull.

bullpen
 See round pen.

bump
1 A Western term for a quick jerk of rein or a quick kick of leg pressure done variously to attract the horse's attention or to encourage it to shift its weight to its hind end. **2** In jumping, a colloquial word for the schooling technique, usually done right before entering the show ring, of intentionally riding a horse to a takeoff spot that will cause its feet to strike the top rail of the fence. The purpose is to encourage the horse to try to be more careful and thus jump a rub-free round. **3** "Jumper's bump" and "hunter's bump" are colloquial terms for sacroiliac subluxation.

bumper pull
A trailer style that attaches to a hitch ball located behind the rear bumper of the tow vehicle. The hitch is not actually attached to the bumper, however; it is attached to the frame of the vehicle.

Burleigh (BURL-ee)
The major international horse trial held on the Marquess of Exeter's estate in Northamptonshire, England. Started in 1961, Burleigh ranks with Badminton, Rolex Kentucky, and the Olympics as one of the world's most demanding three-day events.

bursa
A fluid-filled pouch under the skin; capped elbow or capped hock.

bute
Phenylbutazone, a nonsteroidal anti-inflammatory drug (NSAID) widely used to reduce swelling and inflammation. Some racing commissions and horse show organizations restrict the amount permitted just prior to competition, since it allows unsound horses to perform because they do not feel pain and thus are subjected to the possibility of further injury. Often known by the trade names Butazolidin and Butazone.

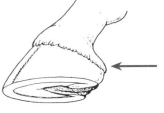

Bulb.

The Lyons Press Horseman's Dictionary **33**

buttbar

The restraining bar across the back of a trailer stall.

Buttermilk

The buckskin mare ridden by Dale Evans, "the Queen of the West," in the Roy Rogers cowboy movies and television series.

buy back

A horse that goes unsold through a public auction because it fails to reach its reserve bid.

buzkashi

An Afghanistani mounted game in which a sheep or goat carcass is carried across the goal line. The successful rider brings honor to himself as well as to his team (which is often his tribe or village).

by

A word indicating a horse's sire. "Secretariat was by Bold Ruler" means that Bold Ruler was Secretariat's sire.

bye day

In foxhunting, an unscheduled day of hunting.

Byerly Turk

Along with the Godolphin Barb and Darley Arab, one of the three Thoroughbred foundation sires, captured from the Turkish forces and imported to England in the mid-17th century by Captain Byerly.

cadence
The rhythm of a horse's stride, often used to describe the regularity of steps.

Cadre Noir
The premier troupe of the French Cavalry School in Saumur, France. The name comes from the riders' black hats and tunics. Composed of 12 officers and 12 noncommissioned men, the Cadre Noir train and present their horses in haute école dressage and in jumping; riders take part in dressage, combined training, and show-jumping competitions.

Calf roping.
© WYATT MCSPADDEN/AMERICAN
QUARTER HORSE ASSOCIATION

cala
A reining competition done by Mexican charros.

calcium-phosphorus ratio (Ca:P)
For good bone health, a horse's diet must contain a balance of calcium to phosphorus at a ratio of 2:1.

calf-kneed
A conformation fault in which the forelegs' carpal joints bend backward. It is considered a serious

Caliente helmet.

conformation fault, since the knee will have a tendency to hyperextend backward. Also known as back at the knee.

calf roping
1 A Western horse show class in which a horse is judged on how well it helps the rider as the rider ropes a calf. In the best-case scenario, the horse springs out of the starting box once the calf is released and maintains a position behind and to the side of the calf. Once the calf is roped, the horse slides to a stop, then backs up to maintain tension on the rope so the calf cannot evade the cowboy while he throws and hogties the calf's legs. **2** In rodeo, the former name for tie-down roping.

Calgary Stampede
A major rodeo held each July in Calgary, Canada.

caliente
A type of sturdy helmet worn predominantly by jockeys and combined training riders; named after Mexico's Agua Caliente Race Track where it was introduced.

C

California reins
Western reins that are closed, as opposed to split, and have a romal.

California style
A type of horsemanship that is based on traditional California vaquero riding and lifestyle.

Camargue
A semi-wild breed inhabiting the marshlands of southern France's Rhône River delta. Barely taller than a pony, with a compact body that is almost always gray in color, the Camargue is the traditional mount of the region's cowboys, called *gardians*.

campaign
To show a horse extensively.

camped out
A position in which the horse stands with its hind legs stretched back and forelegs stretched forward. Most horses assume this position during urination, and some horses may be trained to stand this way in order to show off their conformation in halter classes. Otherwise, it is a sign of a physical problem.
 See also park out.

camped under
A position in which the hind legs or forelegs are held under the horse's body in an abnormal way. It may be a conformational fault, or may indicate pain or soreness somewhere in the body.

canine teeth
A set of four sharp teeth that erupt along the bars of the gums in male horses around the age of four or five. They are only rarely seen in mares. Their purpose is to be used by stallions as a weapon against other stallions. Also called tushes.

cannon
The bone that extends from the knee or hock to the fetlock.

canter
The horse's three-beat gait, a slow or collected gallop known in Western riding as the lope. The sequence of footfalls of a horse cantering on its left lead is right hind, left hind and right fore simultaneously, and left fore. The name purportedly comes from the preferred gait of medieval pilgrims who traveled by horseback to the shrine of Thomas à Becket in Canterbury, England.
 See also lead.

cantle
The elevated rear part of a saddle.

cap
1 A riding hat with the appearance of a helmet, but that does not provide the head protection provided by a helmet. **2** *See* capping fee.

capillary refill time (CRT)
The amount of time needed for blood to return to capillaries after it has been forced out of them (usually done by pressing the horse's gums). The return of the

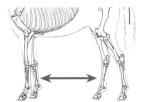
Cannon bones.
© CHRISTINA BERUBE

Horse cantering on its right lead.
© CHERRY HILL

The cantle of a Western saddle.
CREDIT: PHOTOS.COM

A riding cap.
CREDIT: PHOTOS.COM

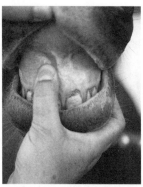

Testing capillary refill time.
© RICHARD KLIMESH

Lipizzaner performing a capriole.
© TEMPEL FARMS

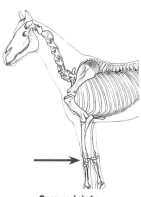

Carpus joints.
© CHRISTINA BERUBE

normal pink color indicates that the capillaries are refilled. Normal CRT is one to two seconds. The test measures certain aspects of the horse's general health.

capped elbow
🐎 *See* shoe boil.

capped hock
An infected swelling at the point of the hock, typically caused by bruising.

capping fee
In foxhunting, the charge paid by nonmembers of the hunt for a day's sport; also called cap.

Caprilli, Federico
Nineteenth-century Italian horseman credited with the development of the forward seat.

capriole
The air above the ground in which the horse springs up out of a piaffe and kicks back with both hind legs while holding the forelegs close to its chest. The word comes from the Italian word for goat.

captive bolt gun
An implement commonly used in animal slaughter, including the slaughter of horses.

card
1 The judge's scorecard. **2** The day's or evening's program of racing. **3** A document indicating a pony's official height for showing purposes.

carpus
The joint in the horse's front leg between the forearm and cannon, more commonly referred to as the knee.

carriage
1 A vehicle designed to carry people in comfort and elegance. **2** The style in which a horse carries itself, especially with regard to the head and neck position.

carrier
A horse that has been exposed to an infectious disease and is able to transmit the disease to other horses, but does not show symptoms.

carrousel
An equestrian spectacle that was popular in 18th-century Europe and that featured mock battles and mounted ballets.

cart horse
Another term for a draft horse.

Caslick's operation
The suturing closed of a mare's vaginal opening to prevent infection caused by foreign material.

cast
1 *adj.* A horse that is lying down on its side or back, wedged against the side of a stall in such a position that the animal cannot rise to its feet without assistance. **2** *v.* To throw a horse down onto the ground with the use of ropes or hobbles.

C

castrate
To surgically remove the testicles of a male horse; geld.

cataract
An opaque growth on the lens of the eye, which restricts vision and may lead to blindness.

catch
In roping, to successfully lasso a calf or steer.

catch ride
To ride a horse that belongs to another owner at a show. A catch rider may or may not be paid for this service.

cathedral
A curb bit having a very high port.

cattle charge
In a Western show or rodeo, a fee assessed to a competitor entering an event that requires the use of cattle.

caulk
A small stud that screws into a hole drilled into a horseshoe and provides traction over wet or frozen ground. Caulks are the equivalents of cleats or spikes on golf or baseball shoes.

cavalier
A mounted knight; an equestrian warrior. The word is now sometimes applied to male riders in a competition.

cavalletti
Training devices made of jump rails supported on low X-shaped holders or on blocks and used primarily as jumping exercises. The name is Italian for "little horses" and, although plural, customarily refers to both one or more than one device.

cavalry
A mounted military unit.

cavesson (CAV-uh-son)
1 The most basic noseband of an English bridle, consisting of a band around the upper part of the nose, above the bit, and a headstall. **2** Close-fitting headgear for the horse, not bitted, used for longeing and in-hand work, usually with a padded noseband bearing one or more metal rings for the attachment of a longe line.

See also dropped noseband; figure-eight noseband; flash noseband.

cayuse (KIE-yoose)
A word that formerly described a Native American horse descended from Spanish horses, now a familiar term for any Western horse, from the Cayuse tribe in present-day Oregon.

CCI
The abbreviation for Concours Complet International—an international-level three-day event run under FEI rules. CCIs are rated using a star system. A CCI* is the FEI equivalent of a USEF Intermediate-level event. CCI** is equivalent to preliminary level,

A horseshoe with caulks.

Cavesson noseband.
CREDIT: J. SHIERS

CCI*** is equivalent to advanced, and CCI****, the highest level of eventing, is a more difficult version of advanced. The only CCI**** events are Britain's Badminton and Burleigh, the United States' Rolex Kentucky, the Olympics, and the World Equestrian Games.

See also CIC.

Centered Riding

A riding philosophy developed by the American instructor Sally Swift and published in 1985 in a book of the same name. Centered riding emphasizes establishing and maintaining rider equilibrium as well as balance between horse and rider. Involves visualization techniques, such as imagining that riders have eyes in their chest that "look" in the direction they want their horses to turn.

Chambon.
© MILLER HARNESS COMPANY LLC

center-fire rigging

A Western saddle with a cinch in the center, around the middle of the horse's belly.

 *Compare to* double-rigged.

cervical vertebral malformation

A condition in young horses in which one or more of the cervical (neck) vertebrae develop incorrectly, causing spinal cord obstruction and muscular incoordination; wobbler syndrome.

chaff

1 The seed husks separated from the seeds by threshing. **2** Chopped hay used as forage.

chain

See curb chain; lip chain; stud chain.

chalk

In racing, the favorite horse among the bettors. The word comes from the former practice of writing odds in chalk on blackboards.

chambon (SHAM-bon)

A type of martingale that influences head and neck position by exerting pressure on the horse's poll.

champion

In horse showing, the horse or rider who wins the most points in a given division at a show.

Champion

The sorrel horse ridden by the cowboy movie and television star Gene Autry.

change of lead

Switching from one canter lead to the other. The transition can be either a simple change of lead or a flying change of lead. Known familiarly as swapping leads.

change of rein

A change of direction. To change to the right rein means to reverse the horse's movement from a counterclockwise to a clockwise direction. Also known as change of hand or change of school.

C

Chapot, Frank

Six-time U.S. Olympic show-jumping rider Frank Chapot won two Olympic silver medals and an individual bronze medal in the 1974 World Championships and rode on a record 46 winning Nations' Cup teams. After his riding career, Chapot became the Team's show-jumping chef d'équipe, guiding the squad to the first-ever Team gold medals in the 1984 Olympics and 1986 World Championships.

Chapot, Mary Mairs

Show jumper Mary Mairs Chapot was the first West Coast rider to win the ASPCA Maclay Championship, the first woman to win a Pan American Games gold medal, and the first woman (with Kathy Kusner) to ride for the United States, in the Tokyo Olympic Games in 1964. She teamed with Frank Chapot as the first husband-wife combination to ride for the United States Equestrian Team.

chaps

Leather leggings originally worn as protection against thorns, brush, and other sharp objects. Although that remains the reason why ranchers wear them, chaps (customarily pronounced "shaps" by Western riders and "chaps" by English riders), especially the snug-fitting "shotgun" variety, are now worn by both Western and English riders for leg support and protection from saddle rubs. Although chaps are considered

informal wear by English riders, they are appropriate, if not mandatory, for certain Western horse show classes. Half chaps are tight-fitting chaps that cover only the lower part of the leg, below the knee, and are commonly worn along with paddock boots by English riders in informal settings.

charger

A horse ridden by a cavalry officer.

charro

A horseman who rides in traditional Mexican equestrian events.

🔵 *See also* cala and colas.
🔵 *Compare to* vaquero.

check

1 *v.* To slow a horse's speed.
2 *n.* In foxhunting, a pause by riders while the hounds search for a fox's scent. **3** *n.* In endurance and competitive trail riding, a required stopping point for rest, water, and veterinary examination.

check ligament

A ligament that connects a tendon to a bone in such a way that the bone is supported without muscular effort by the horse. Check ligaments allow a horse to sleep while standing up.

check rein

In driving, a short strap that runs from the bit to the saddle of the harness to keep the horse from lowering his head. Also called a bearing rein.

Frank Chapot.
COURTESY OF THE U.S. EQUESTRIAN TEAM

Mary Chapot on White Lightning.
COURTESY OF THE U.S. EQUESTRIAN TEAM

Check rein.
© CHRISTINA BERUBE

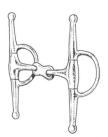

**A full-cheek snaffle
(French mouth type).**

cheek

The arm on some snaffle bits that prevents the rings of the bit from sliding through the horse's mouth. A full-cheek snaffle has arms above and below the ring; a half-cheek has arms only below the ring.

cheekpiece

The strap on a bridle connecting the crownpiece and the bit. It rests against the horse's cheek and is adjustable for correct bit fit.

chef d'équipe

The head coach of the United States Equestrian Team, or any other internationally competitive team. The French words mean "chief of the team."

chestnut

1 A dark red or brownish-red coat, mane, and tail. Although the term is often used synonymously with sorrel, chestnut is properly a slightly darker brown. **2** One of the hard, knoblike growths on the insides of a horse's legs (also called night eye, from a myth that chestnuts help horses to see in the dark). They are the vestigial remains of prehistoric horses' toes. Because chestnuts are as distinctive as human fingerprints, they are used as a mark of identification by breed registries and racing commissions.

Chestnut on a horse's foreleg.
© RICHARD KLIMESH

Cheyenne roll

On a Western saddle, a type of cantle on which the edge is rolled over in back to form a ridge.

Chifney bit

A type of ring bit with a straight, solid mouthpiece, used for leading unruly horses. It can be quite severe and is not designed for riding.

Chincoteague

A breed of feral ponies found on the islands of Chincoteague and Assateague off the coasts of Virginia and North Carolina. According to legend, they are descended from horses and ponies that washed ashore after shipwrecks in colonial times. Although most of the ponies live on Assateague, they are rounded up and swum across to Chincoteague every Memorial Day weekend, where they are auctioned (the proceeds going to the local fire department). The breed received considerable exposure due to the popular children's book *Misty of Chincoteague* by Marguerite Henry.

 See also Misty of Chincoteague.

chin groove

 See curb groove.

chinks

Western chaps that cover the rider's legs above the knees. Worn with high boots that protect the rest of the leg, chinks enable cowboys to kneel while branding or otherwise tending to cattle.

chip

1 In jumping, an extra stride taken close to the fence before leaving the ground. Chipping produces

C

an awkward jump for both horse and rider. **2** Osteophyte; a small bone fragment that has broken off and is "floating" inside the body. Surgical removal generally offers a good prognosis.

chiropractic treatment
An alternative veterinary treatment in which the practitioner manipulates the joints, particularly the vertebrae of the spinal column, bringing them into correct alignment.

choke
n. A condition in which the esophagus becomes blocked, usually by a too-large or unchewed bite of food. Because the horse's trachea and esophagus are separate, a horse suffering from choke can still breathe, but is unable to eat or drink. Veterinary attention may be needed to remove the blockage. After a horse has choked, the resulting scar tissue may make the horse more vulnerable to choke in the future.

choker
A detachable turtleneck-style collar worn with women's ratcatcher shirts. The wearer's monogram stitched on the choker is a traditional touch.

chorioptic mange
 See scratches.

chrome
A slang term for prominent white markings, such as stockings or socks.

chronic
Term describing a long-term illness or condition, possibly lasting the duration of the horse's life. Chronic conditions often also feature acute phases in which the disease or condition becomes active and then recedes again.
 Compare to acute.

chronic obstructive pulmonary disease (COPD)
 See heaves.

chukkar
One of the periods into which a polo match is divided. Outdoor polo has eight chukkars lasting seven and a half minutes each. Arena (or indoor) polo has six chukkars of seven minutes in length. The word comes from the Hindu for "wheel," perhaps referring to the clock on which playing time was kept.

chute
1 The pen from which calves used in calf-roping events are released. **2** The extension to the backstretch or home-stretch portions of some racetracks that permits a straight start instead of a start on a turn. **3** A lane containing a number of fences that a riderless horse is encouraged to jump, the fences serving as a gymnastic exercise.
 See free jump.

CIC
The abbreviation for Concours International Combiné—an international-level one-event run under FEI rules that omits phases

Chincoteague ponies.
© ED CAMELLI

A, B, and C of the endurance test.
◍ *See also* CCI.

cigar
In polo, a type of mallet head in which both ends are tapered.

cinch
The strap on a Western saddle that passes under the horse's belly to hold the saddle in place. Some saddles, especially those used for roping, have two cinches for greater security.

Front cinch.
© RICHARD KLIMESH

circle
An arena figure used in various disciplines, including dressage and reining. In a dressage test or reining pattern, the rider's ability to complete a full, symmetrical circle, maintaining an even bend and without the horse deviating from its arc, exhibits the horse's degree of training.
◍ *See also* opening circle.

circuit
1 Several racetracks within a certain geographic area that have nonconflicting racing dates.
2 A geographical division used with regard to certain horse show awards. **3** A consecutive series of horse shows held at the same facility over a number of days.

claimer
In racing, a horse that is consistently run in claiming races.

claiming price
In racing, the price for which a

horse is running in a claiming race and for which he can be claimed.

claiming race
A race in which any horse so entered may be bought by a licensed owner at a stipulated price or within a range of prices, either directly or through a trainer. Claims can be made until the race begins, with the claimed horse becoming the property of the new owner and the purse (if the horse wins one) going to the previous owner.

class
1 An individual event within a horse show division. **2** In racing, a horse showing the most impressive qualities of breeding and ability of all the horses in the race, as in the expression "the class of the race."

classic format
◍ *See* long format.

classical dressage
A style of dressage riding that is based on the traditional European styles of riding and may include such movements as piaffe, passage, and half-pass, as well as the airs above the ground. Emphasis is placed on the seat of the rider as well as the horse's correct and light obedience to the aids. Today, classical dressage is perfected by the Spanish Riding School of Vienna and the Cadre Noir of Saumur in France.
◍ *Compare to* competitive dressage.

C

clean and fast

In three-day eventing, to incur no penalties in the speed-and-endurance phase. *Clean* refers to the absence of penalties for refusals or falls, while *fast* refers to the absence of penalties for exceeding the time limit.

clean-legged

A horse with legs free from conformation faults, injuries, or blemishes.

clear round

In show or stadium jumping, a round in which the horse incurs no penalties for knockdowns, refusals, or exceeding the time allowed; also known as a clean round.

Cleveland Bay

The breed that originated in the Cleveland area of England's Yorkshire as a coach horse and agricultural worker. Infusions of Andalusian and other Spanish blood gave the horse a refined head and clean legs. As the name suggests, its color is bay. Standing between 16 and 17 hands, the Cleveland Bay is often crossed with Thoroughbreds to produce an outstanding foxhunting horse.

clicker training

A method of training in which the horse is taught to associate a specific sound, made by a small, handheld tool called a clicker, with a food reward. The clicker is then used to reward the horse for correct actions. Clicker training is most commonly used for ground training and trick training, but can also be used for under-saddle work.

clinch

The tip of a horseshoe nail that has been clamped over and down by the farrier.

clinic

A type of intensive group lesson in which a noted trainer or instructor teaches several students, usually over a one- to three-day period. Clinics may involve lectures, demonstrations, and classes, in addition to mounted lessons.

clip

1 *v.* To trim hair from a horse's body in any of several patterns. **2** *n.* A metal projection on the toe of some horseshoes, the purpose of which is to help keep the shoe snugly in place.
 *See* hunter clip, trace clip.

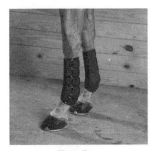

Toe clips.
© MILLER HARNESS COMPANY LLC

clocker

The racetrack official who times horses during their morning workouts.

clone

A genetic duplicate of an existing animal. The world's first cloned equine was a mule named Idaho Gem, cloned by the University of Idaho in March, 2003, while the first cloned horse was a Haflinger named Promotea, born in Italy in August, 2003. Cloning is a controversial topic. The Jockey Club and the AQHA, for example, do not permit cloned horses into their breed registries.

close

1 *v.* To finish in a race. A horse that shows speed after being off the pace is called a quick closer.
2 *adj.* Of a horse's legs, moving near to each other when the horse is in motion, running the risk of frequent interference; as in the phrase "traveling close behind," meaning the hind legs tend to brush each other.

close contact

A jumping saddle with little or no padding in the seat and knee flaps. The phrase refers to the close contact between horse and rider.

closed

1 A breed registry that only accepts offspring of two parents that are both already in the registry.
2 Term describing growth plates in joints (typically knees) that are no longer actively producing bone. Hard work before the young horse's growth plates have closed can lead to joint problems later in life.

closing

In racing, the cutoff time after which nominations or entries are no longer accepted.

clover

A legume grass widely used for hay. White clover may cause excessive salivation, but it is not harmful.

Clydesdale.
© MAUREEN BLANEY

club foot

A malformed hoof that grows excessively upright, with little or no angle in relation to the ground.

clubhouse turn

In racing, the turn of the track that comes after the finish line. It is so named because the preferred clubhouse seats face that part of the track.

cluck

A sound made by a rider or handler by rapidly pulling the tongue away from the teeth and roof of the mouth. The sound is traditionally used to ask a horse to move faster.

Clydesdale

The draft breed that originated in 18th-century Scotland along the River Clyde. The breed was used for agricultural and industrial draft work and by the mid-19th century became Scotland's most popular carriage horse. Standing from 17 to 18 hands and weighing up to 2,000 pounds, the Clydesdale is most typically bay or chestnut and has four white socks up to the knees and hocks, prominent feathers (silky hair on the back of its legs), and a high leg action at the walk and trot. Millions of people recognize the breed from their live and TV appearances pulling the Budweiser beer wagon.

coach horse

An individual or type of horse smaller than a draft horse, yet

C

strong enough to pull a driving vehicle.

coarse

 See common.

coastal hay

Hay made from Bermuda grass.

cob

A type (not a breed) of riding horse, under 15.3 hands, distinguished by its good manners and ability as a saddle horse, especially its ability to carry heavy riders. Developed in Great Britain and Ireland, the cob has a thickset neck and body and short, strong legs.

coffin

A cross-country obstacle composed of an open ditch with post-and-rail fences set in front of and behind slopes on either side of the ditch.

coffin bone

The phalanx bone inside the foot; also known as the pedal (PEED-le) bone.

Coggins test

The test for equine infectious anemia devised by Dr. Leroy Coggins. A negative Coggins is routinely required for interstate shipping and for entering horses in competition.

colas

A Mexican charro event in which the rider grabs and twists the tail of a bull or steer, throwing it to the ground.

cold-backed

Describes a horse that behaves unusually when first mounted, but quickly settles once work begins. It may seem that the horse's back is tender or sore at first, and the horse may hollow or hump its back, attempt to trot off quickly, or even buck or crow-hop immediately after the rider mounts. In some cases, briefly longeing the horse before riding can avert these problems. A cold-backed horse may also be girthy.

cold blood

A horse of all or mostly draft-horse breeding, without Arabian influence. The "cold blood" refers to the characteristically calm animal's Northern European ancestry.

 *See also* hot blood; warmblood.

cold hose

To run cold water over a horse's leg for therapeutic purposes, such as to reduce swelling.

cold-jawed

Unresponsive to bits.

cold shoeing

A farrier's method of attaching pre-shaped shoes, as opposed to shoes that the farrier makes or fits by heating in the hot-shoeing method.

 *Compare to* hot shoeing.

colic

Any irritation, bloating, or blockage of the intestine, including a twisted intestine. Typical symptoms include sweating, lying

Colas competition.
© AMERICAN QUARTER HORSE ASSOCIATION

C

down, nipping at the stomach, and otherwise trying to reduce or escape the pain, and a decrease in appetite and in manure output. The seriousness of colic cannot be overemphasized; immediate veterinary attention is essential. Treatment may consist of doses of mineral oil (to help the horse pass the obstruction, if that is the problem) and intravenous fluids. In some instances, surgery to remove the obstruction or the section of twisted intestine may be required.

Collar.
CREDIT: PHOTOS.COM

collar
In driving, the part of the harness that sits across the withers and shoulders and against which a horse pushes.

collect
1 To put a horse into a more compact frame, usually done to create greater impulsion. Collection is generally accomplished as the rider's legs and/or seat aids urge the horse forward while simultaneously the rider's hands restrain the amount of forward motion. As a result, the horse's body shifts into a more uphill frame, with the hocks well underneath his body, his back lifted, and his weight carried more over his haunches. **2** To gather the semen from a stallion for later artificial insemination of a mare.
 Compare to extend.

colors
In foxhunting, the distinctive attire worn by members of a hunt, especially a colored coat collar and buttons. Foxhunters who have ridden with a hunt for a length of time "earn their colors" and become entitled to wear the hunt's livery.

colostrum
The first milk from a mare after the birth of her foal. Thick and yellow to orange in color, the colostrum is rich in nutrients, antibodies, and globulin, which are essential for the foal's health.

colt
An ungelded male horse under four years old.

combination
In jumping, a series of two or three fences set apart at a total distance of forty feet. A horse that refuses the second or third element of a combination must go back and reattempt all the elements, starting with the first one.

combination bit
A device that functions as both a bit and a hackamore. Rein pressure is distributed over the tongue, bars, and nose.

combined driving
A sport, similar to combined training, in which drivers and their horse or team of horses compete in three phases: dressage, hazards (also called cross-country or marathon), and obstacles (also known as cones).

combined training
An earlier term for eventing.

 See eventing.

common
A pejorative term that indicates a lack of refinement or sharp definition in one or more particular features of a horse's overall conformation; a synonym is "coarse."

competitive dressage
As distinguished from classical dressage, competitive dressage is the style of riding that is seen at USDF and FEI shows. Competitive dressage does not include most of the airs above the ground.

competitive trail ride
A competition in which the object is to finish an overland course of up to fifty miles as close as possible to the predetermined time.

Compare to endurance, definition 1.

complete feed
A pelleted feed that contains all the roughage, concentrates, vitamins, and minerals that a horse needs to thrive. Theoretically, a horse may be fed only the complete feed, without any hay or grass. It is used for older horses with digestive problems, or horses with bad teeth, heaves, or hay allergies.

concentrates
Feeds such as grains, which provide a high level of nutrients in small amounts, as opposed to roughage, such as hay or grass.

concho
A round, usually silver, decoration on a piece of Western tack.

Concours Hippiques
(con-COR ee-PEEK)
French for "equestrian competitions," categories of national and international competitions conducted under Fédération Equestre Internationale (FEI) rules. They are designated as: **CN:** Concours National, or National Competition, an intramural event within a country. **CA:** Concors Amité, or Friendly Competition between two countries. **CI:** Concours International, for more than two countries. **CSI:** Concours International Officiel, with a Nations Cup. The above categories are further distinguished by the following letters at the end: S, for saute (jumping); D, for dressage; CC, for concours complet (eventing); and A, for attalage (driving).

condition
The degree of fitness of a horse. A thin or weak horse is in poor condition, while a well-fed and physically fit horse is in good condition. An obese horse, somewhat counterintuitively, is called overconditioned.

condition book
A list of upcoming races published by the racing secretary, together with the criteria for entering a race and other relevant information.

A decorative concho serving as the ring on a Western bit.
CREDIT: PHOTOS.COM

C

conditioning

The aerobic exercise of a horse to increase his fitness. Often done in preparation for eventing or endurance competitions, conditioning includes long sets of walk, trot, and canter, with short gallop sprints, sometimes while observing the horse's degree of effort with a heart rate monitor.

conditions

The qualifications or eligibility rules for a particular race, such as the horse's age, sex, or the number of previous wins.

cones

 See obstacles.

conformation

An individual horse's physical characteristics in relation to the ideal standards of the animal's breed or type, or compared to any well-made horse. A conformation class in a horse show judges the entries on such standards.

Jumping a coop.
© ED CAMELLI

conformation hunter

A horse show class in which the horse is judged on its conformation as well as performance over fences and on the flat.

conservative

Describes a veterinary treatment plan that is less invasive than another plan, such as surgery.

contact

The degree of rein pressure against the bit in the horse's mouth. Also,

the degree of closeness between the rider's seat and the saddle.

contracted heels

A condition in which the foot and frog become narrow at the heels, causing lameness. The problem may result from faulty trimming or shoeing of the foot and can be corrected with rest (during which time the foot heals) and proper shoeing.

cooler

A lightweight wool or fleece sheet worn by the horse after exercise to prevent catching a chill.

coop

A jumping obstacle with two sloping sides and a flat top, resembling a chicken coop.

Copenhagen

The Duke of Wellington's horse at the Battle of Waterloo. According to his rider, "There may have been many faster horses, no doubt many handsomer, but for bottom and endurance I never saw his fellow."

copper

A metal sometimes used in the mouthpieces of bits. The taste of copper is reputed to be appealing to horses and to encourage salivation and acceptance of the bit.

Corinthian

An obsolete term for an amateur sportsman. A Corinthian hunter class was an appointments class open only to members of recognized foxhunts.

corkscrew

A snaffle bit with a gently twisted mouthpiece.

corn

A cereal plant whose kernels are used for feed.

corns

An injury that develops when shoes are left on the horse's feet for too long, causing pressure because the foot's growth is restricted by the shoe. Corns happen most commonly on the insides of the front feet. Proper foot care will clear up the problem.

coronary band

The part of the foot that joins the hoof wall to the leg and from which the hoof wall grows.

 Compare to hoof.

coronet

A white marking around the coronary band.

corral

A pen, usually round in shape, used to hold or to train horses.

corrective shoeing

A farrier technique to correct foot and leg problems or other conformation flaws by means of specially shaped shoes. Corrective shoeing can help such problems as toeing in and toeing out.

cortisone

The colloquial term for corticosteroids, a class of powerful anti-inflammatory drugs. One common use of cortisone is intra-articular joint injections to treat arthritis, especially in the hocks.

cottonseed meal

The crushed seed of the cotton plant, used as a laxative and a source of protein.

counter-canter

To canter intentionally on the outside lead on a circle or bend, instead of the inside lead; a balancing and suppling exercise for the horse.

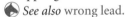 *See also* wrong lead.

count strides

In jumping, to determine how many horse's strides will fit comfortably between two fences. Because four 3-foot human strides equal one normal canter stride, riders before a jumping event will walk the course on foot and measure off the distances in terms of their own strides.

couple

A pair of foxhounds. *Couple* is the unit by which hounds are counted, so seven hounds would be described as three and a half couple. A young hound was often joined by a coupling leash to an older, better-behaved hound, which gave rise to counting in terms of pairs.

coupled entry

Two or more racehorses owned

Corkscrew bit.
© MILLER HARNESS COMPANY LLC

Lipizzaner performing a courbette.
© TEMPLE FARMS

Cow hocks.
© CHRISTINE BERUBE

or trained by the same person and running as a single wagering unit. Success by any horse in an entry will result in a payoff on that entry.

coupling
1 Term for the space between the last ribs and the loin. **2** A type of leash that keeps two hounds side by side.

courbette
The air above the ground in which the horse rears and then performs a series of hops on his hind legs. The word comes from the French for "crow."

course
1 In racing, the track on which the horses run. **2** In jumping, a series of obstacles in a given pattern over which the horse must jump.

courtesy circle
 *See* opening circle.

cover
The act of live breeding, as distinguished from artificial insemination.

covert (COV-ert)
In foxhunting, a thicket, den, or another likely place for hounds to find a fox.

cow
The colloquial term for a bovine other than a bull, whether it is a cow, heifer, steer, or calf.

cowboy
1 A ranch worker who may tend cows, horses, or other livestock, generally while on horseback. **2** A contestant in a rodeo. **3** A slang term for a trainer to whom problem horses are sent to be started or to have difficult training problems resolved.

cowboy mounted shooting
A Western sport similar to barrel racing, with balloons between each barrel. The rider carries a .45 caliber pistol loaded with powder blanks. The powder expelled by the blanks is capable of breaking a balloon at up to 15 feet. The object is to run the barrels while shooting each balloon. Scoring is based on accuracy and speed.

cow-hocked
A conformation fault in which the hocks bow inward and the feet are widely separated.

cowing
Term used to describe a cutting horse that is completely focused on the cow that the horse is working.

cow kick
To kick forward or sideways with the hind legs, as a cow does.

cow pony
Any horse regardless of size that is used in ranch work.

cow sense
The innate (some say inherited) ability of a horse to work cattle as

C

a cutting, roping, or reining horse, most often found in American Quarter Horses and other Western breeds. A horse with this talent seems to anticipate the cattle's every move. Often shortened to "cow."

cowy
Having good cow sense.

CPR
Shorthand for capillary refill test, pulse, and respiration, three exams conducted during a vet check.

Crabbet
The Crabbet Park Stud was an important Arabian breeding operation in England, run by Lady Anne Blunt and her husband, the poet Wilfrid Blunt, starting in 1878. Later maintained by Lady Anne's daughter Lady Wentworth, the stud produced a Crabbet line of small and hardy "desert" types that can be found in the bloodlines of most of the world's Arabian horses.

crack
A vertical split of the wall of the hoof, corrected by letting the foot grow out or with corrective shoeing.

cradle
A device, usually made of wood, that is put on the neck of the horse to prevent it from reaching around to bite or chew bandages or blankets on its body; similar in function to the "lampshade"

collars used on dogs following surgery.

crease
1 *v.* To shoot a horse across the poll in order to knock it unconscious. Creasing was a method used to capture wild mustangs, but often the horses were accidentally killed. **2** *n.* An indentation along the spine between two rolls of flesh, indicative of obesity.

creep feeder
A feed apparatus with bars that are wide enough to allow a foal to eat grain but too narrow to let an adult horse reach in and take the foal's meal.

crepitus
A distinctive crackling or crunching sound heard upon manipulation of a complete fracture.

crest
The upper part of the neck from the withers to the poll.

crest release
The hunter-seat equitation jumping technique in which the rider plants his hands on the horse's crest from takeoff to landing. The position supports the rider's upper body and keeps the hands from interfering with the horse's mouth.
🐎 *Compare to* out-of-hand release.

cresty
Having a pronounced crest, giving the appearance of an arched neck.

Crest.

Crest release.
CREDIT: S. D. PRICE

Stallions and obese horses both often feature a cresty neck.

cribbing

1 A stable vice in which the horse habitually chews or bites the edges of his stall or other solid object. The word is derived from "crib-biting." **2** Wind-sucking, when a horse aspirates and swallows air while biting an object. An acquired habit, it can often be controlled with a cribbing collar.

criollo

A breed found in Argentina, Brazil, and Peru that is descended from Spanish horses. Standing no taller than 15 hands and dun in color, the criollo has a short head and muscular shoulders. It is used for ranch and pack work.

crop

1 The group of foals sired by a stallion in a given season, or a group of foals owned by the same interest. **2** A short riding whip with a wrist loop at the handle end or the curved portion of a hunting whip.

cross-canter

A canter or lope where the horse's forelegs are on one lead and the hind legs are on the other lead. Allowing a horse to cross-canter is bad horsemanship. Also known as cross-firing or disunited canter.

cross-fire

🔘 *See* cross-canter.

crossing the line

In polo, a penalty in which a player crosses the imaginary line made by the flight of the ball. The reason for the rule is to prevent a collision when two or more players are in pursuit of the ball.

crossover

The act of forelegs or hind legs stepping over each other as the horse circles around his front or hind end, respectively. It is routinely seen in spins in reining classes and turns on the forehand or haunches in dressage and general schooling.

crossrail

A jump, usually low, that is composed of two rails that meet to form an X. Crossrails, which can be easily trotted as well as cantered, are most often used for training young horses and novice riders.

cross-tie

To secure a horse by two ropes, extending from opposite walls, to each side of the animal's halter. A horse that is cross-tied has its movement restricted and is thus easier to groom or otherwise handle.

croup

The rump from loin to dock.
🔘 *Compare to* loin.

croupade

An air above the ground in which the horse leaps off the ground and keeps his hind legs close to his

Crossrail.

body; a variation of the capriole.
🐴 *Compare to* ballotade.

crow-hop
Stiff-legged jump made while rounding the back; similar to bucking, but without kicking out the hind legs.

crownpiece
The part of a bridle that rests behind the horse's ears.

crupper
A leather strap that goes under the horse's tail to keep the harness or saddle from slipping forward.

cryptorchid (cryp-TOR-kid)
A male horse with one or two undescended testicles; also known as a ridgeling or rig.

cubbing
The early part of the foxhunting season during which young hounds are introduced into the pack. Cubbing usually begins in late summer and lasts until the beginning of the formal season, which generally starts in October. Riders wear far more informal clothing while cubbing than they do during the formal season. The name comes from efforts to induce fox cubs to leave their parents' den and establish residences of their own (so there will be a wider distribution of quarry around the countryside).

cue
The primarily Western term for a signal from the rider to the horse.
🐴 *See also* aid.

cuppy
In racing, a loose and dry track surface on which horses have difficulty getting good footing.

curb
1 A hard swelling or thickening of the ligament that runs along the hock. It is caused by strain and may or may not cause lameness; it may remain (become chronic) after the animal is rested. **2** One of the two main categories of bits (the other is snaffle). A curb bit's port, shanks, and curb chain or strap create a lever effect on the bars and roof of the horse's mouth, to which the animal reacts by arching its neck and/or stopping. The height and width of the port, the length of the shanks, and the tightness of the chain or strap determine the mildness or severity of the bit. Curbs are traditionally worn by Western horses, saddleseat horses, and upper-level dressage horses as part of a double bridle.

Curb bit with chain.
© MILLER HARNESS COMPANY LLC

curb chain (or strap)
A chain (or strap) worn along with a curb bit under the horse's jaw to increase the bit's leverage effect.

curb groove
The groove in the back of the horse's jaw, behind the lower lip, where a curb strap or chain rests.

curry
To clean a horse with a curry comb.

Curry comb.

Also, a general term for cleaning a horse's body, mane, and tail.

curry comb
1 A grooming tool with stubby, hard rubber bristles, used in a circular motion to remove caked dirt. **2** A metal tool with serrated teeth, used for cleaning bristled brushes.

Cushing's disease
A metabolic disorder common among horses over age twenty, caused by abnormal adrenal gland function. Common symptoms include a long, shaggy coat that does not shed out in the summer, excessive drinking and urination, loss of muscling over the topline and hips, recurring hoof abscesses, and laminitis.

cut
1 To separate a cow or calf from a herd. **2** Colloquially, to geld a male horse.

cut and set
To surgically alter the tailbone of a horse to achieve a higher tail carriage. Sometimes performed on fine harness horses such as Saddlebreds and hackneys.

cutback saddle
1 A saddle that has a recess in the pommel to allow for prominent withers. Dressage and saddleseat saddles often have this feature. **2** A long, flat saddle designed to place the rider's weight over the horse's loins, widely used in gaited horse show divisions.

A cutting horse at work.
© D. R. STOECKLEIN/AMERICAN QUARTER HORSE ASSOCIATION

cutter
1 The rider in a cutting horse event. **2** The driver in cutter and chariot racing.

cutting
A Western horse show class or event in which a horse separates (or cuts) a cow from the herd and then prevents it from returning to the herd. Once the rider indicates to the horse which cow is to be worked, the rider is not permitted to guide the horse. The horse stays between the cow and the herd, blocking the cow's efforts to get back to the herd by moving its body in almost a mirror image to the cow's. The cut ends when either the cow manages to slip past the horse or it is evident that the cow cannot return to the others. Horses, which have two minutes to perform, are judged on their agility and success, with the degree of difficulty of the cow also taken into account. Since certain strains of American Quarter Horses and other Western breeds excel at cutting, the ability is thought to be inherited.
See also alligator; cowing; leak; peel; shape; sour; turnback.

Dally team roping.
© WYATT MCSPADDEN/
AMERICAN QUARTER HORSE ASSOCIATION

D ring

1 A snaffle bit that has rings shaped like the letter D. The purpose is to restrict the amount the rings can turn, which would diminish some of the effect of the reins. **2** The D-shaped rings on a saddle to which a breastcollar or latigo is laced or buckled.

daily dewormer

A pelleted, palatable dewormer that is fed daily along with the horse's feed to prevent intestinal worms.

daisy cutter

An expression for a horse that has a long, low stride.

daisy reins

🔊 *See* antigrazing reins.

Dales

A breed of pony native to the north of England. It was developed in the 18th and 19th centuries as a pack pony. Its strong shoulders and legs make the Dales pony good for riding and driving.

dally

To wrap a lariat rope around the saddle horn after a steer or calf has been roped. The word comes from the Spanish phrase *dar la vuelta,* to make a turn (of the rope).

dally team roping

A Western horse show event in which the horse is judged on its ability to maintain its position relative to the calf as the mount of either the header or the heeler in team roping. In the rodeo event called *team roping*, the fastest time for a pair of riders to rope a steer's head and hind legs determines the winner.

dam

A horse's female parent, or a broodmare.

damsire

A horse's maternal grandfather.

dangerous riding

In polo, a foul committed by a player who rides in a manner that puts other players at risk; for example, by zigzagging up or down the field.

dapple gray
A light gray body speckled with rings of a darker gray. The rings themselves are called dapples.

dandy brush
A brush with stiff bristles used to remove dried mud or dirt from the horse's coat.

dark horse
A horse that wins a race unexpectedly.

Darley Arab
Along with the Byerly Turk and Godolphin Barb, one of the three Thoroughbred foundation sires. Foaled around 1702 and imported to England from the Middle East by a Mr. Darley, the horse was the most important sire of the three in terms of the number of successful racers who sprang from his line.

Dartmoor
A breed of pony native to the Dartmoor Forest in the west of England. Like other native British breeds, it stands between 12 and 13 hands. The Dartmoor has a long, low, comfortable stride, and, because of its Arabian and Thoroughbred blood, is one of the more refined of the native pony breeds.

Dash For Cash
An American Quarter Horse racehorse and an influential sire, named Quarter Horse racing's Racing World Champion in 1976 and 1977, Superior Racehorse in 1976; set two track records.

He won 21 of 25 starts from 1975 through 1978, including nine stakes races. His 1,353 offspring have won in excess of $37 million and include 39 World Champions.

Davidson, Bruce
Five-time Olympic veteran, Davidson has been the U. S. Combined Training Association's (USCTA) "Rider of the Year" a record 14 times. A member of two gold medal Olympic squads, at Montreal in 1976 and Los Angeles in 1984, he was the first American to win a gold medal at the World Three-Day Event Championship in 1974, a victory that he repeated in 1978.

dawn horse
The earliest known prehistoric ancestor of the modern horse; eohippus.

daylight
In tie-down roping, to allow the calf to get up before throwing it down and beginning the tie. A calf that was jerked down by the thrown rope and remains on the ground when the roper reaches it must be daylighted.

dead heat
In racing, two or more horses crossing the finish line simultaneously or too close to tell which one finished ahead of the other or others (there have been examples of triple dead heats). All horses involved in a dead heat are considered as tied for that position.

A dapple gray horse.
CREDIT: PHOTOS.COM

Dartmoor mare and foal.
© CYNTHIA BRANN

Bruce Davidson on Irish Cap.
COURTESY OF THE U.S. EQUESTRIAN TEAM

D

dead weight

In racing, the difference between the amount of weight the horse is assigned to carry and the weight of the jockey. Any difference will be carried as lead bars in the saddle pad, hence the term *dead weight* (as opposed to the rider's live weight).

deciduous teeth

The temporary teeth of a foal, which will fall out and be replaced by permanent teeth; milk teeth.

declaration

Withdrawing an entered horse from a race before the closing of overnight entries.

 See also scratch.

deep

1 In jumping, a takeoff point that is too close to the jump, making the jumping effort awkward for the horse and uncomfortable for the rider. Another term is *tight*. The opposite is *long*. **2** In dressage, a position in which the horse is deliberately ridden with its neck flexed and lowered and the head often behind the vertical. Sometimes used as a warm-up to stretch the back. Also called "round and down."

deep digital flexor tendon

(DDFT)
The tendon that connects the large muscle at the back of the forearm or gaskin to the coffin bone in the hoof. During an episode of acute laminitis, the DDFT may cause the coffin bone to rotate, since the weakened laminae of the hoof cannot counteract its action.

dee ring

 *See* D ring.

defended penalty shot

In polo, a penalty shot which the opposing team may try to block.

 *Compare to* undefended penalty shot.

degenerative joint disease

(DJD)
Chronic and progressive joint damage involving the cartilage and the joint capsule.

De Gogue

Pronounced to rhyme with "rogue," a device used to encourage the horse to flex its head and neck during exercise. For longeing, the cords of the De Gogue attached to the girth, travel up between the front legs and through the bit rings, and connect at the poll. For ridden work, the cords go from the girth through the front legs, up to a pulley at the poll, then down through the bit rings and back to the rider's hands.

den

In foxhunting, a fox's underground lair.

Denhardt, Robert M.

An influential scholar of Quarter Horse characteristics, Denhardt was largely responsible for the formation of the American Quarter Horse Association in 1940, as well as the association's breed registry.

De Gogue.

D

denier

The thread count of fabric. Most often used to describe the outer layer of a horse blanket. A blanket with a higher denier is generally tougher and more resistant to tears.

dental star

The darker dentin that fills a tooth's pulp cavity as the tooth wears down.

depraved appetite

A condition in which the horse compulsively eats something that is not food; for example, wood-chewing and coprophagy (dung-eating).

derby
(DUR-bee in America; DAR-bee in Britain)
1 A hat with a rounded crown and small brim, worn on formal occasions by some foxhunters, dressage riders, and gaited horse riders. **2** Capitalized, any of the classic races for three-year-old Thoroughbreds such as the Kentucky Derby and the Epsom Derby. Like the hat, the race was named for the 12th Earl of Derby, who owned a horse that won the first English Derby.
🦅 *See also* Jumping Derby.

dermatitis

Inflammation or irritation of the skin.

desensitize

As a training technique, to repeat a stimulus, such as a loud sound, over and over until the horse be-

comes accustomed to it and no longer shows a reaction.

desert-bred

An Arabian horse that was born in the Middle Eastern or "Arabian" desert. All horses accepted by the Arabian Horse Association registry must be able to trace their ancestry back to a desert-bred mare.

destrier

A warhorse. The word comes from the Latin for "right," which was the side on which a knight's squire would lead the horse.

destroy

To kill or euthanize (a horse).

dewormer (dee-WORMER)

Oral medication that rids the horse of parasites. The word is used interchangeably with *wormer*.

diagonal

1 Refers to the trot, when the horse's foreleg moves in unison with the opposite hind leg. **2** The rider's posting motion in relation to the horse's trotting steps. When the horse is moving counterclockwise, a rider who rises when the horse's left foreleg and right hind leg strike the ground is posting on the left diagonal. The theory is to lift the rider's weight to free the outside hind leg when the horse is moving in a circle, because that leg provides more of the impulsion. **3** In a riding arena, the distance from one corner to the far opposite corner. Using dressage

Desensitizing a horse.
CREDIT: TOM MOATES

letters, the diagonals are H-K or M-F. The short diagonal is the distance from the midpoint of one long side of the arena to the corner on the opposite side of the arena (E-M, E-F, B-K, or B-F).

digital pulse
The pulse that can be felt in the digital arteries, which run along the backs of the fetlocks. A strong digital pulse is a sign of problems in the hoof, such as an abscess or laminitis.

direct rein
Rein pressure created by the rider's hand being drawn back toward the hip on that side of the horse. The direct rein is the primary way to control speed and direction.
🔹 *See also* indirect rein; neck rein; opening rein.

Turning left using direct rein.
© RICHARD KLIMESH

discipline
1 *v.* To punish. **2** *n.* Any category of equestrian sport; dressage, reining, barrel racing, and show jumping are all examples of disciplines.

dish-faced
Having a concave profile, typical of Arabian horses.

dishing
A gait abnormality in which the horse's hooves swing in an inward arc during each stride, rather than traveling straight; winging in.
🔹 *Compare to* paddling.

disqualification
Removal of a competitor from a show class due to an infraction of the rules.

distaff
A racing term for fillies and mares. A distaff was a spindle used in weaving, considered a task for females.

distance
In jumping, the place from which the horse leaves the ground in relation to the fence's location. Seeing a distance refers to the rider's sensing, in terms of number of strides, where the horse is in relation to the fence. Experienced riders can then shorten or lengthen the horse's stride, if need be, in order to arrive at an optimum takeoff point.
🔹 *See also* deep; long.

distemper
🔹 *See* strangles.

disunited
🔹 *See* cross canter.

division
Any of the major horse show categories. Examples are the hunter division, the conformation division, and the reining division.

DMSO
Dimethyl sulfoxide, a topical anti-inflammatory agent absorbed into the horse's system through the skin, used to administer medication.

Doc Bar
The American Quarter Horse sire

best known for producing sleek and responsive sons and daughters that revolutionized the sport of cutting. In addition, his 485 foals, including 27 AQHA Champions, have won more than 7,000 halter and performance points.

dock
1 *n.* The fleshy root of the tail.
2 *v.* To cut the tail at or above the dock, originally done to carriage horses so their tails would not become entangled in the harness or blow into the driver's face.

Doctor Bristol
A variety of snaffle bit with a double-jointed mouthpiece. The midsection produces pressure on the horse's tongue, while the other two pieces work against the bars of the mouth. Differs from a French link in that the middle section is a flattened plate, the edge of which can press sharply into the tongue.

dog
1 In foxhunting, a pack member of any breed other than foxhound; or a male hound. **2** In racing, one of the rubber cones placed out from the track's rail during training sessions in wet weather to prevent hooves from digging up the inside part of the racing strip.

dog-bone snaffle
The Western term for a double-jointed bit that has a center link shaped somewhat like a dog bone. The similar English bit would be called a French link.

dog cart
A light, open, two-wheeled horse-drawn cart with two back-to-back seats.

doma vaquera
A style of horsemanship that originated in Spain on working cattle farms and is now a performance art. Movements include collected gaits, flying changes of lead, counter-canter, spins, rollbacks, half pass, full pass, turn on the haunches, and turn on the forehand. Andalusians are the traditional breed trained in doma vaquera.
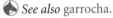 *See also* garrocha.

donkey
Another name for domestic ass.

dope
To illegally drug a horse to enhance its performance in a race or show.

Dorrance, Bill
Widely acknowledged to be the most important figure of "natural horsemanship," Dorrance stressed a resistance-free approach to gentling horses in an era where "breaking" them was prevalent. In the latter half of the 20th century he and his brother Tom were the mentors of many of the current generation of such trainers, including Ray Hunt and Buck Brannaman.

dorsal
A directional indicator that refers to the upper side.
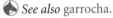 *Compare to* ventral.

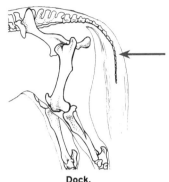
Dock.
© CHRISTINA BERUBE

Doctor Bristol bit.
© MILLER HARNESS COMPANY LLC

D

dorsal stripe

A black or dark stripe that runs along the spine from withers to tail in certain colors or breeds of horse, such as duns and Fjords.

double

1 *n.* In show jumping, a combination of two jumps in a row.

 See also triple.

2 *v.* To pull a horse's head all the way around to one side in order to stop it from bolting.

 See also one-rein stop.

double bridle

An English bridle designed to hold two separate bits in the horse's mouth. The bridle has two crownpieces that pass through the loops of the browband and attach to two separate sets of cheekpieces. One set holds the bridoon bit, while the other holds the curb bit (Weymouth), which lies in the mouth directly below the bridoon. The actions of the bridoon and the Weymouth are controlled through separate sets of reins, permitting the rider a large reining vocabulary for communicating with the horse. Most commonly seen in upper-level dressage and in saddleseat riding. Also known as a full bridle or Weymouth.

Double bridle.
CREDIT: AUDREY L.D. PETSCHEK

double clear

1 In a two-round show-jumping competition, incurring no faults in both rounds. **2** In competitive driving, no time or knockdown penalties in the cones phase.

double-jointed snaffle

A snaffle bit whose mouthpiece has two joints instead of the customary one.

double judged

A class or show in which the entries are evaluated by two judges.

double-rigged

Of a Western saddle, having two cinches.

doughnut

Name for a shoe boil boot.

down

1 The direction toward the ring or arena's gate. To jump down a line (of fences) is to start with the fence farthest away from the gate and head toward the jump closest to the gate. **2** Physically unable to rise. Because a horse's respiratory and digestive systems are designed to function while the horse is standing, a horseman's saying is "a down horse is a dead horse."

 Compare to up.

downhill

1 A conformational type in which the croup is higher than the withers and the stifle is higher than the elbow. Horses that are built downhill have a harder time collecting. A downhill build is undesirable in a dressage horse or a jumper, but is less of a disadvantage in the Western disciplines. **2** Moving on the forehand.

draft breeds

Any of the breeds of large horses used for heavy pulling, such as the Percheron, Clydesdale, and Shire. Descendants of the Flemish Great Horse, all were developed in regions that had abundant and nutritious pasturage that enhanced growth and size. Also known as cold bloods.

drag

1 To bring up the rear of a herd of cattle while moving or driving them. **2** To smooth the surface of an arena before or between rounds of a competition. **3** In driving, a four-wheeled coach with seats on top of and inside the vehicle.

drag hunt

A foxhunt in which the hounds follow an artificial scent that is laid down across the countryside before the hunt begins.

draw

1 The horse's position in a horse show event's starting order or a horse race's post positions. For example, "The favorite drew the eighth post position." The word comes from the positions being randomly chosen by drawing numbers out of a box. **2** In fox-hunting, to search for a fox in a particular area, as in drawing a covert.

 See also covert.

drawing

Describes a poultice or other medication that tends to reduce inflammation.

draw reins

A training device consisting of a pair of reins that passes from the horse's girth either between the forelegs or from each side just below the saddle, and through the bit rings back to the rider's hands. Draw reins are used to encourage a horse to flex its head and neck.

Dreamfinder

As a yearling, this phenomenal Appaloosa stallion won the 1985 grand champion stallion titles at both the National and World Championship Appaloosa shows. His record as a sire of halter and performance winners includes 518 foals who earned more than 17,500 show points, 287 registers of merit, 126 bronze medallions, one bronze superior achievement certificate, and 12 silver medallions.

drench

To give (a horse) liquid medication.

dressage (druh-SAHZE)

Schooling a horse according to principles based on progressive stages of the Training Scale (the idea is that each stage leads out of the preceding stage). The word comes from the French for "train-ing." As a competition sport, horses and riders perform a test of stipu-lated sequences of movements and transitions. Levels of tests range from elementary patterns of walk-ing, trotting, and cantering to

A dressage horse performing an extended trot.
CREDIT: C. MARTIN

D

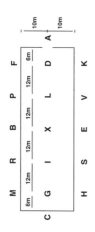

Diagram of dressage letters.

Dressage saddle.

Driving a young horse.

the most advanced tests, which include piaffe, passage, and flying changes of lead. Each movement and transition is scored from zero (not performed) to ten (perfect). The total, plus additional points for regularity of gait, impulsion, rider position, and other factors, determines the entry's score.

🐎 *See also* classical dressage.

dressage letters

A series of letters arranged around the perimeter of a dressage arena, used to indicate where each movement is to be performed during a dressage test. Clockwise around the arena beginning with the In gate, the standard letters are A, K, E, H, C, M, B, F. The "imaginary" letter at the exact center of the arena is X. Less frequently used are the letters D, L, I, and G, which refer to locations along the centerline from A to X to C, as well as the additional letters R, P, V, and S around the outside of the arena (see diagram). Many other disciplines now take advantage of the dressage-letter concept during training and instruction.

dressage saddle

A saddle with a deep seat and long, relatively straight flaps, to allow a long stirrup and steady seat.

dressage whip

A long, thin whip a maximum of 42.3 inches. Its length permits the rider to use it to reinforce leg aids without having to remove the whip hand from the rein.

dress boots

Knee-high, plain-front boots worn in English riding, especially in dressage competition.

🐎 *Compare to* field boots.

drill and tap

The means by which horseshoes are prepared to accept studs or caulks.

driver

In harness racing, the person in the sulky.

driving

1 Directing the speed and direction of a horse pulling a cart or another vehicle by a person in the vehicle being pulled. **2** A method of controlling a horse by means of long reins held by a person who walks behind the horse; the technique is used to train a young horse that has not yet been ridden or a horse that will pull a vehicle; also called long lining. **3** Pushing or directing the movement of a herd of cows or other livestock from horseback. **4** In racing, winning with effort.

driving aids

The combination of a rider's seat and legs that encourages a horse to move forward.

drop a shoulder

An evasion in which the horse falls onto his forehand and drops his inside shoulder, unbalancing the rider. A horse may drop a shoulder to avoid a correct bend or to run out at a jump.

D

dropdown

In racing, a horse that is facing a lower class of competition than encountered in its previous race.

drop fence

A cross-country obstacle, the landing side of which is lower than the takeoff side.

dropped noseband

A noseband that fastens low around the horse's jaw, in front of the bit, to keep the animal's mouth closed so the bit can have greater effect. Also known as a hinged noseband or a hinged dropped cavesson.

dry work

The opening reining phase in a working cow horse class. The dry work is followed by the fence work.

duck

Of a jumping rider, the error of dropping the head and upper body on one side of the horse's neck while in the air. Besides looking awkward, this sudden movement disturbs the horse's balance and may lead to the animal's hitting the fence.

dude

A paying visitor at a guest ranch. The word means a fancily dressed man, so applied because guests often appear in brand-new Western wear.

dun

A horse's coat color that comprises a yellowish or gold body with black or brown legs and tail, a dark dorsal stripe running the length of the spine, and often stripes on the legs and over the withers.

Dutch door

A door that is divided in half horizontally, such that the top can be open while the bottom is closed, or vice versa. The top may be left open to allow ventilation or to allow a horse to see out, or the bottom half may be left open to allow a foal to go into the stall to rest or eat while the mare stays outside.

Dutch Warmblood

A breed native to the Netherlands, originated by crossing Thoroughbreds and European warmblood types with native horses. Strong and athletic, Dutch Warmbloods are used as dressage and show-jumping horses.

dwell

1 Term used to describe a jumping horse that gives the impression of hanging in the air over a fence, usually due to a lack of impulsion, or hesitancy about leaving the ground or landing. **2** In foxhunting, a hound that shows a lack of enthusiasm or drive is said to dwell.

dystocia

Difficulty in foaling, including abnormal presentation.

Drop fence.

Dutch door.
CREDIT: PHOTOS.COM

D

early foot
In racing, showing speed in the early stages of a race.

earth
In foxhunting, a den, especially one in which a pursued fox seeks refuge.

earthbound
A term for a horse that lacks suspension in his gaits; an undesirable quality in a dressage horse.

ease
In racing, to pull up a horse gradually, either because the jockey thinks the horse has no chance to improve its position or because the animal has an injury.

eastern equine encephalomyelitis (EEE)
A very contagious and usually fatal viral infection that affects the horse's brain and spinal cord. Spread by mosquitoes, EEE can be prevented by annual vaccinations.

easy
A verbal command used to ask a horse to settle or to slow down, but without changing gait; as opposed to "whoa," used to ask a horse to halt.

Eclipse
The most outstanding racehorse of his era, Eclipse was foaled in 1764, the year of a total eclipse of the sun. He won 18 races without showing any effort. Owners were reluctant to compete their horses against him, so that eight of his races were walkovers.

Eclipse Awards
Year-end honors given to outstanding horses, jockeys, owners, and others involved in Thoroughbred racing. The award is named after the legendary 18th-century English racehorse.

egg-bar shoe
 See bar shoe.

eggbutt snaffle
A snaffle bit with a fixed joint between the mouthpiece and the oval-shaped rings. The shape of the rings holds the reins in a more direct line with the rider's hands (as opposed to round rings, which

Eggbutt snaffle.
© MILLER HARNESS COMPANY LLC

Elevated poles.
CREDIT: J. SHIERS

let the reins slide around on them more easily). The fixed joint prevents the mouthpiece from sliding on the rings, as in a loose-ring bit, providing a steadier feel in the horse's mouth.

elbow
The joint connecting the foreleg to the bones of the shoulder.

electrolytes
Trace minerals and salts, including sodium, potassium, calcium, and magnesium, that are required for various physiological processes and are especially associated with the absorption of water. Horses can become deficient in electrolytes after prolonged exercise. Electrolytes can be provided to the horse either in the form of a powdered supplement or in a concentrated paste, or "jug." In extreme cases of dehydration, a veterinarian may administer electrolytes intravenously or subcutaneously.

element
In jumping, one of the components of an obstacle or combination, such as the top rail of a fence or the second jump in a double combination.

elevated poles
Ground poles that are lifted a few inches off the ground at one or both ends, to encourage the horse to step higher as he crosses the poles.

Elevator bit.
© MILLER HARNESS COMPANY LLC

elevator bit
A variety of snaffle bit with a series of rings or a long bar on the sides. The reins can be attached to any of the rings, so the bit offers options: the lower the reins are attached, the greater the degree of leverage, for increased flexion and control.

elimination
The involuntary end of competition for an entry that has exceeded a certain standard: for example, in show jumping, incurring more than two refusals or going off course.

emasculator
The implement used for castration.

embryo transplant
(or transfer)
The reproduction procedure in which an embryo is removed from its mother and implanted into the womb of a second (the so-called carrier or surrogate) mare to be carried to term. The purpose is to allow the original mother to be bred again or to continue a competitive career uninterrupted by pregnancy.

endoscope
A veterinary diagnostic procedure in which a small videocamera with a light is sent into the stomach through a nasogastric tube. The camera visually records problems such as obstructions or ulcers. Frequently referred to as a scope.

endurance
1 A type of long-distance competition in which speed as well as

the condition of the horse at the end of the ride are considered (as distinguished from a competitive trail ride). Any breed of horse may compete, but the preferred breed is the Arabian. **2** The ability to withstand exercise for an extended period of time without becoming fatigued.

See also speed and endurance.

endurance day
The second day of a three-day event. In the long or classic format, endurance day consists of four phases: A and C, roads and tracks; B, steeplechase; and D, cross-country. In the short format, only phase D is included.

engaged
Describes a horse that is on the aids and moving with impulsion.

engagement
The action of the horse's hind legs that propels the animal with impulsion; also known as engagement of the hocks.

English
Referring to any of the riding styles that involve a flat, hornless saddle, as distinguished from Western riding. Also, the equipment used in this style. Although the techniques are European in origin and not just British, the name came from the style's association with the predominant style along the eastern seaboard, especially with regard to foxhunting tack. That

is why the style is sometimes referred to as Eastern riding. The English disciplines include dressage, hunt seat, show jumping, and eventing.

enter
1 To enroll a horse in a race, horse show, rodeo, or other competition. **2** In foxhunting, to start using a hound for hunting, to enter into a pack.

enterolith
A large mass that develops around a foreign object in the intestines. Enteroliths can grow to become very large and cause a painful form of colic that may seem to come and go as the enterolith moves around in the intestines. Surgery is required to remove the object.

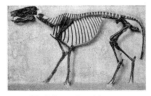

Skeleton of eohippus.

entire
A male horse that has not been gelded; a stallion.

entry
In racing, two or more horses in the same race that have common ties of ownership, leasing, or training.

See also coupled entry.

entry fee
Money paid to enroll a horse in a competition.

eohippus
The earliest true equine, appearing during the Eocene era 55 million years ago. The size of a small dog,

eohippus had four toes on each forefoot and three toes on the back feet (the toes evolved into a single hoof). The word is Latin for "dawn horse."

epiphyseal plates
Growth plates.

EPM
See equine protozoal myelo-encephalitis.

Epsom salts
A coarse-grained salt that may be dissolved in water and used as a drawing agent, such as for soaking an abscessed hoof.

equestrian
1 *n.* A term for a rider or horse-man. 2 *adj.* A term relating to horses or riding.

equine
Any of the species of the family Equidae and genus Equus, in-cluding *Equus caballus* (horse), *Equus asinus* (ass), *Equus burchelli* (common zebra), or *Equus grevyi* (Grevy's zebra), as well as hybrids such as the mule, hinney, or zorse.

equine-assisted psychotherapy
A form of psychological treatment for humans that involves interact-ing with horses in order to achieve self-development.

equine herpes virus (EHV)
A highly contagious and often fatal disease that, under various condi-tions, causes respiratory infection, abortion in pregnant mares, or neurologic disorders.

equine infectious anemia (EIA)
A circulatory disease, also known as swamp fever, caused by bac-teria and producing a decrease in red blood cells that weakens a horse with the disease. There is no known treatment or cure for EIA, which is detected by the Coggins test.

equine polysaccharide storage myopathy (EPSM)
A muscle disorder, most common among draft horses, in which the muscle cells do not properly metabolize carbohydrates. Symp-toms include loss of muscle tone, hind-end weakness, stiffness, and, in severe cases, "shivers" or tying up. Treatment involves feeding a diet low in carbohydrates and high in fat.

equine protozoal myeloencephalitis (EPM)
A noncontagious disease of the central nervous system that causes ataxia, sometimes to the point of inability to walk or stand. The organism responsible for EPM is carried by opossums.

equitation
1 The discipline of horseback rid-ing. 2 A horse show class in which the form and control of the rider are judged, as opposed to the horse being judged. Equitation

classes may be ridden on the flat or over fences.

ergot
A harmless thick callus growth at the back of the fetlock joint. Believed to be a vestigial toe.

 See also chestnut.

ermine marks
Small black markings that often appear on the coronet band.

esophagus
The alimentary canal from the mouth to the stomach.

 Compare to trachea.

estrus
The period during which a mare is sexually receptive; at that time the mare is said to be "in season" or "in heat." The estrus cycle relates to the amount of daylight, increasing during spring and summer months and decreasing during autumn and winter. The length of the cycle averages three weeks, with estrus lasting approximately one week.

ethology
The study of animal behavior.

euthanasia
The killing of an animal in a humane manner, usually by means of a fast-acting drug such as sodium pentobarbital injected intravenously.

evasion
A strategy used by a horse to avoid obedience to its rider.

even money
In racing, odds at which successful bettors receive back as much as they have wagered. Even-money odds are indicated as 1:1 and indicates the betting favorite.

eventing
Formerly known as combined training, eventing is the sport in which the same horse-and-rider combination competes in dressage, speed and endurance (also called cross-country), and stadium jumping. A competition is called a horse trial when it takes place over one or two days, and is called a three-day event if the dressage, cross-country, and stadium jumping take place in that order on successive days. Combined training and eventing was known as the *military* because of the sport's cavalry origins; up until World War II, only cavalry officers took part in Olympic three-day eventing, even though the sport had been one of the equestrian Olympic sports since 1912.

ewe-necked
A conformation fault in which the topline of the neck curves downward, with a greater muscle mass on the underside than along the crest; "upside-down neck."

exacta
In racing, a type of wager in which the horses that finish first and second must be selected in that order; also known as perfecta.

E

exercise rider
In racing, a person who is licensed to gallop horses during morning workout training sessions.

exhibitor
A participant in a horse show.

Exmoor
A breed of pony native to the Exmoor moorlands in the west of England. The oldest of the native British pony breeds, the hardy Exmoor measures only some 12 hands, but is strong enough to carry an adult rider.

exsanguination
Massive blood loss resulting in death.

extend
To increase the length of the horse's stride, accomplished by the rider's increasing the driving aids and relaxing rein pressure.
🜂 *Compare to* collect; *see also* move up.

extruded feed
A type of concentrated feed made by a process of pressure-cooking various ingredients and shaping them into pellets.

E

A farrier shaping a horse's hoof with a rasp.
CREDIT: TOM MOATES

Falabella
 See Miniature Horse.

farrier
A person who shoes horses; also known as horse shoer or blacksmith; from *fer,* the French word for "iron."

fast
In racing, a track surface that is dry and even; the optimum condition for a dirt tack (the turf equivalent is firm).

fault
1 The unit of penalties in jumper classes for knocking down or refusing to jump an obstacle, or for exceeding the time limit. Each knockdown counts as four faults. The first refusal counts as four faults; the second results in elimination. **2** A flaw or blemish in a horse's conformation. Conformation faults occur in degrees: some can be so severe they affect the animal's way of going, while other less severe faults are simply cosmetically unattractive.

feather
In foxhunting, when a hound wags its tail in excitement at the sight or scent of a fox. The word presumably comes from the image of a waving plume.

feathers
The long hairs on the fetlocks of certain draft breeds and ponies.

fecal egg count
The veterinary analysis of a horse's feces to determine the population levels of various intestinal parasites by counting their eggs.

Fédération Equestre Internationale (FEI)
The international governing body of officially recognized horse sports competitions, including the Olympics; located in Lausanne, Switzerland.

feed bag
A fabric container that holds grain or pellets. It fits over the horse's muzzle and is used for feeding when the horse is not in his stall.

feelers
The long, whiskerlike hairs around the eyes.

FEI

 *See* Fédération Equestre Internationale.

FEI-level

1 A horse or rider that competes internationally. **2** In dressage, the levels above Fourth Level: Prix St. Georges, Intermediare I, Intermediare II, and Grand Prix. **3** In eventing, CCI or CIC events.

Fell

A breed of pony native to the northwest of England. Influenced by the Friesian horse, this sturdy, predominantly black pony stands approximately 14 hands and is equally adept at being ridden or driven.

fenbendazole

A dewormer effective against tapeworms, whipworms, roundworms, and hookworms. Brand name is Panacur.

fence

An obstacle for a horse to jump, which may be natural or man-made.

fence judge

In the cross-country phase of eventing, a person who stands near one of the jumps to watch each competitor and note whether they negotiated the jump successfully or not. Fence judges are often volunteers.

fence work

The second phase of the working cow horse class, in which the horse maneuvers the cow down the long side of the arena, then into the center where the cow is made to turn in both directions. The horse must be able to work close to the cow to influence the cow's movements and not let the cow escape.

See also dry work.

fender

The wide panel between the seat and stirrup of a Western saddle. It protects the rider's leg from rubbing against the horse's side.

feral

Describes an animal of domestic heritage that has become wild. American mustangs are technically feral horses, not wild horses, since they are descended from domestic animals that belonged to settlers.

fescue

A variety of hay grass. An endophyte fungus, toxic to some horses, can infect fescue, leading to problems with pregnancy, including abortion, in some mares, as well as lethargy in geldings.

fetlock

The joint between the pastern and the cannon bones.

fever rings

Horizontal bands visible on a horse's hooves that are indicative of stress. Fever rings may be caused by fever, founder, or a sudden change in diet. Also called founder rings.

Turning a cow during fence work.
© WYATT MCSPADDEN/
AMERICAN QUARTER HORSE ASSOCIATION

Fender.

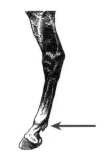

Fetlock.

F

The fiador is the white rope visible behind the bosal.
© CHERRY HILL

Field boot.

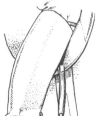

Fillis stirrup.

fewspot
Describes the coat pattern of an Appaloosa that is almost entirely white or solid-colored, with only a few spots. An Appaloosa with no spots is described as a no-spot or solid Appaloosa.

fiador (FEE-a-dor; sometimes THEE-a-dore)
The part of some hackamores that goes over the horse's poll and knots behind the jaw to keep the bosal in place.

field
In foxhunting, the collective term for riders (other than the hunt staff) who follow the hounds.

field boots
Knee-high riding boots with laced ankles; traditionally worn in hunt-seat shows.

field hunter
A horse that is used for foxhunting, as distinguished from a show hunter.

field master
In foxhunting, the member of the hunt staff who is responsible for leading the field, especially with regard to keeping the field from riding too close to and interfering with the hounds.

fifth leg
The ability of certain horses to extricate themselves and their riders from a bad approach to a jump.

fifth-wheel hitch
On a towing vehicle, a fifth-wheel hitch is the system of rails and hitch ball in the bed of the truck that allow a gooseneck trailer to be attached.

figure eight
1 A type of noseband made of two pieces that cross over the horse's nose and buckle behind the bit rings. It is especially effective in keeping the horse's mouth closed, and thus increasing the bit's influence, without impeding the horse's breathing. **2** An arena pattern comprised of two circles joined at a common point. One circle is ridden clockwise, the other counterclockwise.

filled
Term meaning *swollen*; said of the tendons in the lower legs.

Fillis stirrup
An English-style stirrup with slightly rounded sides. The most widely used style today, it was invented by James Fillis (1834–1913), English circus rider, trainer, and author.

filly
A female horse under the age of four and that has not had a foal (if she has foaled, the horse is called a mare, no matter what her age).

find
In foxhunting, when hounds first pick up the fox's scent.

Fine Harness
A horse show division for three-gaited Saddlebreds that pull a light, four-wheeled vehicle. The horse is judged on its action, elegance, and manners.

finishing brush
A grooming tool with relatively soft bristles, used to put a final sheen on the horse's brushed coat.

firing
🔹 *See* pin firing.

firm
In racing, a turf surface having solid, compact footing; the turf equivalent of a dirt track's *fast*.

First Level
In dressage, the level above Training Level, in which the horse demonstrates balance and throughness. Test movements include serpentines, 10- and 15-meter circles, lengthenings, leg yields, simple changes of lead, and counter-canter.

first-year green
A show hunter that is in its first year of showing in the hunter division. Fences in these classes are set at 3 feet 3 inches.

fistulous withers
A deep infection at the withers due to a break in the skin that has become contaminated with bacteria. Treatment involves cleaning the wound so it can heal properly and treating the infection with antibiotics.

fit
In excellent physical condition.

fittings
Term for saddle accessories, such as the girth, stirrups, and leathers.

five-gaited
Describes American Saddlebreds able to move at the walk, trot, canter, slow gait, and rack.
🔹 *Compare to* three-gaited.

fixture card
In foxhunting, the list of locations where hunts will start out throughout the season. Fixture cards are distributed at the beginning of the hunting year.

Fjord pony
A breed of pony native to Norway. Invariably dun in color, with its mane trimmed to stand upright, the Fjord pony is noted for its compact shape and rugged constitution. It is used for both riding and driving.

flag
1 *n.* A training device consisting of a piece of material, such as a scrap of cloth or a plastic bag, attached to the end of a whip or stick. The trainer, usually unmounted, uses the sight and sound of the flag to induce the horse to move away. **2** *v.* To elevate the tail. Flagging can indicate excitement, or, in a mare, a readiness to breed.

F

Flak jacket.

Flank.

Flash noseband.
© CHERRY HILL

flagman
In polo, an appointed semi-official who signals when a goal has been scored by waving a flag above his head, or when a goal has not been scored by waving the flag toward the ground.

flake
A section of baled hay, usually measuring from eight to twelve inches wide.

flak jacket
The familiar term for the protective safety vest worn by jockeys, combined training riders during the cross-country phase, and many other riders.

flank
The area of the horse's body between the ribs and the hip.

flap
The panel on an English saddle that covers the billets and protects the rider's leg from being rubbed by them.

flare
The quality of a hoof that spreads out somewhat sideways as it grows, rather than growing vertically.

flash noseband
A standard cavesson noseband with the addition of a strap attached to the bottom of the noseband that fastens around the muzzle in front of the bit. The strap encourages the horse to keep his mouth closed and holds the bit up in the correct part of the horse's mouth, while the noseband permits the use of a standing martingale.

flat
In English-style riding, riding in an arena without jumping, as in the expression "working on the flat." Also, as a verb, to exercise a horse without jumping.

flat racing
A term used to distinguish racing that is not harness (Standardbred racing) or over fences (steeplechase or hunt racing).

flax
A seed fed to horses as a supplement to improve coat, skin, and hoof quality and as a source of omega-3 fatty acid. The oil from flax seed is called linseed oil.

flaxen
The color of a light gold mane and/or tail, typically on a horse with a darker body color.

flea-bitten gray
Describes a gray coat with tiny dark flecks or spots.

flehmen face
An expression made by the horse in which he lifts his nose, curls his upper lip back exposing the teeth, and wrinkles the nostrils in response to a strong or unusual odor. A stallion will typically make a flehmen face after smelling a mare's urine.

F

Flemish Great Horse

The medieval mount of knights in armor, originating in present-day Belgium. When a large and robust steed was needed to carry warriors wearing up to one hundred pounds of armor, selective breeding of the biggest animals to be found produced the Flemish Great (or War) Horse. Many were exported to other parts of Europe. When the age of chivalry ended, descendants of these warhorses were used to breed draft horses to pull plows and wagons.

flex

A dressage or training technique in which the rider causes the horse to bend its head at the poll while simultaneously the animal's jaw accepts the bit. It is one aspect of putting a horse on the bit.

flexion test

A veterinary technique used to determine lameness in which a joint, most often the hock, is flexed to its fullest extent and held that way for several minutes. The horse is then immediately trotted out while the vet watches for increased lameness.

float

To file down the sharp edges of a tooth to keep the edges from cutting into the inside of the horse's mouth. A rasp file or power float is used for this procedure.

flocking

The padding material that fills the panels of a saddle. The material can be wool, a wool-synthetic blend, cotton, foam rubber, felt, or air pockets.

flying change of lead

A switch of leads at the canter, lope, or gallop without breaking stride to the trot or walk. It is accomplished (on a horse that has been so trained) by the rider's shifting his weight to ask the horse to shift its weight, then applying the canter aids for the other lead.

🔊 *Compare to* simple change of lead.

flying pace

A gait particular to Icelandic horses, similar to a pace, in which the legs on one side move together, with a moment of suspension between strides.

fly mask

A mesh covering for the horse's eyes, face, and sometimes ears to protect the horse from insects and bright sun.

fly predators

Tiny, nonstinging, wasplike insects that kill the larvae of flies. Also called fly parasites, the insects are commercially available and are released by farm owners to control nuisance fly populations.

fly sheet

A light, sometimes mesh, blanket worn in warm weather to shield against insects.

Flehmen face.
CREDIT: PHOTOS.COM

Floating a horse's teeth.
© RICHARD KLIMESH

Flying change of lead.

A fly mask and fly sheet.
CREDIT: J. SHIERS

F

fly spray
A liquid product applied to the horse's coat to repel insects.

fly whisk
A whiplike device having a clump of horsehair at one end, used to brush away insects during a ride.

foal
A colt or filly under the age of one year. As a verb, to give birth to a horse.
  See also suckling; weanling.

footing
1 The material that comprises a riding surface, such as sand, shredded rubber, or crushed stone. **2** The condition of an arena or racetrack. Also known as *going*, as in the expression "hard going."

foot weights
Weighted rings placed on the forefeet of a horse to cause a high-stepping action. Used on Saddlebred show horses.

fore
Short for foreleg or fore foot, meaning *front*.

forearm
The portion of the foreleg between the elbow and the knee.

forehand
The part of the horse in front of the barrel.
  See also heavy on the forehand.

Foal.
CREDIT: PHOTOS.COM

forelock
The portion of the mane between the ears and over the forehead.

forging
An interference in which the hind feet strike the soles of the forefeet.

fork
The part of a Western saddle just behind the pommel.

form
1 In racing, an evaluation of a horse's ability, based on breeding, past performance, and current workouts. A horse that is considered competitively fit is said to be "in good form." **2** The jumping style of a horse, particularly a hunter. A hunter that jumps with high, square, and tight knees, a round bascule, a graceful neck position, and tidy hind legs is considered to have good form.

formal season
The part of the foxhunting year from the end of the cubbing season to the end of the hunting year (usually when winter weather makes hunting difficult to impossible or, in warmer climates, the beginning of spring when foxes give birth to their cubs).

forward
1 The quality of a horse that desires to move with impulsion and responds enthusiastically to the rider's driving aids. **2** In jumping, a distance between two related jumps that must be ridden with a

greater pace in order to fit in the correct number of strides, as in "the outside line is a forward five."

forward seat

1 In English riding, the position for jumping in which the rider inclines her upper body at the waist so it can be held over the horse's center of gravity (which is above or ahead of the withers during a jump). **2** A close-contact saddle designed to facilitate a forward seat position.

foul

In racing, a prohibited action by a horse or jockey, such as cutting off another horse. If the patrol judge and/or the stewards feel that the action affected or might have affected the outcome of the race, the offending horse will be disqualified and the order of finish changed accordingly.

foundation sire

A stallion to whom the lineage of all members of a breed can be traced back. Foundation sires include Janus for American Quarter Horses, Justin Morgan (also known as Figure) for Morgans, and, for Thoroughbreds, the Byerly Turk, Godolphin Barb, and Darley Arabian.

founder

Advanced and severe laminitis. The sole may separate from the hoof wall, and in some cases the coffin bone may rotate.

Four Horsemen of the Apocalypse, the

In the Book of Revelations, chapter six, four riders traditionally named Pestilence (mounted on a black horse), War (on a red horse), Famine or, alternatively, the Anti-Christ (on a white horse), and Death (on a pale horse).

four-in-hand

In driving, a vehicle pulled by four horses, two leaders in front and two wheelers behind them.

Fourth Level

In dressage, the level above Third Level, in which the horse demonstrates a high degree of suppleness, impulsion, throughness, lightness, and balance. Test movements include collected walk, quarter- and half-canter pirouettes, walk pirouettes, flying changes, and zigzag half pass at the trot and canter. Fourth level is the highest level of competition before the FEI divisions.

foxhound

The breed of dog used in the sport of foxhunting. There are two strains, the American and the English, with the latter somewhat smaller in size.

foxhunting

The pursuit of foxes by hounds, which are in turn followed by riders. Foxhunting arose in 18th-century Britain when Parliament ordered that fields be enclosed. Wood and brush fencing and

Driving a four-in-hand.
© ED CAMELLI

earthwork banks and ditches proved to be appealing jumping obstacles for riders, who began to follow hounds that hunted foxes as a method of predator control (foxhunting is also known as riding to hounds). British colonists introduced the sport to America; Washington and Jefferson were avid hunters. Centuries-old traditions of dress are scrupulously observed, such as the scarlet (called pink) coats worn by members of the hunt staff. Some hunts pursue coyotes instead of or together with foxes. More than 150 hunts in North America include drag hunts that pursue artificial scent instead of live quarry.

Foxhunting is now banned in England.

fox trot
A gait in which the back feet trot while the front feet walk. Typically done by the Missouri Fox Trotter breed, the gait provides a smooth and comfortable ride.

frame
The outline or overall shape of a horse. "In a frame" or a "round frame" refers to a horse whose hind legs are stepping up under its body to generate impulsion (as opposed to being strung out behind) and whose neck is flexed. "In a frame" is comparable to "on the bit."

free choice
Any feed that is provided to the horse constantly, so he can choose when and how much to eat. Water and a mineral salt block should always be provided free-choice, and many horsekeepers also offer free-choice hay. Grain and other concentrates should never be fed free-choice, since the horse is likely to overindulge, leading to obesity and possibly colic and/or laminitis.

free jump
To school a horse over fences without a rider, either on a longe line or in a jumping chute.

free longe
To longe a horse in an enclosed area without the use of a longe line. The horse responds to the verbal commands, gestures, body position, and whip aids of the handler. Also called free-school or longe at liberty.

 See also longe.

free rein
An extension of the reins to almost their full length, to allow the horse to lower and extend its neck as a relief from work at a more controlled, collected position. Many dressage tests end with the horse leaving the arena on a free rein.

freestyle
An upper-level dressage or reining test in which the riders design their own sequences of movements and transitions; they are judged on both their horses' performances and the creativity of their tests.

free walk
In a dressage test, a movement performed at the walk in which the horse is given a long rein. The horse should stretch its head and neck forward and down, while proceeding in a straight line with swinging, relaxed, ground-covering strides.

French link
A type of double-jointed snaffle bit, similar in construction to the Doctor Bristol, but with a figure-eight-shaped center link, or, in some versions, a bean.

fresh
1 Of cattle, not been previously used for cutting or team penning. **2** Frisky.

Friesian
An ancient breed characterized by its black coat, fetlock feathers, long full mane and tail, and high leg action. Related to the Flemish Great Horse, the breed has influenced the Shire, Oldenburg, and several of the British native ponies. The Friesian, whose name comes from the Friesland region of the Netherlands, has typically been used for driving, but recently is becoming popular for riding.

frog
The elastic, V-shaped portion of the sole of the foot, located between the bars; absorbs concussion and provides traction.
 Compare to hoof.

front-runner
In racing, a horse that runs on or near the lead at the start and then tries to hold or improve that position.

full board
A stabling arrangement whereby the fee for the boarded horse includes a stall, stall cleaning, feed, and turnout.
 Compare to rough board.

full brothers/sisters
Horses having the same sire and dam.
 See also half brothers/sisters.

full-cheek snaffle
 See also cheek.

full cry
In foxhunting, the collective sound made by an entire pack of hounds in pursuit of a fox.

full mouth
Having all the permanent teeth. A horse will grow from 36 to 44 teeth: 24 molars, 12 incisors, and anywhere from none to four each of canine and wolf teeth.

full pass
A lateral movement in which the horse moves sideways without forward motion. Also known as side pass. Used in dressage tests and as a general suppling exercise.

Fulmer bit
A full-cheek snaffle with loose rings.

Friesian.
© KENTUCKY HORSE PARK

F

furlong

One-eighth of a mile or 220 yards; the standard unit of measurement for flat racing.

furosemide

A diuretic medication used to treat bleeding by shrinking the capillaries in the lungs, widely known under its trade name Lasix.

fuse

Term meaning to join together. Joints can fuse in very advanced arthritis, which eliminates pain but causes the joint to be inflexible. In some cases, a veterinarian may deliberately induce joint fusion in order to relieve pain.

futurity

1 A stakes race for two-year-olds for which owners pay a nominating fee and then additional fees as the race approaches. **2** Any of certain horse show competitions for two- or three-year-olds.

Horses are born knowing how to gallop.
© CHERRY HILL

gag snaffle

A snaffle bit attached to a cheek-piece that draws upward and pulls the bit's mouthpiece into the corners of the horse's mouth while simultaneously putting pressure on the poll. Widely used in polo and show jumping for its slowing and stopping power, it is considered a severe but often useful piece of tack.

gait

One of the distinctive leg movements of a horse in motion. These include the walk, the jog or trot, the lope or canter, the gallop, and certain others such as the single-foot, rack, pace, and fox trot.

gaited horses

The familiar collective term for horses with a natural, inherited ability to perform other gaits than the basic walk, trot, and canter. Gaited breeds include American Saddlebreds (rack and slow gait), Tennessee Walking Horses (running walk), Missouri Fox Trotters (fox trot), Rocky Mountain Horse (singlefoot or rack), Standardbred (pace), Icelandic Horse (tolt), Paso Fino (paso fino, paso corto, and paso largo), and Peruvian Paso (paso llano and sobreandando).

Galiceño

The product of Spanish horses brought to North America by Cortez, the breed was used first in Mexico and then in the United States for ranch work and as pack horses. At under 14 hands at maturity, but nevertheless classified as a horse, the Galiceño is compact in build and possesses great stamina for an animal of its size.

gall

A sore resulting from pressure or chafing, such as a girth gall.

gallop

1 The horse's natural running gait.
2 In racing, to exercise a horse, usually during the morning workout period.

galloping boot

In racing, a covering for the ankle, shin, and tendons that protects against abrasion caused by the racetrack surface.
See also brushing boot.

G

Galvayne's groove

The groove in the upper incisor teeth that grows longer as a horse ages. It appears when the horse is ten, reaches approximately halfway down the tooth by age 15, and reaches the bottom at age 20. Named after the 19th-century British horseman Sydney Galvayne, the indentation is valuable in accurately estimating a horse's age.

Gambler's Choice

A type of show-jumping competition in which fences are assigned numerical value according to their difficulty. Riders jump them in any order they wish (but no fence more than twice) within a time limit. Clearing a fence adds its number of points to the rider's total; a knockdown receives no score. The highest score wins the class. There is often a bonus "joker" fence that can be attempted at the end of the round: clearing it gains additional points, but a knockdown results in subtracting the point value from the rider's total score.

gaming

Participating in mounted games.

See also gymkhana; playday.

garrocha

The long pole used in some forms of doma vaquera. Traditionally the garrocha was used to guide cattle, but it is now part of the performance art of doma vaquera.

gas colic

A colic resulting from excess gas in the intestines. Gas colic often will resolve on its own, which can be aided by hand-walking the horse.

See also colic.

gaskin

The part of the hind leg between the stifle and the hock; second thigh.

gastric torsion

A type of colic in which the horse's intestine twists, cutting off the digestive tract and causing intense pain. Surgery is required within a matter of hours to correct the twist, or death will result.

gastritis

Inflammation of the stomach.

gate

See starting gate.

gaucho

A cowboy horseman of Argentina and Brazil who works cattle on the vast *estancias*, or ranches.

gee

The verbal command made to ask a driven horse to turn left.

See also haw.

geld

To castrate a male horse, which is then called a gelding. The procedure renders the animal easier to manage.

Gelderlander

A breed native to Gelder province of the Netherlands. Standing

Galvayne's groove visible in the upper incisor of a twelve-year-old gelding.
© RICHARD KLIMESH

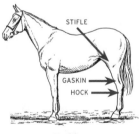

Gaskin.

approximately 16 hands and chestnut in color, the Gelderlander is used primarily for carriage driving.

gelding
A castrated male horse.

Geneo JJ
Before becoming the all-time leading Appaloosa racing sire, calculated by number of wins, number of winners, and dollars earned, Geneo JJ earned the 3-year-old and 4-years-and-older race colt titles in 1986 and 1987 respectively. He went on to sire 117 race starters who have accumulated more than $3.2 million on the track, as well as winners in halter, hunter-in-hand, and hunter-under-saddle classes.

gentle
To tame a wild or unhandled horse.

German martingale
A martingale whose straps run from the girth up between the front legs and through the bit rings, and then snap onto the reins of the bridle.

gestation
The period between conception and birth, approximately 11 months for a horse.

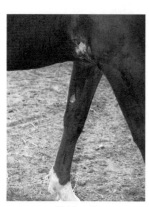

Girth gall.
© RICHARD KLIMESH

get
The offspring of a stallion. The offspring of a mare is called produce.

gig
1 A two-wheeled driving vehicle with a single seat. **2** A Western term for spurring a horse.

ginger
v. To insert an irritant, such as ginger or pepper, into a horse's rectum to cause a high tail carriage. Now illegal under most show rules, gingering was once used on Saddlebreds and similar breeds of show horses.

girth
1 The circumference of a horse's body behind its elbow. **2** A strap that passes under a horse's belly to secure the saddle in place. The word usually describes the piece of English tack and the rear cinch on a Western saddle.

girth extender
A piece of tack that buckles onto the girth to increase its length.

girth gall or girth sore
A blister or raw sore caused by the continuous rubbing of an ill-fitting girth or cinch, treated by antiseptic and rest and preventable by tack that is correctly fitted and adjusted. Long-term aggravation may lead to a severe abscess. Treatment includes cleaning and dressing the wound (and draining any trapped pus or blood), followed by rest until the wound has healed. Properly fitting tack prevents the condition from occurring. Also known as cinch sore.

girthy
Describes a horse that habitually

reacts in a negative way to the tightening of the girth or cinch. A slightly girthy horse may simply pin his ears, shuffle his feet, or threaten to bite as the girth is tightened, while an extremely girthy horse may rear, pull back, kick, or strike out. The response may be due to pain or to previous bad experiences.

give tongue
Of a foxhound, to bark enthusiastically, especially when scenting a fox.

glass eye
A blue eye.

glaucoma
A chronic eye disorder characterized by increasing pressure within the eyeball. May lead to blindness.

glucosamine
A complex sugar that is used in the body's production of cartilage. A common component of joint supplements, it is believed to have a beneficial effect on arthritis due to its anti-inflammatory, pain-relieving, and possibly healing effects.

Godolphin Barb
Along with the Byerly Turk and Darley Arab, one of the three Thoroughbred foundation sires. The stallion was purchased in Paris by Edward Coke in 1729 (according to the story, the horse was discovered pulling a cart), who then took the horse to England.

The horse was then acquired in 1733 by the Earl of Godolphin.

gogue (rhymes with "rogue")
🐎 *See* De Gogue.

going
🐎 *See* footing.

going away
In racing, winning by an ever-increasing margin as the horse approaches the finish line.

Goldstein Engle, Margie
American show-jumping rider who holds the record of 10 American Grandprix Association Rider of the Year titles. She was also a member of the United States Equestrian Team's show-jumping squad at the 2000 Olympic Games in Sydney, Australia.

Go Man Go
This American Quarter Horse was named World Champion three times from 1955 to 1957, including becoming the first two-year-old to be so designated. He set three track records and one world record, equaled another world record, and then went on to become an important sire of racehorses.

gone away
In foxhunting, when the fox leaves the covert.

good
In racing, a surface footing that is slightly damper and thus slightly slower-going than a fast track.

G

good bone
See bone.

gooseneck
A trailer style that has an extended portion in the front that hitches to the center of the bed of a pickup truck, rather than to the back bumper. Many people consider gooseneck trailers to be more stable. Due to the weight distribution, any trailer that hauls more than three horses must be a gooseneck.

See also bumper pull; fifth-wheel hitch.

goose rump
A pronounced slope of the hindquarters from croup to dock. Many horsemen believe a goose rump indicates a horse with an aptitude for jumping.

go-around
At a hunter pace or organized trail ride, the alternate route that allows a rider to choose not to jump or negotiate other obstacles.

go-round
In Western horse shows or rodeos, a sequence in which all or certain qualified entrants in the class or event compete.

go to ground
In foxhunting, a fox that disappears into a burrow or another hole is said to have gone to ground.

grab
A colloquial term for overreaching, as in "The horse grabbed himself in his near foreleg."

Gracida, Carlos
Mexican-American polo player, ranked at a 10-goal handicap for more than 15 years and the only player to win the Grand Slam of Polo three times. He won the Player of the Year title five times (only his brother Guillermo "Memo" Gracida has also done so) and holds the record for most tournament victories.

grade
A horse of no specific breed, the "mutt" of the horse world; also, a horse that will not be accepted for registration by a breed organization.

graded race
Races that have been categorized according to quality of horses and/or purse sizes. Grade I (abbreviated to GI) is the highest category, grade II (GII) the next, and so on to grade IV. Group races are the European equivalent and are indicated by Arabic, not Roman, numerals.

grain
The seeds of certain cereal grasses, used as horse feed; concentrates.

Grakle or Grackle noseband
See figure-eight, definition 1.

granddam
The mother of a horse's dam (also known as the "second dam").

Grand National

The well-known steeplechase race held each spring at the Aintree race course in Liverpool, England. The course is 4 miles, 860 yards in length and includes 30 obstacles, including the formidable Beecher's Brook and The Chair, where many falls occur. Popularized by the book and film *National Velvet,* the Grand National is widely considered the world's most difficult steeplechase.

grand prix

1 A show-jumping class involving the horse show's most demanding course and offering large amounts of prize money; the phrase is French for "great [rich] prize." **2** Capitalized, the highest level of FEI dressage tests, requiring such advanced movements as piaffe and passage.

Grand Prix Special

An upper-level dressage test involving more collected movements and more demanding sequences of movements than a Grand Prix does.

grandsire

The father of a horse's sire.
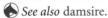 *See also* damsire.

granulation

The first tissue to grow over a healing wound. Excessive granulation tissue is called proud flesh.

grass founder

Laminitis caused by consumption of too much fresh green grass. Common in ponies.

gravel

A hoof infection that travels up through the white line and erupts through the coronary band.

gray

A mixture of white hairs with any other colored hairs. Appearances to the contrary, there are no white horses (except for albinos, which are a genetic mutation); horses that appear to be white are in fact light gray, with dark pigmented skin.

gray horse melanoma

A skin disorder particular to gray horses, in which benign tumors develop, especially around the tail and face.

grazing bit

A curb bit with rear-curving shanks, so called because the shanks permit the horse to put its head closer to the ground than a curb bit with straight shanks would (some riders object to their horse's eating while working, while other riders do not).

greasy heel

 See scratches.

green

1 An untrained horse, or one that is just beginning its training. **2** An inexperienced rider. **3** The color of the prize ribbon awarded for sixth place.

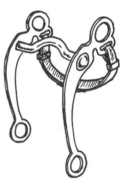

Grazing bit.
© CHERRY HILL 2000

G

green-broke
The minimum degree to which a horse has been trained to accept and respond to a rider.

green hunter
1 A show hunter in its first or second year of showing, that is, First-Year Green or Second-Year Green. **2** An American Quarter Horse that has not yet earned more than ten points in working hunter or jumping classes.

Greyhound
A gray Standardbred gelding, Greyhound was the outstanding trotting horse of his day and arguably the most outstanding in harness racing history. In 1938 he lowered the mile record to 1:55 1/4, a mark that stood until 1969. He trotted 25 two-minute miles and at one time held 14 world records. Following his death in 1965, Greyhound was honored as harness racing's Horse of the Century.

Grisone, Federico
A 16th-century Italian horseman who, in Naples, established the first modern riding school. He was the author of the first systematic training manual, *Gli ordini di cavalcare* (1550), which presented a more systematic approach to schooling than previous trainers had taken.

grob (rhymes with rob)
Spelled "grab" in German and pronounced to rhyme with "rob,"

Walking over ground rails.

a jumping obstacle consisting of a ditch at the bottom with typically a vertical fence at the top of the descent slope, another over the ditch, and a third at the top of the ascent slope. Since the word is German for "grave," some horsemen avoid the ominous connotation by referring to the obstacle as a sunken road.

groom
1 *n.* A person whose job is to clean, feed, and otherwise care for horses. **2** *v.* To clean a horse.

grooming halter
A halter that consists of only a noseband and headstall, with no throatlatch, so that the underside of the head may be more easily groomed and clipped.

grooming mitt
A rubber mitten covered with raised bumps, used for grooming a horse.

ground hitch or ground tie
Of a riderless horse, trained to stand with no more restraint than the ends of the reins touching the ground. The need for such discipline came from the lack of a fence, tree, or other object to which a cowboy could tie his horse when he needed to dismount, perhaps to examine a calf, out on the range.

ground line
In jumping, the actual or perceived base of a fence that a horse

and rider will use to judge at which point to leave the ground.

ground pole or ground rail

A pole of the size used to make jumping fences that is placed directly on the ground, to be walked, trotted, or cantered over.

Ground rails are useful in helping a horse and rider learn to regulate the length of strides or how to see a distance.

groundwork

1 The type of schooling when the trainer is standing on the ground, as distinguished from when the horse is being ridden. **2** Training the horse "on the flat," as distinguished from being worked over fences.

growth plates

The cartilage at the end of a bone from which new bone is produced as a young horse grows; epiphyses. Riding or heavily working a young horse too early can result in damage to the growth plates.

grullo

A smoky or mouse-colored body color (not a mixture of black and white hairs, but each hair mouse-colored) with black mane and tail and usually a black dorsal stripe and black on lower legs.

Grunsven, Anky van

A superstar of the dressage world, this Netherlands rider won the Individual gold medals in the 2000 and the 2004 Olympic Games and the Individual silver medal in the 1996 Games. She was on the squad that won the 1992, 1996, and 2000 Team silver medals. She took first in the World Cup Finals from 1995 through 2006, except for 1998 when she finished in second place, and she won the 2006 World Championships gold medal in the Grand Prix Kür and the silver medal in the Grand Prix Special.

The horses that carried van Grunsven to most of her successes were Gestion Bonfire and Gestion Salinero.

gullet

1 On a Western saddle, the arched open part below the horn or pommel; on an English saddle, the open center panel that runs the length of the saddle's underside. **2** The esophagus.

gut flora

The beneficial intestinal bacteria that assist in digestion.

gymkhana (jim-CON-uh)

A program of mounted games, such as pole bending and musical chairs. From a Hindu word for "ball-house," gymkhanas were a popular training exercise among British cavalrymen stationed in India who then brought the idea back to Europe. The games are now a feature of Pony Club and other competitions in which youngsters take part.

gymnastic

In jumping, a series of low fences

G

set at specific distances to encourage a horse to lengthen or shorten
his stride. Gymnastic work also
encourages a horse to use his back
and hind legs and to jump in a
balanced and athletic fashion.

gyp rope
Old-fashioned term for longeing,
most often heard in the context
of racing.

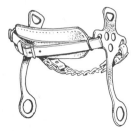

Mechanical hackamore.

Half pass in dressage.

habit
An outfit of clothes for riding, a term now used primarily to describe the coat and long skirt worn by sidesaddle riders.

hack
1 A pleasure ride. **2** The familiar term for an under-saddle hunter class. **3** A riding horse.

hackamore
A bitless bridle that controls the horse by means of pressure from the bosal on the animal's nose. A mechanical hackamore has long metal shanks and a curb strap or chain that creates a curblike lever effect to tighten the bosal. Hackamores are most often seen on horses that have been schooled to neck-rein.

🜂 *See also* bosal; fiador; mecate.

hack barn
A stable where horses are rented for pleasure rides.

Hackney
The name Hackney applies to both a breed of horse and of pony. Both are noted for their high-stepping action at the walk and trot and, accordingly, are used for driving, especially in horse show classes. Hackney horses and ponies were both developed in 18th-century England through the crossing of Thoroughbreds with trotting horses. The animals have relatively small heads, long and curved necks, and compact bodies of a solid color. In American horse shows, Hackney ponies are driven in four-wheeled roadster carts or in sulkies, and are judged primarily on their animated gaits at the walk and trot.

The word *Hackney* is thought to come from a French word for "nag." Hackney horses and the hired carriages they once pulled is the reason why "hack" became a slang term for a taxicab.

Haflinger
The breed of pony originating in the Austrian Tyrol. Standing slightly under 14 hands and with a coat that ranges from chestnut to palomino, the sure-footed and hardy Haflinger is prized as a riding and driving animal. Members

H

of this especially long-lived breed have had healthy and productive lives well into their 40s.

half brothers/sisters

Horses having the same dam but different sires.

 See also full brothers/sisters.

half chaps

Leather chaps that extend from the rider's ankles to just below the knee. They are (literally) cooler than full chaps.

half-cheek snaffle

 See cheek.

half halt

Application of the rider's hand and leg aids to achieve a momentary rebalancing of the horse, or as a signal to the horse to prepare for a change of gait or pace. It is accomplished by a combination of the rider's hand and seat aids while maintaining impulsion with the legs, all done within a single stride.

half pass

A lateral movement in which the horse simultaneously moves sideways and forward, while bent in the direction of travel.

half-round

A horseshoe that is convex on the underside.

half school

The classical term for a change of direction while moving, made by reversing toward the center of the arena and thus making half of a figure eight.

half seat

The hunter-seat equitation position where only the rider's lower legs are in contact with the horse; the rider's seat is lifted out of the saddle so that the horse's hind end will carry less weight at the canter or gallop. Also known as two-point contact, the half seat is an excellent way for a rider to develop balance and leg strength.

halloo

In foxhunting, the signaling shout that a fox has been sighted. Also, view halloo.

halt

The term for asking a horse to stand still, or the position of a motionless horse.

halter

1 A head piece with a noseband and throatlatch but without reins, used to lead or restrain a horse. Because hitching a horse by the reins can lead to a mouth injury if the horse rears back, using a halter is the customary way to secure a riderless horse. 2 A term for a horse show conformation or breeding class.

Hambletonian

One of the foundation sires of Standardbred trotters, Hambletonian produced more than 1,300 foals in 24 years, between 1851 and

A full halt.
CREDIT: S. D. PRICE

A horse prepared for a halter class.
CREDIT: PHOTOS.COM

1875. Through four of his sons, 99 percent of all of the harness racing horses in North America today trace their bloodline to him. The most prestigious race for three-year-old trotters is named for him and is held at The Meadowlands raceway in New Jersey.

hame
Part of a harness that attaches the collar to the traces.

hammerhead
An English spur with a blunt, square neck.

hand
The unit by which horses are measured from their withers to the ground. One hand equals four inches, so a horse that stands 15 hands high (abbreviated hh) measures 60 inches to the withers. A horse that is 15.2 hands measures 15 hands and 2 inches.

hand gallop
A gait that is faster than a canter, but not as fast as a full gallop. The implication is that the horse's speed is under the control of the rider's hand.

handicap
1 A race in which weights are assigned according to the horses' past performance and present form. The goal is to create a theoretical dead heat among all horses in the race. **2** To determine the relative merits among the horses in a race by using such data as breeding, past performance, latest workouts, and record of recent successes of the horse's jockey and trainer. **3** In polo, 🔷 *see* rating.

handicapper
The racetrack official, usually the racing secretary, who assigns the weights that the horses will carry.

handily
In racing, winning easily, with little effort from the jockey.

handle
1 In racing, the total amount of money passing through the pari-mutuel machines for one race, the entire day's racing, or another period. **2** In Western parlance, describes the quality of a horse that is well broke and easy to ride and work with, as in the phrase, "to put a handle on a horse." **3** To work with a horse from the ground in day-to-day tasks such as haltering, grooming, and leading.
🔷 *See also* unhandled.

hand-ride
In racing, urging the horse by the use of the jockey's hands and body weight without using the whip. A jockey will hand-ride a horse that is winning so easily and eagerly that it needs no greater urging.

hands
The degree of skill and finesse with which a rider uses the reins. To have "good hands" is a high compliment.

hand-walk
To lead a horse from the ground as a form of light exercise. Hand-walking is often an important part of the recovery process for a horse that has suffered an injury.

hang a leg
Of a jumping horse, to let one foreleg dangle below the other over the top of the fence. Because it is an indication of an unsafe jumping style (the horse might hit that leg against the top of the obstacle), hunter class judges will penalize a horse that hangs a leg.

Hanoverian
A warmblood breed that originated in the 18th century in the German province of Hanover. The breed's solid body and powerful legs make Hanoverians excellent dressage and show-jumping horses, their primary use today.

hard and fast
A rope that is tied solidly to the horn of a saddle, as opposed to being dallied (wrapped).
 See also dally.

hard mouth
The mouth of a horse that has been ridden in harsh bits or by a heavy-handed rider, until the bars of the mouth are desensitized, making the horse less responsive to normal rein aids.

harness
The system of straps and metal hardware that is used to attach a horse to a cart, carriage, plow, or other driven vehicle.

harness racing
Standardbred trotting and pacing racing, as distinguished from flat racing and steeplechasing.

Hatley, George
Known as "Mr. Appaloosa," Hatley was instrumental in the breed's achieving prominence in the horse industry. He served as executive secretary of the Appaloosa Horse Club from shortly after its founding until 1978, and as editor of *Appaloosa News* (now *Appaloosa Journal*) from 1949 through early 1966. He published the first Appaloosa Stud Book and helped develop the Chief Joseph Trail Ride.

haunches
The hindquarters of the horse.

haunches-in
A two-track movement in which the horse travels with his croup closer to the center of the ring than his shoulders are carried.

haute école (oat ay-COLE)
The French phrase for "high school." It is applied to upper-level dressage training.

haw
The verbal command made to ask a driven horse to turn right.
 See also gee.

hay
Dried grass fed primarily as a

Hand-walking.
CREDIT: PHOTOS.COM

Harness.

H

source of roughage. A horse at work requires approximately 1 to 2 percent of its body weight in fresh grass or hay, or a daily average of 10 to 20 pounds. Hay comes in two categories: legumes, which includes alfalfa and clover, produce nitrogen and are rich in protein and calcium; grasses, including timothy and red tip, are richer in carbohydrates. As a general rule, horses are fed a mixture of legume and grass hay to get the fullest benefit from this important dietary staple.

hay analysis
The laboratory analysis of a hay sample to determine its levels of nutrients.

hay cubes
Hay that has been compressed into cube-shaped pellets. Packaged in easy-to-store bags, cubes lack the dust that regular hay can have, and so they are preferable for horses with heaves or other breathing or allergic conditions. However, cubes are more expensive than regular hay.

hay grass
Any of various species of grass rich in carbohydrates, as distinguished from protein-rich legumes.

hay net
A feeding container made of knotted string or light rope and suspended in a stall to hold a quantity of hay.

Hay net.

hazard
In combined driving, a cross-country obstacle. Among the most popular with course designers are water hazards (ponds or streams through which the entries are driven) and mazes made of logs.

hazer
A rider who rides alongside a cow or bronc at a rodeo to cause it to run in a given direction, such as to keep a steer running in a straight line for the roper.

head
1 *v.* To place a horse in front of a cow to stop or to force the cow to change directions. **2** *n.* In racing, the margin between horses equal to the length of a head. **3** *n.* A single animal, in counting livestock. For example, 50 head of horses means 50 horses.

head bumper
A cushion that attaches to the crownpiece of a halter to protect the horse's head, such as during shipping.

head collar
The British term for a halter.

header
1 In team roping, the contestant who ropes the steer's horns or head. **2** In chariot racing, the assistant who makes sure the horses are facing straight ahead at the start of the race.

headshaking

A disorder in which the horse tosses or shakes its head compulsively, especially while under saddle. Headshaking may be due to an insect, pollen, or dust allergy; a pinched facial nerve; or photosensitivity.

headshy

Describes a horse that is afraid of movements near or contact with its head. Such a horse may have been abused in the past, or may have a medical condition.

headstall

The Western bridle excluding the bit.

"heads up!"

The traditional warning to be aware of an approaching horse.

heart

The quality of a horse that is bold, competitive, and seems to have an innate desire to win or to please its rider.

heart-rate monitor

An electronic device that records and displays heart rate. Used by event, competitive trail, and endurance riders during conditioning.

heat

1 In racing, one of a series of qualifying races to determine eligibility in the finals of a race. **2** Increased temperature in the leg or hoof that is noticeably higher than normal. Detected by touch, heat is an indication of a possible injury or illness because of the increased blood flow that raises the temperature of tissues. **3** The condition of a mare that is receptive for breeding: ovulating or in estrus; the mare is said to be "in heat."

heave line

The distinctive muscular buildup, caused by coughing, along the ribcage of a horse that suffers from chronic heaves.

heaves

A disease, similar to asthma in humans, marked by difficulty in breathing, coughing, and loss of energy. The cause is exposure to dust, molds, and other allergens. Changing the horse's environment and/or administering medication to help the animal breathe are the treatments. A horse that suffers from the condition is referred to as "heavy" (HEE-vy).

heavy

1 In racing, a track surface that is drying out, somewhere between muddy and good. **2** Describes the hands of a rider who uses excessive rein pressure.

⬤ *See also* soft, definition 2.

heavy on the forehand

Describes a horse that travels in an unbalanced way because it is carrying too much of its weight on its forequarters, which restricts the ability to move forward with optimum impulsion. The solution is a half halt or more prolonged combination of rein and driving aids.

The horse in the background is leading by a head.
CREDIT: PHOTOS.COM

H

heel
The rear portion of the foot.

heeler
In team roping, the contestant who ropes the steer's hind legs.

helmet
Protective headgear for the rider, with a chin strap, and often but not always covered with black velvet or velveteen.

herbs
Any of several plants that can be fed as a supplement to treat various ailments or promote health.

herd
1 *n.* A group of horses. **2** *v.* To move a group of animals all together.

herdbound
Describes a horse that is very reluctant to leave its equine companions. The herdbound horse is anxious when its companions are out of sight, pacing and calling if loose or becoming unruly under saddle. Also known as "buddy sour."

herpes virus
⬥ *See* equine herpes virus.

herring-gutted
A conformation fault marked by flat sides that extend sharply from girth to stifle.

heterozygous
When a breeding animal has one gene (of a total of two genes) that codes for a given characteristic. There is a 50 percent chance that such an animal will pass on the gene for that characteristic to an offspring.
⬥ *See also* homozygous.

high hooking (or high sticking)
In polo, a foul in which the player lifts the head of his mallet above his shoulder and then makes contact with an opponent.

high school
The translation of the French phrase *haute école*, referring to the most advanced dressage movements, such as passage, piaffe, and the airs above the ground.

hind
Short for hind foot, hind leg, or hindquarters.

hindquarters
The portion of the horse behind the torso, or barrel, including the croup.

hinney
The offspring of a horse and a female ass.

hip
The joint that connects the thighbone to the pelvis. Visible as a bony protrusion on each side at the top of the haunches.

hippodrome
A race course for chariot racing.

hippology
The study of horses, ponies, and other equines.

hippotherapy
The use of horses in the care of people with physical or mental disabilities.
🔹 *See also* therapeutic riding; equine-assisted psychotherapy.

hip-shot
A way of standing in a relaxed manner with one hind leg cocked, resting the toe on the ground.

hitch
1 The device on the back of a truck or another towing vehicle to which the trailer is attached. **2** To fasten a horse to a driving vehicle. **3** To tie a horse to a post, tree, or another stationary object to keep the horse from wandering off.

Hitchcock, Thomas, Jr.
This American polo player is considered one of the greatest of all time. Rated at 10 goals, the highest handicap, he led four teams to U.S. National Open Championships in 1923, 1927, 1935, and 1936.

hit the wall
Used in reference to endurance horses, it means to reach the limit of stamina.

hives
Raised welts on a horse's skin that may or may not itch or ooze pus.

Usually caused by an allergic reaction or insect bites.

hobble
A restraining strap attached to a horse's legs to keep it from wandering off (not to be confused with *hopple*).

hock
The joint of the hind leg between the gaskin and the cannon bones. The hock is the source of a horse's "rear engine" impulsion.

hog
To cut a mane shorter than a roached mane.

hog's back or hogsback
A jumping obstacle composed of three parallel poles of which the middle pole is the highest.

hog-tie
To tie a calf or steer by three legs after the animal has been thrown down. Such a tie marks the end of a tie-down roping go-round.

"hold hard!"
In foxhunting and elsewhere in the horse world, the command to come to an immediate halt.

hold out
In jumping, to remain on the track (usually along the arena's rail) until the horse is lined up with a fence set inside the track. Lining up a jump permits the most direct straight route to the obstacle.

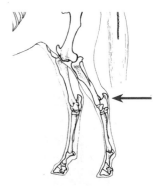

Hock.
© CHRISTINE BERUBE

H

Hood.

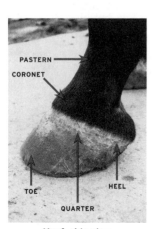

PASTERN
CORONET

TOE   HEEL
        QUARTER

Hoof, side view.
© RICHARD KLIMESH

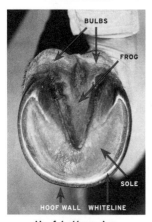

BULBS

FROG

SOLE

HOOF WALL   WHITELINE

Hoof, bottom view.
© RICHARD KLIMESH

Hollywood Dun It

The outstanding sire of reining horses, the sons and daughters of this buckskin stallion have earned more than $4,000,000 in National Reining Horse Association events, as well as winning gold medals in United States Equestrian Team competition and winning American Quarter Horse Association World Championships.

Holsteiner

A warmblood breed that originated in the 17th century in the German province of Holstein. Originally a coach horse, the Holsteiner benefited from subsequent infusions of Thoroughbred blood to become a valuable modern dressage and show-jumping horse.

homebred

A horse bred by its owner or in the breeder's home state.

homeopathy

A mode of alternative medicine in which highly diluted compounds, often plant-based, are used to treat various ailments.

home stretch

 See stretch.

homozygous

When a breeding animal has two genes for a given characteristic. Such an animal will always pass on the gene for that characteristic to its offspring.

See also heterozygous.

honda

A small loop at one end of a rope, through which the bight is passed to create a throwing loop.

Honorary Secretary

In foxhunting, the official who sends out fixture cards, collects capping fees, and performs other of the hunt's administrative duties.

hood

A covering worn over the horse's head and neck to protect the animal from dirt, insects, or inclement weather.

hoof

The hard outside part of the foot. Like the human fingernail, the horse's hoof must be trimmed when it grows too long, a chore that typically must be done every six to eight weeks. Many horses wear metal shoes that protect their hooves from pavement, rocks, and other hard surfaces and objects. Hooves are made of keratin, a protein substance, which dogs find tasty (which is why barn dogs gather around a blacksmith who is trimming hooves).

hoof boots

Tough rubber or plastic covers that fit tightly over the bottom of hoof. They are used to protect barefoot hooves from rough or hard terrain.

hoof dressing

A petroleum compound applied to moisturize dry hooves and to treat certain foot conditions.

The substance also has cosmetic use; hooves of a show horse are painted with dressing right before entering the arena.

hoof knife
An implement used by a farrier to cut away excess material on the frog, sole, and bars of the hoof.

hoof pick
A hooked metal tool used for cleaning wadded hay, manure, bedding, small stones, and so forth from the underside of the hoof.

hoof testers
A pinching implement used by a veterinarian to put pressure on the sole of the hoof in order to localize the source of pain.

hook
A sharp protrusion on a cheek tooth, routinely filed away in a process called floating.

hooking
In polo, the legal tactic of reaching with the mallet head to catch the head of an opponent's mallet.

hooking on
In natural horsemanship during groundwork, especially free longeing, the moment when a horse chooses to follow the human's lead. The horse may turn or step toward the trainer, indicating an interest in and desire to respond to the trainer's body language.

hoolihan
A toss of the lariat without any preliminary swings of the rope over the roper's head. (The word is likely to have been the name of a cowboy who had mastered the technique.)

hopples
In harness racing, leather straps worn on the legs of pacers to keep them from breaking into a trot or gallop.

horn
1 The upright projection on the front of a Western saddle, especially designed to wrap a rope. 2 The short instrument (the hunting horn) blown by the huntsman to signal hounds and the foxhunters, or the longer instrument (the coach horn) blown by some horse show ringmasters to signal the beginning of a class. 3 The hard material that makes up the hoof wall.

 See also dally.

The horn of this saddle is wrapped with a band of rubber to prevent the rope from slipping.
© CHERRY HILL

hors de concours (HC)
In dressage, a test that is ridden in order to get a score and the judges' comments, but without being considered for a ribbon and without gaining points for year-end awards.

horse
A member of the species *Equus caballus* that measures more than 14.2 hands.

 See also pony, definition 1.

horse gentler
A term for a practitioner of

H

Hunt cap.

resistance-free training. To gentle a horse is in contrast to the former practice of breaking a horse by harsher methods, such as outlasting the animal's bucking.

Horse Latitudes

An area of light winds between 30° and 35° North latitudes, so named because sailing ships carrying horses to America or the West Indies were often obliged to lighten their loads by casting the horses overboard when becalmed in these latitudes.

horseman

A person of either gender who has a thorough working knowledge of riding and horse care. Although the term *horsewoman* is widely used, objection to the collective term *horseman* is rare.

horsemanship

Riding skill, especially with regard to form and control.

horse whisperer

A term that is somewhat equivalent to a natural horsemanship practitioner, but is not commonly used by natural horsemen themselves. The term implies that the horse whisperer has a supernatural ability to communicate with and control difficult horses.

hot

Term for an excitable horse.

hot blood

Horse with pure or a majority of

Hunters and foxhounds.
© ED CAMELLI

Thoroughbred or Arabian bloodlines. The phrase derives from the high-mettled, excitable nature of such breeds and types.

🐎 *Compare to* warmblood; cold blood.

hot shoeing

The method of making or fitting shoes by heating them in a forge.

🐎 *Compare to* cold shoeing.

hot walker

A person or a machine that leads a sweating horse after exercise until the animal is cool. The hot-walker machine, to which one or more horses are attached to long vanes, is powered by a small motor and leads the animal(s) around in a circle, thus freeing humans to do other duties.

hound

A canine used for foxhunting, the foxhound.

Houyhnhnms

The race of horses in *Gulliver's Travels* by Jonathan Swift. Their intelligence and culture stood in marked contrast to their human servants.

hunt

1 *n.* An organized group of people who foxhunt; a foxhunting club. Often used in the name of such organizations, e.g., Blue Ridge Hunt and Myopia Hunt. **2** *v.* Slang term for jumping with ease and grace, like a show hunter. **3** *v.* Of a reining horse, to "hunt a circle" is to follow the curve of a circle without guidance from the rider.

hunt cap

Sturdy, velvet-covered headwear traditionally worn by the Master of Foxhounds and hunt staff and by competitors in hunter-seat horse show classes and at lower levels of dressage and eventing. Like any other protective headgear, the cap should include a well-fitting chin harness.

hunter

A horse show division in which horses are judged on whether their style of moving and jumping ability are suitable for the foxhunting field: standards include a ground-covering stride, an athletic and tidy form over fences, and a quiet, pleasant disposition. The term also applies to a horse or a person involved in the sport of foxhunting.

hunter clip

A pattern in which all the horse's body hair is trimmed except for a patch under the saddle (to absorb sweat) and the lower legs (to protect against thorns).

hunter hack

A horse show class in which horses are first judged over two low fences and then at the walk, trot, and canter.

hunter/jumper

English-style riding and showing that involves training and exhibiting in hunter, equitation, and jumper divisions, as distinguished from saddleseat, combined training, dressage, and so forth.

hunter pace

A competition in which teams of two or three riders cover a cross-country course of several miles. The course may or may not include jumps. The winner is the team that completes the course closest to the optimum time as established by the event's organizers.

hunter's bump

The colloquial term for sacroiliac subluxation, which results in the prominence of the sacral tuberosity, appearing as a bump on the top of the horse's hundquarters; jumper's bump.

🔊 *See also* sacroiliac subluxation.

hunter trial

A competition in which horses are judged over a cross-country course of fences on the athletic ability needed by foxhunting mounts.

hunter under saddle

A horse show class in which the horse is judged on its ability to move at the walk, trot, and canter as a hunter-type horse. Judges look for a ground-covering walk, a long, low, daisy-cutter trot that doesn't break at the knee, and a smooth canter. Manners will also be taken into consideration.

A pony hunter competing over fences.
CREDIT: PHOTOS.COM

Hunter under saddle class.
© AMERICAN QUARTER HORSE ASSOCIATION

H

Hunt, Ray

A student and protégé of Bill Dorrance, Hunt is largely responsible for the spread of Dorrance's "natural horsemanship" concepts and techniques through many clinics and other appearances. His book, *Think Harmony with Horses: An In-Depth Study of Horse/Man Relationship*, is a collection of sayings that reflect Dorrance's and his own approach.

hunt seat

The English-style riding position designed for jumping; also known as hunter seat.

hunt-seat equitation

(also hunter-seat equitation) A horse show class in which riders are judged on the form and control of their hunt-seat horsemanship.

huntsman

The member of a foxhunt's staff who is responsible for working the pack of hounds and supervising kennel activities. The Master of Foxhounds often acts in this capacity.

hunt staff

In foxhunting, the huntsman and whippers-in.

hurdle race

A jumping race in which the obstacles are brush-topped bundles of sticks. The name comes from portable fencing once used to separate fields in which sheep were kept.

hyaluronic acid (HA)

A joint lubricant naturally produced by the body. Arthritic horses may be given supplemental HA either by injection or by feeding.

hybrid

The product of the mating of a horse and another equine species, such as an ass or zebra. Hybrids are almost always sterile.

hybrid vigor

The tendency of a crossbred animal to be more hardy and healthy than a purebred animal.

hydrogen peroxide

A topical antiseptic commonly used for first-aid care of wounds.

hyperflexion

1 Extreme and abnormal flexion of any joint. **2** A position in which the horse is ridden with extreme flexion of the neck, holding the head low and behind the vertical, often with the nose almost touching the chest. A controversial dressage training and warm-up technique, hyperflexion is also known as Rollkur.

hyperkalemic periodic paralysis (HYPP)

A muscular disorder that is an inherited affliction of American Quarter Horse bloodlines related to the stallion Impressive. Symptoms include twitching or tremors, sweating, and hind-end weakness or collapse. Horses with

HYPP are also noted for having the pronounced musculature favored in halter classes, so they were extensively bred before the inherited nature of the disease was fully understood. Because there is no known cure, efforts have been made to eliminate the disorder through selective breeding. Horses related to Impressive are now blood-tested and may be identified as H/H (homozygous; will pass on the disease to all of their descendants if bred), N/H (heterozygous; will pass on the disease to 50 percent of their descendants), or N/N (do not have the genetic mutation that causes the disease and will not pass it on to descendants).

H

Icelandic horse

The breed of pony native to Iceland. (Although standing 13 hands high or less, the breed is referred to as *horse* in Iceland.) It may well be the world's purest breed because no outside blood has been added since around the year 1200. It moves at five gaits: the walk, trot, gallop, pace, and the tolt, the comfortable running walk for which the breed is famous. Icelandic horses are among the world's most rugged, able to thrive on the island's sparse vegetation, and able to cover great distances over the most demanding terrain with no discernable effort.

icthammol

A thick, dark ointment used as a skin emollient or as a drawing salve for hoof abscesses.

identification

A system of recognizing and verifying individual horses by means of several features that are noted on registration certificates, such as the animal's coat color, markings, lip markings, pattern of the chestnuts, scars, and brands.

Idle Dice

Among America's greatest show horses, especially during the 1970s, this Thoroughbred won more than $400,000 in his show-jumping career, which by today's standards could equal triple that amount. Among "Ike"'s 31 grand prix victories were the American Gold Cup three times and the American Invitational; he was the only horse to win the President's Cup at the Washington International Horse Show twice. He is most closely associated with rider Rodney Jenkins.

IM

An abbreviation for intramuscular, or into the muscle.

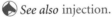 *See also* injection.

impaction

A type of colic caused by a blockage in the intestinal tract, in some cases precipitated by dehydration or overeating. A mineral oil drench may help resolve an impaction. Veterinary assistance is required.

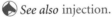 *See also* colic; enterolith.

imprinting

The process of desensitizing a

Icelandic horse.
© KENTUCKY HORSE PARK

newborn foal to various stimuli within the first 24 hours after its birth. Imprinting is believed to make the foal easier to handle and train later in life.

impulsion
Energy generated by the horse's hindquarters to produce a forward thrust.

in-and-out
In jumping, a combination of two fences set one cantering stride, or approximately 24 feet, apart. The combination comes from foxhunting, where horses might be asked to jump over a fence out of a field, across a narrow road, and over a second fence into the next field.

Incentive Fund
A program run by the AQHA in which stallions and their offspring (before the age of 24 months) are nominated (enrolled). The lifetime enrollment makes horses eligible to receive money at the end of each year according to how many points the horse earns in AQHA shows. The total amount of money is divided between the nominator of the stallion (10 percent), the original nominator of the horse (10 percent), and the current owner of the horse (80 percent).

incisors
The upper and lower front teeth, used for biting.

Incitatus (In-kie-TAH-tus)
The favorite horse of the mad Roman emperor Caligula, who named the animal a priest and a consul. Incitatus lived in an ivory stall and drank from a golden bucket. The name means "spurred on."

incubation period
The amount of time between exposure to a disease-causing agent, such as bacteria, and the development of observable symptoms. Depending on the disease, horses may or may not be contagious during the incubation period.

independent aids
The rider's ability to use the various aids (each hand, each leg, and seat) without affecting any of his or her other body parts.

independent seat
A rider's ability to maintain a proper body position without relying on the reins for support.

indirect rein
Rein pressure created by the rider drawing his hand back toward his opposite hip, used to straighten or turn the horse by displacing the animal's weight. An example would be the rider's drawing the right rein toward his left hip, thus causing the horse to shift its hind end to the left.

indoor arena
A large building constructed around and covering a riding arena, so that horses may be ridden during inclement weather.

Indoors

Informal name for the important autumn hunter/jumper shows in the Northeast: the Washington (D.C.) International, Capital Challenge (Upper Marlboro, MD), Pennsylvania National (Harrisburg, PA), and Syracuse Sport Horse Invitational (Syracuse, NY). So called because all the shows take place in covered arenas.

inflammation

The swelling of body tissue, usually accompanied by heat, redness, and pain.

influenza

A highly contagious viral disease. As with humans, symptoms include coughing, muscle soreness, loss of appetite, and decreased resistance to secondary infections. Vaccination reduces the chance of contracting the disease, for which rest is the primary treatment.

in front

Term relating to the forelegs.

🐎 *See also* behind.

in front of the rider's leg

Describes a horse that is moving with sufficient impulsion to give the rider the feeling that the animal is ahead of and carrying the rider, as opposed to the feeling that the source of energy is lagging behind.

infundibulum

The dark depression in the biting surface of a horse's tooth that grows larger as the horse ages; cup.

In gate

The entrance to an arena. Large arenas have both In and Out gates to avoid traffic congestion, while smaller rings use a single gate for both entrances and exits. The In-gate area is traditionally where riders, trainers, owners, and other interested parties gather to watch the action in the company of other like-minded people.

in hand

Term for when a horse is held or worked by someone who is standing on the ground. *In hand* is also another term for a halter class.

injection

The introduction of a substance into the horse's body by means of a needle and syringe. There are three common types of injections: intramuscular (into the muscle; IM), intravenous (into the vein; IV), and intra-articular (into the joint). Experienced horse people with the proper training sometimes administer IM injections, and occasionally IV injections as well, but intra-articular injections are only performed by veterinarians. Any kind of injection, if administered incorrectly, can have harmful or fatal effects on the horse.

inquiry

In racing, an investigation instituted by the stewards to see whether a foul was committed.

🐎 *See also* objection.

inside

1 The side of the horse or rider that is closer to the center of a riding ring or arena. The left side would be the inside when a horse is traveling counterclockwise.
2 In racing, a position closer or closest to the track rail.

interference

The striking of any part of one leg with the hoof of another leg. Interference may include brushing, forging, or overreaching.

Intermediare

In dressage, the two FEI levels above Prix St. Georges but below Grand Prix. Intermediare I tests include two-tempi flying changes and full canter pirouettes. Intermediare II tests include one-tempi flying changes, piaffe, and passage. Sometimes called Intermediate.

intermediate

1 The second-highest level of national competition in eventing. It is intended to prepare horses and riders for international Two Star (CCI**) events. The dressage test may include canter to halt and walk to canter transitions, turns on the haunches, simple changes, and counter-canter. The cross-country phase includes banks, ditches, or water with narrow elements, a bounce combined with other elements, or corners in a combination. The cross-country course will incorporate 28 to 32 obstacles over a distance of 2,600 to 3,200 meters, to be ridden at 550 meters per minute. Fences may be up to 3 feet 9 inches in height, with spreads of up to 5 feet 3 inches and drops of up to 5 feet 11 inches. The show-jumping course includes 12 to 14 obstacles with heights up to 3 feet 11 inches and spreads of up to 4 feet 9 inches. **2** A rider who is more experienced than a beginner, but not as experienced as an advanced rider.

See also beginner novice; novice; training; preliminary; advanced.

interval training

A system of conditioning in which the horse is given increasingly more rigorous exercise immediately followed by rest periods to allow the animal's heart rate and lungs to recover, as a way to increase stamina.

intra-articular

Term meaning into the joint.

See also injection.

Introductory

In dressage, the lowest level of competition. The horse demonstrates acceptance of contact, straightness, and accuracy. Test movements are walk and trot only, including free walk and 20-meter circles.

intubate

To insert a long tube through the nostril, down the esophagus, and into the stomach. Done by a veterinarian either to administer medication or other substances or to remove the stomach contents.

invitational
A race or horse show class open only to those horses that have been asked to take part.

iodone
A dark red liquid with antibacterial properties, often used in first-aid care for wounds or fungal skin infections.

Irish bank
A type of cross-country jump that consists of a wide, flat-sided hill made of dirt. The horse must jump up onto the bank and then down off the other side.

Irish Draft Horse
(also Draught)
A native breed of Irish heavy horse. Although called a draft horse, the breed is far smaller and lighter than the Clydesdale, Percheron, or other draft breeds that are larger due to the infusion of Arabian and Thoroughbred blood. Standing between 16 and 17 hands and with bone and substance, the Irish Draft Horse is a steady and agile jumper, which makes it suitable for breeding to Thoroughbreds to produce the Irish hunter, a crossbred used primarily as a foxhunting mount.

Irish knit
A type of cooler made of thick, white, loosely woven cotton. May be used during hot weather as an antisweat sheet.

irons
The colloquial word for stirrups on an English or racing saddle.

IV
Abbreviation for intravenous, meaning into the vein.
See also injection.

ivermectin
The active ingredient in many dewormers; effective against large and small strongyles, pinworms, ascarids, hair worms, stomach worms, threadworms, and bots.

jack
A male donkey.

jackpot
Money paid by exhibitors at the
beginning of a show or rodeo that
is collected and then given to the
winner at the end of the event.

jack spavin
A visible bone spavin.

jail
In racing, the 30-day period after
a horse has been claimed during which time it must run for a
claiming price 25 percent higher
than the price for which it was
claimed.

jenny
A female donkey.

jibbah
The characteristic bulge on an
Arabian horse's forehead.

jig
An uncomfortable jerky and
bobbing part-walk/part-jog trot.
Horses often jig when excited or
just feeling good.

jockey
1 A rider in a horse race.
2 To maneuver a horse during a
race. 3 A dark or black marking
that appears on a saddle or other
leather tack due to wear, such
as under the stirrup leathers.
4 On a Western saddle, the leather
flap that covers the top of the
fender.

**A jockey on the way
to the starting gate.**
CREDIT: PHOTOS.COM

Jockey Club
The regulatory body of Thoroughbred racing. There are Jockey
Clubs in every country that has
such racing, with functions that
include maintaining the stud book,
accepting and approving registration and names of foals, and
providing officials as stewards or
judges.

jockey's agent
A representative of a jockey hired
to arrange mounts for the rider.
An agent is said to hold the jockey's book.

jodhpur boots
Low footwear secured with an
ankle strap and traditionally worn
with jodhpurs.

J

jodhpurs
English riding pants that extend to the ankle, worn by riders of gaited horses and by young children. The name comes from the Indian province (now state) of Jodhpur, where the native dress included similar leggings.

jog
The Western term for trot, especially a slow, collected trot. Riders sit to the jog, but they post to what Westerners call the long trot.

Jog.
© CHERRY HILL

joint
1 The flexible connecting point between two bones. **2** The flexible connecting point between links in a single- or double-jointed bit.

joint block
 See block, definition 1.

joint injection
 See injection.

Joint Master
In foxhunting, one of two or more Masters of Foxhounds simultaneously supervising the operations of a hunt.

jousting
Today, a sport in which galloping riders try to spear a small ring suspended six to eight feet above the ground. Inspired by the activity of medieval knights in armor, jousting is the state sport of Maryland.

jumper
A horse show division in which

Jumper class.
© WYATT MCSPADDEN/
AMERICAN QUARTER HORSE ASSOCIATION

horses are scored on their ability to clear fences and other obstacles without regard to the form or style of horse or rider. Also known as show jumping.

Jumping Derby
A demanding show-jumping competition where the permanent course includes banks, sunken roads, and other natural obstacles. The best-known derbies are held at Aachen (Germany), Hickstead (England), and Spruce Meadows (Canada).

jumping hackamore
A type of bitless bridle made of leather that uses pressure on the nose to control the horse.

jump-off
In show jumping, an additional tie-breaking round.

junior
1 A rider below the age of 18. **2** In AQHA shows, a horse five years old or younger.

jumping chute
 See chute, definition 3.

juvenile
In racing, a two-year-old. Races for juveniles are usually sprints so the young animals are not overtaxed.

J

keeper
A leather loop on bridles and saddles into which the end of a strap is inserted to keep the end from flapping. Also used on full-cheek snaffles to stabilize the upper cheek by connecting it to the bridle.

keg shoe
A premade horseshoe, as opposed to one that is formed by the farrier.

Kellogg, William K.
American manufacturer and breeder of Arabian horses. In 1932, Kellogg donated his ranch in Pomona, California, to the University of California. Kellogg's extensive collection of literature about the breed is now housed at California Polytechnic University, a leading institution for equine studies.

Kentucky Derby
The first of the Triple Crown races, held on the first Saturday in May at Churchill Downs, Louisville, Kentucky. First held in 1875 and run at a distance of a mile and a quarter, the Derby is arguably the most famous horse race in the United States.

keratin
The type of protein that makes up hair and hoof walls.

keys
Small metal pieces that hang from the center of a bit to entertain a mouthy horse.

kick
To strike out with a hind leg.

kicking chain
A light, thin chain attached to the horse's hind legs with a leather strap, which hits the horse in the leg when he tries to kick. Used to correct horses that kick their stall walls.

kick up
Another term for bucking.

Kimberwicke
A bit with a curb chain and a mouthpiece shaped into a low port. The Kimberwicke combines the actions of the snaffle and curb by means of a single set of reins.

Kimberwicke bit.

K

King

Widely considered to be the most important sire of American Quarter Horses, he produced 20 AQHA champions and innumerable other award-winners during the 1950s. His outstanding conformation was instrumental in setting the standard for American Quarter Horse judging.

kissing spines

Describes an impingement of the dorsal spinous processes. Two or more of the vertebrae touch or rub together, causing sudden, intermittent back pain. May be due to conformation or trauma.

Klimke, Reiner

German dressage rider Reiner Klimke's six gold and two bronze medals stand as the Olympic record for the equestrian events. He won Team gold in 1964, 1968, 1976, 1984, and 1988 and the Individual gold in 1984. His two bronze medals came in the individual event in 1968 and 1976. He also won six gold medals at the World Championships, two Individual (1974 and 1982), and four Team (1966, 1974, 1982, 1986). Most of Klimke's successes came aboard his horse Ahlerich.

knacker

A person who collects and disposes of horse carcasses.

knee

The joint in the foreleg between the forearm and cannon bone.

knee roll

The padding on some English saddles against which the rider's knee rests for support.

knuckled over

A congenital defect involving hyperflexion of the fetlock joint.

kur (KUHR)

A freestyle dressage competition performed to music that has been selected by the rider. The word is German for "choice."

Kusner, Kathy

Show jumper Kathy Kusner was one of the first women selected to represent the United States Equestrian Team in Olympic competition. After riding at the 1964 Olympic Games in Tokyo and the 1968 Games in Mexico City, Kusner played an integral part in the USET's Team silver medal victory in 1972 at Munich. In 1968 she became the first licensed woman jockey in the United States, and later, in several other countries. She was also the first woman to ride in the Maryland Hunt Cup.

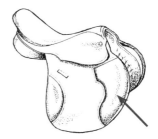

Knee roll.

K

lactic acid
A waste substance produced by the muscle cells during exercise. Insufficient cooling out can result in a buildup of lactic acid, leading to sore muscles or, in extreme cases, tying up.

La Guérinière, François Robichon de (La GAIR-in-ee-yair)
The 18th-century French horseman and author who was an influential contributor to classical horsemanship. An adherent of the idea of school riding for its own sake (not just as training for the cavalry), he is credited with the invention of the shoulder-in, flying change of lead, and counter-canter.

lame
Showing an irregular gait, usually due to pain in one or more limbs. A mechanical lameness is an inability to move correctly that is not due to pain, such as a fused joint.

laminae
The tissues of the foot that attach the wall of the hoof to the coffin bone.

laminitis
An inflammation and separation of the laminae due to faulty blood circulation, causing severe pain. In severe cases the coffin bone begins to rotate. A major cause is overeating, especially rich food. Other causes include stress, ailments such as Cushing's disease, and obesity. Treatments include long-term and total rest, anti-inflammatory medication, and corrective shoeing. Chronic or severe laminitis is known as founder.

Lamri
The mare ridden by King Arthur. The name means "the curveter" or "one that prances or frolics."

landau
In driving, a four-wheeled two-seat vehicle with a folding top; named after a town in Germany.

lariat
A long rope with a loop at the end used for roping cattle, horses, or other livestock.

larking
In foxhunting, unnecessarily (and

Hooves of a horse with chronic laminitis.
© RICHARD KLIMESH

Lariat.
CREDIT: PHOTOS.COM

annoyingly) jumping fences when hounds are not running.

Lasix
 See furosemide.

lateral gait
Any gait in which the two legs on the same side move in unison. The most commonly known lateral gait is the pace. A lateral walk is considered to be a fault.

lateral movement
Any movement, such as the half pass or the two-track, in which the horse moves simultaneously forward and to the side (the exception is the full or side pass, which has no forward movement).

latigo (LAT-ig-oh)
The strap that fastens the cinch on a Western saddle.

lay up
To send a horse for rest or recuperation, or the period of such recovery.

lead
1 *n.* The foreleg that consistently and most visibly precedes the other foreleg in striking the ground at the canter/lope and the gallop. When traveling counterclockwise, the horse should be on its left lead, and on the right lead in the other direction, for optimal support and balance.

Determining which lead the horse takes is the responsibility of the rider, who applies the appropriate aids (or cues) to ask for that

Adjusting a latigo.
© RICHARD KLIMESH

gait. **2** *v.* To guide a horse from the ground by means of the reins or lead rope.

See also counter-canter; cross-canter; flying change of lead; simple change of lead; wrong lead.

leader(s)
In driving, the horse(s) hitched in front of the others.

See also wheeler(s).

leading rein
See opening rein.

lead-line class
A horse show class in which young children ride ponies that are led by adult handlers.

lead pony
In racing, a ridden horse (not a pony) that escorts racehorses to the post. Being led in this fashion tends to reassure and relax the runners.

lead rope
A rope that is attached to the halter, usually with a clip, for leading or tying. May be made of nylon, leather, cotton, or other material.

leak
Term used when a cutting horse loses the advantage over a cow by moving toward the animal instead of staying back and waiting for the cow to move forward.

leaning into a distance
Term used when a jumping rider

inclines her upper body too far forward during the approach to a fence. Leaning increases the likelihood of being out of balance when the horse leaves the ground.

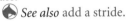 *See also* distance.

leaning on the bit

The effort by a horse to have its forequarters supported by the rider's hands, as opposed to carrying itself without such help.

lean-to

A three-walled shed with a roof, often used as a shelter for horses.

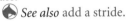 *See also* run-in shed.

leaping horn

The hooklike projection on a sidesaddle over which the rider rests her forward leg.

lease

To rent a horse on a long-term basis. A half-lease, also known as part-board, is when the owner shares riding time with the leaser.

leathers

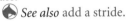 *See* stirrup leathers.

leave off a leg

Term used to describe when a jumping horse leaves the ground with one foreleg noticeably trailing the other. This unbalanced position, which can lead to the horse's hitting the fence or falling on landing, can be caused by the rider's restraining the animal's head at the takeoff point.

leave out a stride

Term used in jumping when the number of strides between two fences is decreased by one, accomplished by increasing the horse's length of stride. Its purpose is typically to save time in a jumper class.

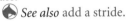 *See also* add a stride.

left behind

Term used in jumping to describe when the rider is thrown backward by the horse's jump and thus out of position; also called getting left.

legume

Any of the nitrogen-rich grasses used for hay, such as alfalfa.

leg up

1 A boost into the saddle by someone standing on the ground, as jockeys are hoisted onto their horses. **2** To exercise a horse in order to bring him back to peak condition, usually done after a horse has been laid up.

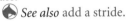 *See also* lay up.

leg wraps

Protective cloth material that snugly encircles a horse's legs for support or to prevent injuries.

leg yield

A lateral movement in which the inside fore- and hind legs cross in front of the outside legs while the horse progresses both sideways and forward. The horse's body is bent slightly away from the direction of travel (that is,

L

in a leg yield to the left, the horse is bent to the right).

lengthening
A term in dressage that describes the horse taking longer strides within a gait than in the typical working gaits, but not as big as in the extended gaits.

leopard Appaloosa
An Appaloosa with dark spotted markings all over its body.

lespedeza
A legume grass used for hay.

levade
The air above the ground in which the horse bends its haunches and raises its forehand until its body reaches and maintains an angle of less than 45 degrees.

Liberty
1 A horse show class in which horses individually run free around the arena to music and are judged on their grace and presence. 2 A circus act in which a group of horses circle, halt, and rear in response to the trainer's gestures and verbal commands.

A 1634 etching by Jacques Callot showing King Louis XIII executing a levade.

liberty, at
Describes a horse that is loose in an enclosed area.
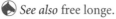 *See also* free longe.

liberty horse
A riderless circus horse that performs in a group, doing such movements as circling around the

ring or rearing on a command from the trainer.

lift
In foxhunting, to gather hounds and move them to another spot.

ligament
Fibrous tissue that connects bones, as well as supporting and strengthening joints.

light horse
An obsolete British expression for a saddle horse that was not a pony or a draft or draft-cross horse. Light horses were used by the cavalry, where speed was essential.

limit
A class for riders or horses that have not won more than three classes in that division at recognized horse shows.

line
1 A term used in jumping to describe a series of two or more fences set apart at related distances. 2 "On the line" is another term for shown in hand.
 *See also* in hand.

linebreeding
A breeding program that produces progeny descended from a common ancestor.

liniment
A liquid or gel applied to the skin to reduce inflammation or to soothe sore muscles.

L

linseed meal or linseed oil

A meal or oil made from flax seeds, used as a laxative or as a source of protein and omega-3 fatty acids.

lip chain

1 A severe method of controlling a horse in hand by running the chain of a lead line from the ring of the halter on the far side, through the horse's mouth, over the upper gums, and through the halter ring on the near side. Often used by handlers at racetracks.
2 A twitch made of chain.

Lipizzaner (LIPPIT-zahner)

The Austrian breed most widely known for its association with the Spanish Riding School. The breed was created from Spanish horses imported to Austria in the 16th century. Between 15 and 16 hands high, stocky in build, and usually light gray in color, Lipizzaners are used for classical dressage and, to a lesser extent, for driving.

lipstick

In dressage, a slang term for the white foam that gathers on the lips of a horse that is working well on the bit.

Little Brown Jug

The most prestigious race for three-year-old Standardbred pacers, it is held in September in Delaware, Ohio.

live foal

(or live foal guaranteed)
A provision in a breeding contract whereby the stud fee is due only if and when the mare delivers a live foal.

liver chestnut

Describes a dark chestnut coat, the color of fresh raw liver.

Liverpool

A jumping obstacle composed of one or more rails over a shallow man-made pool or tray of water, named for such a fence at Aintree, Liverpool, the site of the Grand National steeplechase.

Liverpool bit

A bit used for driving that has a straight mouthpiece and long, straight shanks with several slots to attach the reins.

Llanero (YAH-nairo)

A native breed of Venezuela descended from Spanish stock. Slightly smaller than other Central and South American breeds, with an arched neck and small feet, the Llanero is widely used for ranch work.

local hunter

A horse show class open only to hunters that live within (usually) 50 miles of the show. The underlying reason is to exclude better horses from farther away from competing against and defeating animals from the show's vicinity.

locking stifles

See upward fixation of the patella.

Lipizzaners performing a quadrille.
© TEMPEL FARMS

Loin.

Longe.

lockjaw
 See tetanus.

loin
The part of the back between the saddle and the croup, unsupported by the horse's rib cage.
 See also coupling.

long
A term used in jumping that describes a takeoff spot that is uncomfortably far away from the obstacle, the opposite of *tight* or *deep*.

long and low
A manner of riding in which the horse's back is elevated and stretched and the head and neck are held in a relaxed, lowered position approximately level with or slightly higher than the withers. Used in many disciplines to warm up a horse and is desirable in the show ring for hunters under saddle.

longe; lunge
(both pronounced "lunge")
To exercise or train a horse by encouraging it to circle around its handler at the end of a rope called a longe line, which is 15 feet or longer. Encouragement may come from a longe whip, five feet long and with a five-foot lash. Longeing is often used as a warm-up exercise for a horse. Riding a horse that is being longed is an effective way for a rider to develop a deep, secure seat, with or without stirrups and without the use of reins.

long format
The traditional format for a three-day event, which includes the full speed-and-endurance phase: roads and tracks, steeplechase, and cross-country. Also called the classic format.
 Compare to short format.

long reining
The procedure in which the trainer walks behind the horse and guides the animal with driving reins. Although used to teach a horse to be driven in harness, long reining is also used to school young horses before they are ridden. Also known as ground driving or long lining.

long stirrup
In hunter/jumper competition, a hunter or equitation division for older riders, typically with jumps up to 2 feet in height. The age limit depends on the particular show, but often the minimum age for long stirrup is 14.
 See also short stirrup.

long toe/low heel
An undesirable hoof conformation in which the heel is low and possibly underrun, while the toe grows too long. Caused by natural conformation or poor trimming, the long toe/low heel hoof creates stress on hoof and leg joints, possibly leading to lamenesses such as navicular disease.

long trot
A Western term for an extended or rapid trot, as distinguished from

the slower and more comfortable jog. Western riders usually post the long trot and sit to the jog.

long yearling
A horse that is between 18 and 24 months old.

loose
Not held by a lead line, tie rope, or other type of restraint.

loose-ring bit
A snaffle bit, the rings of which are able to slide through the mouthpiece, allowing the horse to move the bit slightly in its mouth.

lope
A slow or collected three-beat gait, the Western term for the gait called the canter by English riders.

lop-eared
Having ears that naturally flop downward and to the side.

lose
Of a cutting horse, to allow the selected cow to escape and return to the herd. Losing a cow will be heavily penalized in cutting horse competitions.

loss of use
An equine insurance contract provision providing for compensation in the event the horse cannot take part in its intended activity.

loud
Describes an Appaloosa or a pinto that has a very bright, flashy coat

pattern with a lot of white.

lower leg
The rider's leg from calf to anklebone.

low ringbone
 See ringbone.

Lusitano
The native breed of Portugal, virtually identical in conformation to the Andalusian and, like that breed, used as a riding and a carriage horse.

Lyme disease
A disease caused by a bacteria that is transmitted by deer ticks. The bacteria infect various body parts, especially the joints. Symptoms vary but may include vague, intermittent lameness, general stiffness, an aversion to being touched, and an irritable attitude. Treatment with antibiotics can reduce the symptoms. If Lyme disease goes untreated, long-term joint damage can result.

Lusitano performing the Spanish walk.
© STEVEN D. PRICE

lymphangitis
A chronic infection of the lymph nodes, characterized by massive swelling of one or more legs. The swelling may recede temporarily, but the horse will always have the disease (chronic), and the swelling may return during acute episodes.

L

magnet therapy
Treatment for pain and inflammation using strong magnets applied over the affected area. It is believed that the magnets encourage blood flow.

magnetic resonance imaging (MRI)
A veterinary diagnostic technique in which a combination of magnets and radiation are used to create a detailed, three-dimensional image of the inside of the body, including bones, soft tissue, and fluids. Due to the large size of horses, MRI use is limited mainly to the head and limbs.

maiden
1 A horse of either sex that has never won a race. **2** A horse show division for horses or riders that have not won a class in that division at a recognized show. **3** A mare that has never had a foal.

maintenance
A balance of feed and exercise that results in the horse maintaining a consistent weight, rather than losing or gaining weight.

mallet
In polo, the stick with which the player strikes the ball. Mallets measure approximately four feet in length with a tapered cylindrical head of various shapes and sizes and a wrist strap at the handle end. The ball is struck with the side, not the end of the mallet head. A mallet is also called a stick.

malocclusion
A deformity of the mouth in which the upper and lower sets of teeth do not align properly, such as parrot mouth or undershot jaw.

mane comb
A small metal comb with relatively wide spaces between the tines, used to clean a mane without breaking off the hairs.

Mane comb.

manège (ma-NEGZH)
An enclosure, usually covered, for training horses and riders. By extension, the word can apply to formal school dressage in general. The word comes from the French for "enclosure," from the same root as the word menagerie.

M

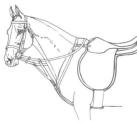

**Standing martingale
(Western type).**
© CHERRY HILL

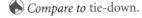

Running martingale.
© CHERRY HILL 2000

manège movements
See school movements.

manners
Ground training of the horse, especially regarding respectful behavior toward humans. A horse with good manners is easily handled and led, moves when asked and stands still otherwise, is not pushy, and does not bite or kick.

Man O'War
Widely considered to have been the greatest horse in American Thoroughbred racing, Man O'War won 20 of 21 races during his two-year career in 1920 and 1921, setting three world, two American, and three track records in the process. Ironically, he lost that one race to a horse named Upset. He was equally impressive as a sire, producing 64 stakes winners, including Triple Crown winner War Admiral. (Man O'War did not race in the Kentucky Derby, but won both the Preakness and the Belmont Stakes.)

manties
A type of large, rectangular pack carried by a pack horse.

marathon
The cross-country phrase of combined driving. Distances can range up to 17 miles and include such hazards as ponds and maze-line gates.

mare
A female horse four years or older, or a female horse of any age that has given birth.

mare motel
A slang term for a system of pipe corrals or gate panel sections arranged to form outdoor stalls, often covered with a roof. The name is derived from the fact that breeding farms sometimes use these pens as temporary housing for visiting broodmares.

Marengo
The gray Arabian stallion ridden by Napoleon Bonaparte at the Battle of Waterloo. The horse was named for the town in Italy where, in 1800, Napoleon defeated the Austrian army.

markings
The pattern of (usually) white hair on a horse's head and legs that help in identification. Common patterns include blaze, snip, star, socks, and stockings.

martingale
A strap attached from the girth and running between the horse's forelegs to either the cavesson (standing martingale) or the reins (running martingale). A martingale is used to restrict a horse's head movement and thus increase the rider's control.
Compare to tie-down.

mash
Crushed bran mixed with hot water and served warm to aid bowel regulation or post-exercise

digestion. Mash is also given to horses with poor teeth.

mask
In foxhunting, the fox's head, awarded to a member of the field who is close to the hounds at the kill.

massage therapy
Treatment of muscle soreness or stiffness by pressing and rubbing the muscles and ligaments to release knots and increase blood flow.

Master of Fox Hounds (MFH)
The presiding official of a foxhunt, who often assumes financial responsibility for the upkeep of the hounds and other expenses.

match race
A challenge race between two horses, most often between two celebrated horses to determine which is the better of the two.

maternal grandsire
The sire of a horse's dam.

mature
1 A term meaning fully grown. 2 Describes a horse five years old or older.

maverick
An unbranded and unclaimed calf. The word comes from Samuel Maverick, a 19th-century Texas rancher who neglected to brand his cattle.

McClellan saddle
A saddle with a flexible tree, designed by Civil War general George McClellan to fit a wide range of horses. The saddle was and is today used primarily by the cavalry and mounted police.

mecate (meh-KAT-ay)
A set of reins, traditionally used with a Western snaffle bridle or bosal, made of a single long horsehair or nylon rope. The excess serves as a lead rope when the rider is dismounted.

mechanical hackamore
🐎 *See* hackamore.

mechanical lameness
🐎 *See* lame.

meconium
The first feces produced by a newborn foal.

medal class
1 The familiar term for the USEF Hunter-Seat Medal equitation qualifying classes and final championship event in at the Pennsylvania National Horse Show in Harrisburg, Pennsylvania. 2 Any other so-designated equitation class, generally implying that it is a qualifying class for a year-end final championship.

medication list
In racing, a list kept by the track veterinarian and made available to identify horses that have been treated with permissible medication.

medicine hat
The term that describes horses

Mecate reins.
CREDIT: TOM MOATES

with all or predominantly white bodies and color on their ears and top of the head, the pattern resembling a bonnet or hat. Many Native American Plains tribes considered such horses able to provide mystical protection to their riders in battle.

medium
In dressage, a gait with bigger strides than the working gaits, but not as big as the extended gaits.

meridian
The paths of energy around the body that are stimulated during acupuncture and acupressure treatments.

methylsulfonylmethane
(MSM)
A sulfur supplement that is a natural anti-inflammatory and also promotes healthy hair and skin.

microchip
A tiny computer chip containing a unique identification number, which can be injected into the neck of a horse. If the horse is lost or stolen, the chip can be scanned and used to identify the animal when it is found.

military
A European term for three-day eventing. The name comes from eventing's cavalry origins.

milk teeth
See deciduous teeth.

Miniature horse.
CREDIT: PHOTOS.COM

Millar, Ian
He is the most successful show jumper in Canadian history. With his horse Big Ben, Millar won more than 40 Grand Prix titles worldwide and the World Cup in 1988 and 1989. Millar has been a member of every Canadian Olympic Equestrian Team and World Show Jumping Championships team since 1972.

Miniature Horse
Reputed to be the world's smallest equine, the breed was created by the Falabella family of Argentina by inbreeding Shetland ponies for size. The American Miniature Horse Association requires that Miniatures not exceed 34 inches in height when full grown, though other registries allow horses of 38 inches. Miniature Horses are typically kept as pets or as harness ponies.

minimal white
Describes the coat pattern of a Paint or pinto that is mostly a solid color, with a small amount of white above the knees or hocks.

minus pool
In racing, a pari-mutuel betting pool that happens when a horse is so heavily bet on that, after state and track deductions, there is not enough money in the pool to pay the legally prescribed minimum amount on each winning bet. In such case, money from the track or the state racing association pays the difference.

M

Missouri Fox Trotter

An American breed noted for its fox trot, a comfortable sliding gait in which the horse walks in front and trots with its hind legs coming well underneath its body. Similar to other gaited horses, the Missouri Fox Trotter was bred to be able to easily carry a rider over rough terrain. The breed, which was developed in the 19th century, is also noted for its flat topline, powerful hindquarters, and amiable disposition.

Misty of Chincoteague

A real pony made famous by a 1947 children's book of the same name by Marguerite Henry. Set on the coast of Virginia, the story involves the annual "Pony Penning" roundup and auction of wild ponies that live on nearby Assateague Island to benefit the local fire department. The roundup and auction (unsold ponies make the short swim back to Assateague) continue to be held the last week of July.

mixed sale

A sale consisting of more than one type of horse, such as yearlings, broodmares, and horses in training.

mob

Australian term for a herd of horses.

mobile starting gate

In harness racing, a car or other vehicle with a long barrier mounted across its rear end. The horses trot or pace up to the barrier as the vehicle moves so that the horses get an even start on gait as they and the vehicle cross the starting line. The vehicle then accelerates away.

model

A horse show term for a conformation or halter class.

modern pentathlon

 See pentathlon.

moment of suspension

The point in a horse's stride when none of his hooves are touching the ground. The walk and jog do not have a moment of suspension, nor does the trot in many horses. The canter, the gallop, and, in some horses, the trot have a moment of suspension.

Monday-morning disease

 See azoturia.

monkey mouth

The conformation fault of an undershot jaw.

 Compare to parrot mouth.

moon blindness

An inflammation of the iris in the eyeball. The severe pain causes the horse to blink, tear, and rub the eye. If untreated, blindness is likely. Treatment includes antibiotic or cortisone ointment and confinement in subdued lighting. Known more formally as periodic opthalmia, or recurrent uveitis, the term *moon blindness* refers to the old belief that the disease's recurrence was somehow related to phases of the moon.

M

Morab

A Morgan/Arabian crossbred horse. Morabs make especially good mounts for endurance riding and other long-distance activities.

Morgan

Morgan.
© JAN SYNICK/AMERICAN MORGAN
HORSE ASSOCIATION

A breed of horse that originated in New England in the late 18th century. The foundation sire, thought to be a Thoroughbred, was named Figure and owned by a Vermont schoolteacher named Justin Morgan (the horse was often referred to as Justin Morgan, too). Figure matured into a stallion that was a compact but powerful saddle and driving horse that also hauled timber and pulled a plow. In addition, he became a remarkably prepotent sire, endowing his get with his conformation, speed, and stamina. The Morgan has retained the crested neck and compact, well-rounded body, as well as great versatility as a riding and driving horse. In fact, the Justin Morgan class at horse shows requires the same horse to perform under saddle, in harness, and pulling weight.

morning glory

In racing, the sarcastic expression for a horse whose performances during races never equal its morning workout times.

morning line

In racing, the odds on a horse as determined by the track handicapper, based on his or her estimation of odds likely to be determined by the bettors.

morning workout

In racing, the exercise period that lasts from dawn until mid- or late morning. Then the track is closed to prepare for the day's racing.

Morris, George

The most influential American trainer of hunter-seat equitation and show-jumping riders, Morris rose to prominence by winning equitation finals at the age of 14 and then as part of the gold medal–winning United States Equestrian Team squad at the 1959 Pan American Games and the silver medal–winning squad at the 1960 Olympic Games.

Morris's many successful students include Conrad Holmfeld, individual silver medalist at the 1984 Olympics, and Chris Kappler, winner of the individual silver medal 2004 Games. He is now the USET's show-jumping coach.

motion

The rider's upper body position in relation to the horse's center of gravity. A rider who is in balance with the horse is said to be riding "with the motion." Riding "behind the motion" is appropriate when using the driving aids to encourage the horse forward. Riding "ahead of the motion" disturbs the horse's balance by placing too much of the rider's weight on the animal's forehand.

mount

1 *n.* Term designating a saddle

horse. **2** *v.* To get onto the back of a horse.

mount fee
In racing, the flat fee earned by a jockey who has not ridden any of the top three finishers in a race (when he would have earned a percentage of the purse).

mounting block
A step or platform over 2 feet high used to facilitate getting on a horse.

mouthpiece
The part of a bit that goes into the horse's mouth.

move up
In jumping, to ask the horse to extend its stride and cover more ground with each stride, done when the distance to the takeoff spot appears too far away from the fence.

Mr. Ed
The "talking" horse of the 1960s television series. The human voice-over was synchronized to Mr. Ed's lip movements, a stunt accomplished by his enjoyment of the peanut butter applied to the inside of his mouth.

muck out
To clean a stall of manure and soiled bedding.

mudder
In racing, a horse that performs well on a wet track.

muddy
In racing, a track surface that is soft and wet but without pools of water, as distinguished from sloppy.

mud fever
 See scratches.

mud knot
A loose knot tied in a horse's tail. The shorter length keeps as much mud as possible out of the tail hair. Mud knots are most often seen on horses that race on rainy days.

mule
The offspring of a jackass and a mare. Standing approximately 15 hands tall, mules are used primarily as pack animals, although they can be used for riding and occasionally appear in horse shows and dressage competitions. Like hinnies (and most other interspecies crosses), mules are almost always sterile.
 Compare to hinney.

mullen mouth
A nonjointed snaffle bit with a straight or curved solid mouthpiece.

Murray, Ty
Ty Murray holds the record for winning the most World All-Around Rodeo Champion titles—seven of them (1989–1994, 1998). He was also the top money-winner in Bareback, Saddle Bronc, and Bull Riding events for those years. He is now a television

Mullen mouth bit.
© MILLER HARNESS COMPANY LLC

M

analyst for rodeo and bull riding competitions.

mustang

The feral horse native to the Western United States. Descended from escaped or stolen Spanish horses brought to North America during the colonial era, the present-day mustang is a small (approximately 15 hands) and rugged animal that continues to roam the West's remaining rangeland in herds.

mutton-withered

The term for the conformation defect of poorly defined, flat withers.

mutual grooming

Two horses grooming each other by nuzzling, licking, and gently biting each other's coats, usually at the withers. Mutual grooming strengthens the bond within a herd.

muzzle

The part of the face between the nostrils and the upper lip.

Mutual grooming.
CREDIT: PHOTOS.COM

M

nag

1 *n.* A slang term for an old or worn-out horse. **2** *v.* To use the same aid or cue over and over, to the point that the horse begins to ignore it.

nappy

adj. Describes a horse that is balky or reluctant to move forward.

narky

An uncomplimentary slang term for a horse that is behaving in an erratic manner, as if under the influence of a mood-altering narcotic.

Narragansett Pacer

A now-extinct breed developed in colonial New England. Its influence can still be found in such breeds as the Standardbred, Morgan, and Saddlebred. According to legend, Paul Revere rode a Narragansett Pacer on his famous midnight ride.

nasogastric tube

A long, flexible tube that is inserted into the stomach by way of a nostril; used to administer medication or fluids.

National Show Horse

A breed created by crossing Arabians and Saddlebreds. Standing approximately 16 hands high, the horses have gracefully arched necks, fine features, and elevated and elegant gaits.

National Velvet

The 1935 novel by Enid Bagnold; the story of a young English girl, Velvet Brown, who trains and rides her horse, The Pie, to first place in the Grand National steeplechase. However, in an era when only male jockeys were permitted to compete, horse and rider are disqualified when race officials discover that Velvet is a girl.

Nations Cup

An international team show-jumping competition involving two rounds of jumping. The three best scores of each team's round (four horses customarily compete) count toward the overall scores.

Native Costume

An Arabian horse show class in which riders wear such clothing as flowing capes, pantaloons, head

N

dresses, scarves, sashes, and other items that evoke Bedouin desert regalia.

natural aids

The rider's legs, hands (via the reins), seat, and voice.

See also aid; artificial aids.

Natural Balance shoe

A patented horseshoe design with a square, rolled toe intended to mimic the hoof shape found in a barefoot horse.

natural horsemanship

An eclectic philosophy of horse training. Although precise methods vary among its many practitioners, the essential themes include the use of the horse's instincts and natural body language to communicate and develop respect; application of pressure to request an action and the subsequent release of pressure as a reward for correct responses; extensive groundwork to prepare for under-saddle training; and desensitizing the horse to various stimuli.

navicular disease

A degenerative condition of the front feet caused by faulty blood flow to, or pressure on, the navicular bone and the surrounding area. This common cause of lameness appears as a choppy movement of one or both front feet. Treatment involves corrective shoeing to take the pressure off the front of the foot, anti-inflammatory medication, and reduced work.

near side

The left side of a horse. Because such activities as leading, mounting, and dismounting are done on or next to the horse's left side, that side of the horse is nearer to the person doing the activity.

The tradition of mounting and dismounting on the near side arose in the days when men carried swords; most people were right-handed and carried their swords on their left hips, which made mounting and dismounting from the left side less cumbersome. Hence the old expression about mounting that "the left side is the right side, and the right side is the wrong side."

Compare to off side.

neatsfoot oil

An oil made from the hooves and leg bones of cattle, used to condition leather.

neck

1 The part of the body that connects the head to the shoulders.
2 In racing, the margin between two horses equal to the length of a neck.

neck rein

Rein pressure created when one rein is pressed against the horse's neck, used as a cue to turn to the other side. For example, neck reining against the left side of the neck asks for a right turn. Western horses have been traditionally and routinely taught to neck rein so cowboys can ride one-handed,

Neck rein.
CREDIT: JAMES C. WOFFORD

N

using their free hand to rope. Also known as bearing rein.

neck rope
In calf roping, a loop around a horse's neck through which one end of the rider's lasso passes from the saddle horn to the rider's hands. This arrangement acts as something of an anchor to keep the horse from running off after the roper dismounts.

A neck shot.

neck shot
In polo, a stroke in which the player's mallet makes contact with the ball under the pony's neck. It is used primarily to send the ball off at a right angle.

neck sweat
 See sweat.

neigh
A loud call made by a horse. Horses may neigh to one another when separated or upon meeting, or may neigh to humans, as a greeting and often in anticipation of being fed.

neonatal
A term relating to a newborn foal.

nerve block
A diagnostic procedure in which a veterinarian injects a temporary anesthetic into a given point on a lame horse's leg. The horse is then trotted out, and if the nerve block produces soundness, the veterinarian can assume that the numbed joint is the source of the

horse's pain. Sometimes called a joint block.

nerving
The largely obsolete procedure in which a nerve in the horse's leg is cut or removed. It was performed on animals with lower leg or foot problems to eliminate pain. However, nerved horses would then work beyond the capacity to do so safely, and the animals would break down. The technical term is "neurectomy."

neurologic exam
A veterinary examination in which the vet looks for symptoms of a problem in the central nervous system. The exam may include such tests as turning the horse in a tight circle to watch for improper hoof placement and pulling the tail to the side as the horse walks to check whether the horse can compensate for being pulled off balance, as well as general lameness evaluations.

neurologic symptoms
Symptoms of a disease or injury that affects the central nervous system. Neurologic symptoms include ataxia, aimless wandering, head pressing, hind-end weakness, paralysis, stumbling, walking in circles, muscle twitching, a head tilt, muscle atrophy, and many others.

Newcastle, William Cavendish, duke of
Seventeenth-century English

N

military leader, riding master, and author. His book, *Methode et Invention Nouvelle de dresser les Chevaux*, advocated abandoning the harsh training methods of the Renaissance in favor of a more gentle and understanding approach.

New Forest

A pony breed native to the New Forest area of Hampshire in England. The largest of the British native ponies, the New Forest stands up to 14.2 hands high, making it suitable to carry most adults as well as children.

Newmarket boots

Tall canvas and rubber boots designed to be worn in wet weather. Named after the English racing center of Newmarket.

New Zealand rug

An extremely heavy-duty canvas turnout blanket, usually green in color and lined with insulation.

Nez Percé horse

Pronounced, "nez per-say," a crossbred of Appaloosa and Akhal-Teke, established as a breed in 1995 in an effort to restore the Appaloosa as originally created by the Nez Percé tribe.

 *See also* Appaloosa.

nick

A merger of bloodlines that is likely to produce a particularly desirable offspring, especially for racing.

nicker

A soft, throaty, grunting sound made by a horse. Horses may nicker to one another or to humans as a greeting or to express affection. Many horses nicker in anticipation of being fed. Stallions nicker to mares in season, and mares and foals nicker to each other as well.

nictitating membrane

A translucent, retractable flap of tissue that covers, protects, and moistens the eyeball within the eyelids; third eyelid.

night blindness

An inherited vision problem that renders horses virtually or actually blind in low light. Symptoms include a reluctance to move in the dark and cross-eyes when viewed from the front. There is no known cure.

nighteye

Another name for the chestnut (see definition 2) on the inside of a horse's legs.

nippers

A farrier's tool used to cut the clinches off the nails before removing a horseshoe and to trim the hoof horn before shaping it with a rasp.

nitrofurazone

A bright yellow antibacterial agent commonly used in first-aid ointments and sprays for treatment of minor wounds.

N

nod

1 In racing, a lowered head at the finish line that crosses the wire just ahead of another horse. The expression "gets the nod" refers to a horse that wins in such a fashion. Also called bob. **2** An unnatural up-and-down movement of the head at the trot due to lameness. The horse's head will drop down when the sound leg touches the ground, and go up when the lame leg touches the ground. **3** In Tennessee Walking Horses, a desirable movement of the head seen when the horse is working in the running walk.

non-pro

In Western horse showing, an amateur; a nonprofessional.

nose

1 The front part of the head below the nostrils. **2** In racing, the distance between racehorses equal to the length of a nose, the shortest distance by which one horse can beat another. **3** In foxhunting, a hound's ability to detect scent.

nose bag

A bag that is applied over the horse's muzzle and attached with a strap over the poll, used to feed grain.

noseband

The part of a halter or bridle that is strapped around the horse's muzzle above the nostrils and below the cheekbones. Bridles may have many different types of nosebands, including cavesson, figure-eight, dropped, and flash.

novice

1 The second level of national competition in combined training events. The dressage test includes walk, trot, and canter and 20-meter circles. The cross-country phase includes a drop and a jump out of water. The cross-country course will incorporate 16 to 20 obstacles over a distance of 1,600 to 2,000 meters, to be ridden at 350 to 400 meters per minute. Fences may be up to 2 feet 11 inches in height, with spreads of up to 3 feet 3 inches and drops of up to 3 feet 11 inches. The show-jumping course includes 9 to 11 obstacles with heights up to 2 feet 11 inches and spreads of up to 3 feet 9 inches. **2** The division for riders or horses that have not won more than three classes in that division at recognized horse shows. **3** An inexperienced rider.

See also beginner novice; training; preliminary; intermediate; advanced.

nuchal ligament

A large, long ligament that runs along the crest from the poll to the withers.

nuclear scintigraphy

A diagnostic technique in which a harmless radioactive substance is injected into the horse's blood. The blood concentrates the substance in areas of increased inflammation, especially in

N

bone disorders. An X-ray of the horse's body will reveal these concentrated points, allowing the veterinarian to locate the exact source of a lameness. Commonly known as a bone scan.

Number 1
In polo, the player whose primary function is to spearhead the drive on the opposing team's goal.

Number 2
In polo, the player whose primary function is to back up the Number 1 player.

Number 3
In polo, the player whose primary function is to direct the team's scoring attacks. Normally the team's best player plays the Number 3 position.

🐎 *See also* back, definition 3.

numnah (NUM-na)
British term for a saddle pad that is shaped like an English saddle, as opposed to a square saddle pad.

nurse mare
A mare who "adopts" and feeds a foal whose dam has rejected it, has died, or produces insufficient milk.

nuts
A British term for pelleted grain.

N

oats
A cereal grain widely used as feed.

objection
In racing, a claim made by a jockey, trainer, or owner before the race has been declared official that their horse had been interfered with during the running of the race. If the stewards sustain the objection, the order of finish will be altered accordingly.

See also inquiry.

obstacles
The final phase of a combined driving competition, in which vehicles negotiate a course of pairs of traffic cones set slightly wider than the vehicles' axles. Tennis balls are balanced on the tops of the cones, and any ball that a vehicle dislodges results in penalty points. Also known as cones.

occipital bone
The back of the skull; the poll.

odds
In racing, a figure based on how much money bettors will collect on a particular horse based on either handicappers' estimation of the horse's chance of winning (the morning line) or the actual amounts of money bet on all the horses in that race.

See also pari-mutuel.

odds-on
In racing, odds of less than even money by which the payoff profit will be less than the amount wagered. For example, a horse that wins at 1-2 odds will pay $3, the $2 bet plus the $1 profit.

off
adj. Slightly lame.

offset oxer
In jumping, a spread fence of which the rear element is lower than the front element. Offsets are illegal on horse show grounds because the optical illusion traps horses into hitting the back rail, which is in fact the purpose of such fences.

See also bump, definition 2.

offset stirrup
English stirrups with longer inside arms that cause the treads to slope

Obstacles phase of a combined driving competition.

O

Oldenberg.
© ED CAMELLI

inward. The purpose is to help riders keep the weight of their feet on the inside of the stirrup.

off side
The right side of a horse. "Off" refers to the custom of saddling and mounting from the horse's left, or near, side, so, in relation, the off side is farther off.
🐾 *Compare to* near side.

off stride
In harness racing, breaking into a gallop instead of trotting or pacing. A horse that goes off stride must be pulled down to the trot or pace within several strides or else be disqualified.

off the pace
In racing, to run behind the leaders at the early stages of the race.

off the track
A horse that was once a racehorse (Thoroughbred, Standardbred, or Quarter Horse) and is now being used for other purposes, such as pleasure or showing.

off-track betting
Wagering in legal outlets other than a racetrack.

Ohl, Cody
Tie-down roping champion Cody Ohl set a world record at the 2003 National Finals Rodeo, a time of 6.5 seconds. That came after spending a year recovering from surgery following a devastating injury to knee tendons two years earlier.

Oldenburg
A German warmblood breed, originally based on the Friesian horse. Later, the Oldenburg was modified with infusions of Cleveland Bay, Hanoverian, and Thoroughbred blood until the horse became the largest in size of all the German warmbloods. Standing between 16 and 17 hands high, with a deep body, strong shoulders, and good bone, it is widely used as a show jumper.

Olympic Games
Equestrian events in this quadrennial international competition are show jumping, dressage, three-day eventing, and the riding phase of the modern pentathlon.

Olympic martingale
A training device composed of leather straps, one end of which is snapped onto the rings of a running martingale and passed through the bit rings; the other end is attached to the rein some twelve inches from the bit. When the horse raises his head, the straps pull downward and put pressure on his mouth.

omnibus
An annual publication produced by a horse show organization, which lists the recognized shows and events for that year, as well as the rules and test patterns.

onager
An Asian species of wild ass.

one-ear bridle

A Western bridle that has a strap around one ear instead of a browband.

one-rein stop

Used to stop a bolting horse, this "emergency brake" involves pulling hard on one rein, which forces the horse to turn in a circle, slow down, and stop.

one-sided

Term used when a horse is able to work more comfortably and effectively in one direction than the other. Because a one-sided horse is limited in athletic ability, such suppling exercises as the shoulder-in and leg yield are useful.

on the bit

A description of a horse that is flexed at the poll, accepting the bit, responsive to the rider's aids, and moving with impulsion. Although the term comes from dressage, the concept is found in all equestrian disciplines.

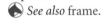 *See also* frame.

on the buckle

Term for riding a horse on a very long rein, with the rider literally holding the buckle at the end of a set of English reins.

on the dressage score

In eventing, to finish "on one's dressage score" is to complete the event without incurring any faults during the cross-country or stadium jumping phases, so that the dressage score is the competitor's final score.

on the muscle

Term used for a strong or frisky horse.

open

1 A class or division at the highest level of difficulty in that category, such as open equitation, in which riders who have won more than three classes in that division are eligible. **2** A class, division, or competition in which both professional and amateur or non-pro riders are eligible. **3** A class, division, or competition in which horses of all breeds are eligible. **4** A broodmare that has not been bred.

open-front boots

Boots used on jumpers to protect the tendons, but with only thin straps across the fronts. The purpose of the exposed front is to let the horse feel the strike if he hits a jump, so he will be more inclined to lift his legs higher in the future.

opening circle

In jumping, a wide circle made between entering the arena and approaching the first fence. Its purpose is to establish pace and impulsion. Also known as a courtesy circle or hunter circle.

opening rein

A rein aid created by the rider's moving the rein hand out to the side away from the horse's

One-ear bridle.
© CREDIT: PHOTOS.COM

shoulder, used to turn the horse in that direction without slowing his forward progress. Also known as leading rein.

opthalmia
🐎 *See* moon blindness.

orchard grass
A type of bunchgrass commonly used to make hay.

O-ring
🐎 *See* loose-ring bit.

osselet
A bony growth on the outside of the ankle joint caused by a wound, bruise, or strain. Symptoms are puffiness of the fetlock joint, soft tissue, and/or lameness. If lameness persists, the osselet may need to be surgically removed.

ossification
The abnormal transformation of tissue into bone, often in response to trauma or repetitive stress.

osteochondritis dissecans (OCD)
Inflammation of the joint cartilage, resulting in fragmentation of the cartilage. Occurs in young, growing horses and may be caused by nutritional deficiencies or excesses. Treatment may involve joint injections and stall rest, or surgery to remove cartilage fragments.

ostler
An old term for stablehand.

out of
Indicating a horse's maternal relationship. The phrase "Secretariat was out of Somethingroyal" indicates that Somethingroyal was Secretariat's mother.
🐎 *See also* by.

out-of-hand release
In jumping, a release in which the rider's hands follow the horse's head from takeoff to landing. The reins remain in a direct line from the rider's elbow to the horse's mouth. Also called an automatic release.
🐎 *Compare to* crest release.

out of the money
In racing, finishing worse than third. So called because bettors do not win on a horse that finishes worse than third.

outrider
In racing, the mounted escort that leads the field to the starting gate and, in flat or steeplechase racing, catches the loose horse of a jockey who is thrown before or during a race.

outside
1 The side closer to the rail of a riding ring or arena; the right leg of a rider who is moving counterclockwise around a ring is the outside leg. 2 In racing, a position away from the track's inner rail.

outside course
In horse showing, a hunter course in a large, open field with relatively

long, and therefore usually unrelated, distances between jumps.

🔹 *See also* related distance.

over at the knee

A conformation defect in which the upper leg arches forward from the knee when viewed from the side. If a straight line were dropped from the knee down, it would hit the ground in front of the hoof.

overbent

Describes a horse moving forward with too much sideways arc; this can be corrected by a rider's co-ordinating rein and leg aids. Also, used to describe a horse that is overflexed.

overface

In jumping, to present a horse at a fence or another obstacle that is too high or otherwise too difficult for the horse's ability or level of training. Overfacing a horse is a quick way to create long-term problems with regard to refusals and other disobediences.

overflexed

Too much bend at the poll, as indicated by the horse's face carried behind the vertical. The correction is to relax rein pressure while applying or maintaining the driving aids.

overgirth

🔹 *See* surcingle, definition 2.

overlay

In racing, higher odds than, in the handicapper's opinion, the horse's past performance would suggest. Considered to be a good bet.

overmounted

Riding a horse that is too difficult for that rider's ability.

overnight

In racing, a race for which entries close 72 hours or less before the first race on the day that particular race is to be run. Such a time frame allows trainers to make last-minute decisions about whether to enter their horses.

overo (OH-vairo)

A Paint or pinto coat of a dark color with white patches. The opposite of *tobiano*, which is a white coat with dark patches.

overreach boots

Protective covering for the backs of a horse's front feet against injury in case the hind feet brush against them; bell boots.

overreaching

A form of interference in which the horse strikes his front hooves, heels, or lower legs with his own hind hooves.

override

1 In foxhunting, to ride too close to the hounds, especially when they are checking, or to ride in front of the Field Master. Neither is considered proper behavior. **2** To ride a horse with aids that are too strong for that particular horse.

Overo.
© RICHARD KLIMESH

Oxbow stirrup.
© RICHARD KLIMESH

overtrack
At the walk or trot, to reach so far forward with the hind legs that the hind hoofprint lands partially or completely in front of the front hoofprint. Desirable in a dressage horse.

ox
In the pedigree of a warmblood or other crossbred horse, "ox" next to a horse's name indicates that the horse is a purebred Arabian.

 See also xx.

oxbow
A relatively narrow Western stirrup with a rounded bottom.

Oxer.
© STEVEN D. PRICE

oxer
In jumping, an obstacle made of two or more sets of standards to create width. The word comes from the reluctance of oxen and other bovines to jump width, the reason why rows of double fencing were used to separate fields. (Although a Liverpool and water jump test the ability to jump width, they are not considered oxers.)

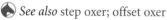 *See also* step oxer; offset oxer

O

pace
A two-beat lateral gait natural to some Standardbreds and, with some variations, to the Pasos and certain other breeds. The right foreleg and hind leg move simultaneously, as do the left foreleg and hind leg. The tendency to pace is largely inherited, although training can develop and enhance the ability.
 *See also* amble.

pacer
In harness racing, a Standardbred that paces, or a race for such horses. Pacers are generally faster than trotters.

pacey
A movement fault in which the horse's legs tend to move in lateral pairs.

pack
1 In foxhunting, the group of hounds used to hunt on a given day. Also, all the hounds owned by a foxhunt. 2 A wrapped bundle carried by a horse or mule.

packer
A horse with a kind temperament, one that will carry an inexperienced or inept rider safely and without objection.

pack horse
A horse that accompanies a traveler to carry supplies. The pack horse is led, not ridden.

pad
1 A fabric blanket worn between the saddle and the horse's back to cushion the back against the weight of the saddle and rider and also to absorb sweat. 2 A hard plastic or rubber sheet that covers and protects the sole of the foot against rocks and other hard objects. 3 In foxhunting, a fox's foot.

paddling
An undesirable movement in which one or more feet swing to the outside, similar to the motion of a canoe paddle. Also known as paddling out or winging out.

paddock
1 In racing, the enclosure where horses are saddled before a race. 2 A fenced area in which horses are turned out for free exercise or rest.

Pad for hoof.
© RICHARD KLIMESH

paddock boots

Low, laced or zipped riding footwear.

 Compare to jodhpur boots.

Paint

The American breed distinguished by patches of white and another color above its knee and also having at least one parent registered with the American Paint Horse Association, the Jockey Club (Thoroughbreds), or the American Quarter Horse Association. Although Paints and pintos resemble each other in coloration, the distinction is in their ancestry.

 See also overo *and* tobiano.

pair

Term used in driving to describe two horses hitched side by side.

palfrey

A small saddle horse of the Middle Ages and Renaissance that paced or ambled.

Palomino

Any horse having a golden yellow coat with white or cream mane and tail. When the word is capitalized, it refers to a member of that registered breed. As a color type (as distinguished from a breed), palomino individuals appear in many breeds, such as the American Quarter Horse and Paso Fino. The most prized color is that of a newly minted gold coin.

palpation

Manual examination by a veterinarian.

Pan American Games

The equestrian events in this quadrennial competition among teams from the Western Hemisphere are show jumping, dressage, and three-day eventing. Often abbreviated to Pan Am Games.

panel

1 One of the two padded sections under the cantle of a saddle that rest against the horse's back. **2** A solid, boarded portion of a fence line, often encountered in the foxhunting field.

panic snap

A special type of safety clasp used on the ends of cross-ties, trailer ties, and some lead ropes. The snap is easily released in case of emergency by pulling on it.

panniers

A pair of basketlike packs, usually made of canvas or nylon, strapped on either side of a pack horse.

papers

Common term for a registration certificate.

parade

A Western horse show division in which horses are judged at the walk, jog, and lope. The degree of eye-catching animation is taken into consideration, as well as the ornate (often silver-mounted) bridle, breastplate, and saddle that the horse wears.

Paddock boots.
© MILLER HARNESS COMPANY LLC

P

para-equestrian
A horse sports designation applying to riders with physical disabilities. Para-equestrian dressage is included in the USET High Performance sports.

parasite
An organism that sustains itself by living on or in and feeding from another organism. Internal parasites include intestinal worms and bots; external parasites include ticks and lice.

pari-mutuel
In racing, the predominant method of wagering at racetracks, in which all money bet is divided among holders of winning tickets after governmental and/or racing agencies deduct their share. From the French *parier mutuel,* meaning "mutual stake" or "betting among ourselves."

Side view of parrot mouth.
© RICHARD KLIMESH

park gait
In pleasure driving, a stylishly elegant medium trot.

park out
To stand with the hind legs stretched out behind, back hollowed, and head high. Some horses, such as Morgans, Arabians, and Saddlebreds, are taught to park out on command to display their conformation in the show ring. The practice derives from harness horses, who were taught to park out when stopped to take on or leave off passengers, because it is more difficult for them to shift

or move around when in such a position.
In horses not so trained, parking out can be a sign of abdominal pain.

parlay
In racing, a wager in which the winnings from a preceding race are reinvested in the next race.

parrot mouth
The conformation fault of an overshot upper jaw.
 Compare to monkey mouth.

part-board
 See lease.

pas de deux (pah de deuh)
A dressage exhibition or test in which two riders perform a pattern that offers a "mirror image" of each other's movements and transitions. From the French "step of, or for, two."

paso corto
The shorter, more collected gait of a Paso horse.

Paso Fino
The breed of laterally gaited horse that developed in the Caribbean from horses brought to Santo Domingo on Columbus's second voyage. Standing about 14 hands, with fine features that reflect their Arabian and Barb forebears, the Paso Fino is characterized by a brilliant yet comfortable four-beat lateral pacing gait in which only one hoof strikes the ground at a time. As distinguished from the

Peruvian Paso, the Paso Fino is somewhat smaller with a somewhat shorter stride. Paso Finos are used as show horses and as pleasure mounts.

paso largo
The longer, more extended gait of a Paso horse.

paso llano
 See Peruvian Paso.

passage (pah-SAHZ)
In dressage, a highly collected trot in which the horse appears to be floating across the ground.

pastern
The portion of the lower leg between the fetlock and the foot.
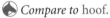 *Compare to* hoof.

past performances
1 In racing, published information that gives complete details on a horse's previous races and workouts for handicapping purposes.
2 In horse showing, the record of a horse's points and awards.

pasture
1 A large, grassy field for grazing horses. **2** The grass in such a field.

pasture board
A boarding arrangement in which the horse lives outdoors full-time, usually with a run-in shed for shelter.

pasture-sound
Describes a horse that is chronically lame and can no longer be ridden, but is comfortable and stable enough to be turned out.

patrol judge
In racing, an official who stands on an elevated platform and observes the running of the race in order to report possible rule violations, such as rough riding, to the stewards.

patron (pah-TROHN)
In polo, the sponsor of a team on which he customarily plays. The word is pronounced in the French or Spanish fashion.

pattern
The prescribed series of movements in certain Western classes, including reining, horsemanship, and equitation.

peacock stirrup
 See quick-release stirrup.

peanut roller
A derogatory term for a Western pleasure show horse that has been trained to carry its head extremely low, as if rolling peanuts along the floor.

peat moss
A dense, springy, highly absorbent plant that grows in swamps and is sometimes used as bedding for horse stalls.

peck
Describes a landing from a jump when a horse pitches forward or stumbles, thrusting the head toward the ground (as if pecking like a bird).

P

pecking order
In a group of horses, the order of status among the herd members. Every herd establishes a pecking order, with one horse being the alpha (dominant) horse.

pedal bone (PEE-dal)
 See coffin bone.

pedigree
A record of a horse's ancestry and breeding.

peel
A term used when cattle in a cutting competition move single file around the cutting horse and back to the rest of the herd.

Pegasus
In Greek mythology, the winged horse tamed and ridden by Perseus when he rescued Andromeda from the Minotaur.

Pelham bit.
© MILLER HARNESS COMPANY LLC

pelham
A two-rein bit that combines a curb and a snaffle.

pelham converter
Two straps, one on each side of a pelham bit, that connect the curb and snaffle bits, enabling the rider to use one rein instead of the two normally required when using a pelham (one rein is less likely to slip between the rider's fingers).

pelleted bedding
A highly absorbent processed wood product made of sawdust compressed into small pieces and used for bedding in stalls.

pellets
Feed that has been processed and compressed into small pieces. Usually made of grain or other concentrates, but hay or beet pulp pellets are also available.

pen
An enclosure for animals. In Western competitions, the riding arena is called the show pen.

penalty
In polo, the result of a foul. Depending on the severity of the foul, penalties range from automatic goals to defended or undefended shots at various distances from the penalized team's goalposts.

penning
 See team penning.

pentathlon
A five-phase competition that includes show jumping (the other phases are running, pistol shooting, fencing, and swimming). The event calls for all the skills once needed to deliver a military message.

Percheron
A draft breed, originating in the La Perche region of northern France. Infusions of Arabian and Barb blood gave the Percheron the most refined features of all the draft breeds. Predominantly colored from light to very dark gray,

P

Percherons have prominent withers, sloping shoulders, and short, powerful legs. The largest horse on record was a Percheron that measured 21 hands and weighed in excess of 3,000 pounds.

perfecta
In racing, a type of wager in which the bettor must select the first two horses without stipulating the order in which they will finish.
See also exacta.

perfect course
The result of a show-jumping class in which the number of horses in the jump-off round equals the number of prize ribbons being offered in that class. Abbreviated to PC.

performance
A horse show division in which the horses or riders are judged on their ability and skills, as opposed to a halter class. Typically refers to the Western disciplines of reining, cutting, roping, and so on.

periodic opthalmia
See moon blindness.

Peruvian Paso
The breed of laterally gaited horse that developed in Peru from horses brought by Spanish explorers and colonists. Standing between 14 and 15.2 hands, the Peruvian Paso is slightly larger than its Paso Fino cousins. It moves at two distinctive gaits: the paso llano, which has an evenly

spaced four-beat cadence; and the sobreandando, a faster and slightly more lateral movement. Peruvian Pasos are enjoyed as show horses and for pleasure riding.

pesade
In classical dressage, movement similar to a levade, but with an angle of 45 degrees or greater.

Pessoa, Rodrigo
The Brazilian show-jumping rider holds the distinction of having won three consecutive World Cup championships (1998–2000). He also won the 1998 World Show Jumping championship and, by disqualification, the 2004 Olympic Individual gold medal.

phaeton
In driving, a light four-wheeled carriage with one or two seats that face forward. Phaetons often have a high back and are fancifully and ornately decorated. The name comes from the Greek mythological figure, the son of Apollo, who drove the chariot of the sun so close to Earth that Zeus was obliged to strike down Phaeton with a thunderbolt to prevent the planet from catching fire.

phantom
In breeding, an artificial mare used to collect a stallion's semen for artificial insemination.

phenylbutazone
See bute.

Percheron.
© PERCHERON HORSE ASSOCIATION OF AMERICA

Peruvian Paso.
© DEBBIE PYE

P

photo finish

In racing, the end of a race in which two or more horses finish in such close order that only a high-speed photograph can reveal the exact order. Photos can be used to determine not only the winner, but the horses that finished second or third.

Piaffe.
CREDIT: AUDREY L. D. PETSCHEK

photosensitization

Hypersensitivity to sunlight. Can result from ingesting certain plant toxins and appears as red, flaky skin and hair loss.

piaffe (pee-AFF)

A highly collected trot in place. Found in upper-level dressage tests and also performed in haute école exhibitions, the piaffe requires the highest degree of impulsion and collection. The word is from the French, "to paw the ground in annoyance."

pick out

1 To use a hoof pick to clean a horse's feet. **2** To rid a stall of clumps of manure and urine-soaked bedding.

pick-up man

A rider in a rodeo who assists bronc riders in dismounting from the bucking horses.

piebald

A pinto or Paint coat consisting of patches of black and white.
Compare to skewbald.

Pigeon-toed horse.
© RICHARD KLIMESH

pigeon-toed

A conformation defect in which the toes of both forelegs angle in toward each other and affect the horse's stride.

pig-eyed

A conformation fault in which unattractively tiny, round eyes are set too close together.

piggin' string

A length of rope used by calf ropers to tie the calf's legs together.

pillars

Two vertical posts between which a horse is tied while learning the haute école movements of classical dressage.

pillion

The style of riding, most often found in Spanish folkloric events, in which the woman sits on the horse's rump behind the saddle and holds onto the male rider's waist.

pin firing

The technique of applying heat to a leg with hot needles, done to increase blood flow and thus promote healing. Thanks to more modern methods of stimulating blood flow by means of medications, the procedure is now rarely done.

pinhook

v. In racing, to buy a young, usually unraced horse with the purpose of trying to resell the animal at a profit.

pink

The color of the prize ribbon awarded for fifth place.

Pink

The familiar name for the scarlet coat worn by those male foxhunters who are entitled to wear one (the hunt staff plus gentlemen members of the hunt), commonly believed to be the name of the London tailor who originated the garment. Also known as hunting pink (not capitalized).

pinto

Any horse with a coat of patches of white and another color above its knee. Although multicolored horses are most closely associated with Western riding, they have been prized over the centuries throughout the world; pintos can be seen in art ranging from Japanese scrolls to paintings of the 17th-century Spanish artist Velasquez.

🖤 *See also* Paint; overo; tobiano.

pinworm

A small parasite that infests the intestines and the rectum. A sure symptom of infection is the horse's rubbing its tail against a fence post or another solid object in an attempt to relieve the anal itch. The remedy is to administer deworming medication.

pipe-opener

In racing, a short vigorous gallop intended to clear the horse's lungs.

pirouette

In dressage, a movement in which the horse's forequarters circle around the hindquarters in the walk or canter, while all four legs maintain the correct sequence of footfalls for the gait.

pivot

In reining work, a 90-degree turn with one stationary hind foot acting as a pivot.

place

1 In racing, second position at the finish. **2** To win a ribbon at a horse show.

placing judge

In racing, the official in charge of determining the order of finish. Photo-finish cameras, instant TV replay, and other technological aids assist in making such decisions.

plait

🖤 *See* braid.

plantar

The ligament below and behind the hock joint.

plate

In racing, a horseshoe most typically made of aluminum. Because of their lightness, plates are the usual shoes worn by flat and harness horses.

playday

A rodeolike contest that does not include events involving cattle or broncs. May include barrel racing, pole bending, goat tying, and gymkhana games.

Pinto.

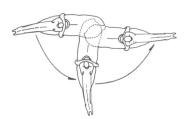

**Making two pivots
for a 180-degree turn.**
© CHERRY HILL 2000

P

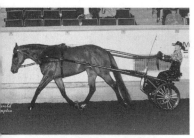

Pleasure driving.
© AMERICAN QUARTER
HORSE ASSOCIATION

Plow horses.
CREDIT: PHOTOS.COM

Black points on a bay horse.
CREDIT: PHOTOS.COM

Point-to-point race.
© ED CAMELLI

pleasure driving

A horse show class in which horses pull a four-wheel cart and are judged on their movement and manners. Piloted by drivers wearing formal clothing, the horses perform at the walk, park trot, and road trot.

plow horse

Any breed of draft horse historically used to pull farming implements. Today it is a derogatory term used for an unattractively heavy or poorly moving animal.

Pluvinel de la Baume, Antoine

The 17th-century French trainer and author whose books described several haute école movements, including the courbette and capriole. Pluvinel was also the first to introduce pillar work to encourage collection and the airs above the ground.

PMU foal

A foal produced as a by-product of the Premarin industry, which uses the urine of pregnant mares to create a hormone replacement therapy drug for women. The foals are often draft crosses and are sometimes sold to private buyers in the United States.

Poco Bueno

Second only to his father, King, on the American Quarter Horse Association's leading sire list during the 1950s, Poco Bueno earned many grand champion titles and is widely considered to be the most outstanding cutting horse sire of all time.

point

1 The widest part of a body feature, such as point of hip, point of shoulder, or point of hock. 2 A sharp edge on a cheek tooth, routinely filed away by floating. 3 The mane, leg, and tail colors or markings, when different from the body color. 4 In showing, a numerical value assigned to placings in a class. Points usually accumulate over the show season to be tallied for year-end awards.

point-to-point

A hunt race that takes place over a course of obstacles such as hedges, post-and-rails, and other natural obstacles routinely encountered while foxhunting. Entries are traditionally horses and riders who hunt with the foxhunt that sponsors the race.

pole

1 In jumping, to rap the hind legs with a bamboo pole when the horse is in the air over a fence. Considered illegal by most governing bodies, poling discourages a horse from hitting subsequent fences. 2 In racing, any of the markers around a track that indicate distances from the finish line, such as the quarter pole or mile pole.

pole bending

A timed Western horse show event

in which a horse-and-rider team weaves between six poles in a slalomlike pattern. The pattern begins with a gallop to the pole farthest from the start/finish line; the team circles around that pole and slaloms through the others, then weaves up through the poles, rounds the last one, and gallops across the start/finish line.

pole position

In racing, the starting-gate position of the horse closest to the inside rail.

poll

The highest portion of a horse's head, behind its ears.

poll evil

A bacterial infection of the bursa in the poll area. The symptoms are swelling and drainage of the infection. Antibiotics are the treatment.

polo

A mounted sport in which two opposing teams attempt, with long-handled mallets, to drive a ball between the other team's goalposts ("hockey on horseback" helps to explain the object). Teams consist of four players in outdoor polo and three players in arena, or indoor, polo. Originating in Asia (polo is a Tibetan word for "ball"), the sport was introduced to Europe by British cavalrymen who learned to play in India during the 19th century. An American newspaperman and sportsman, James

Gordon Bennett, brought polo to the United States in 1876.

The so-called golden age of American polo took place during the 1920s and 1930s, when large crowds lined polo fields to watch professionals, amateurs, and celebrities play. The button-down-collar shirt was devised to keep collar ends out of the eyes of polo players, while the familiar short-sleeved collarless polo shirt relieved players from similar upper-body restraint and distractions.

Polo is now played in this country on the international, club, intercollegiate, and interscholastic levels.

See also mallet; penalty; backhand; neck shot; tail shot.

polo wrap

A type of bandage that extends from the fetlock almost up to the knee. It provides support and protects against the impact of polo balls as well.

polyvinylchloride (PVC)

A hard, durable, white synthetic material commonly used to make fences and jumps.

pommel

The elevated front part of an English or Western saddle.

pony

1 *n.* A horse of any breed that measures no higher than 14.2 hands at maturity. **2** *n.* A member of any pony breed, which should not measure higher than 14.2 hands,

Pole bending.
© WYATT MCSPADDEN/
AMERICAN QUARTER HORSE ASSOCIATION

Polo.
© ED CAMELLI

Ponying.
CREDIT: PHOTOS.COM

although individuals of the breed may grow taller. (For example, a purebred Welsh pony that matures at 14.3 hands is still a pony.) Show ponies are divided into three categories: large, measuring between 13.2 and 14.2 hands; medium, between 12.2 and 13.2; and small, under 12.2. Ponies compete against others of the same category. **3** *n.* A horse of any size used in polo. **4** *n.* In racing, a horse of any size used to lead the racehorses out to the track. **5** *v.* As a verb, to lead another horse from horseback.

Pony Club

An educational and recreational equestrian organization for young people under the age of 21. Stressing theoretical and practical knowledge of riding and horse care, the U.S. Pony Club was modeled after the British version and incorporated in 1954. Local chapters are often sponsored by foxhunts. Every Pony Club member is tested and rated at levels that range from D, the most elementary, up to A, which is so demanding that only a few dozen youngsters annually qualify for this level.

pony goal

In polo, a goal scored when a pony, not a player, causes the ball to pass between the goalposts.

pony jock

In hunter/jumper showing, a strong young or small-statured rider who is hired by a pony's owner to ride the pony at a show.

Rider in the rise portion of the post.
© RICHARD KLIMESH

Pony of the Americas

A breed of American pony distinguished by its Appaloosa markings, striped hooves, and mottled muzzle. The breed originated in 1956 when an Appaloosa mare was bred to a Shetland pony stallion. The result, named Black Hand, was a miniature Appaloosa that became the new breed's foundation sire.

Ponies of the Americas are used for riding, especially the Western variety.

pony-strided

Of a horse, having a short stride.

pony trekking

Sightseeing on horseback. The phrase—and the concept—is used primarily in Britain, Ireland, and other Western European countries where vacationers ride ponies and horses for escorted full- or half-day outings.

port

The arched portion of the mouthpiece of a curb, Pelham, Kimberwicke, and similar bits. The port acts against the roof of the horse's mouth, causing the animal to flex its head as well as to shift its weight back to its hindquarters as an aid in slowing or halting.

post

1 To rise out of and sink back into the saddle in rhythm with the trot in order to make the gait more comfortable for the rider. English-style riders routinely post, as do Western riders when their horses are doing the long trot. The word is derived from *postillion*, the rider who sat on one of a team of coach horses to assist the driver in controlling the horses.

🐎 *See also* diagonal, definition 2.

2 In racing, term meaning the starting line.

post entry

A horse whose owner or trainer has been able to enter the animal in a race or other competition right before the competition begins.

posting trot

A trot to which the rider posts, as distinguished from a sitting trot. Also called a rising trot.

post-legged

A conformation fault marked by overly straight angulation between the gaskin and cannon, with a correspondingly straight hock joint.

postmortem

An autopsy to determine the cause of death.

post parade

The pre-race procession in front of the grandstand that gives spectators the chance to view the horses.

post position

In racing, the order of horses in the starting gate, indicated by numbers that begin with the stall closest to the rail. Post positions are assigned by the racing secretary, who draws them randomly by pulling numbered pills out of a box.

post time

In racing, the time when a race is scheduled to begin, at which point no further wagering is permitted.

Potomac horse fever

A debilitating viral infection first identified in the mid-Atlantic states but now found elsewhere in the United States. The cause has not yet been determined. Symptoms include high fever and very loose bowels, often accompanied by laminitis. Treatment involves administering fluids and electrolytes, antibiotics, and anti-inflammatory medicine for the laminitis.

poultice

A thick paste applied to the lower legs and then wrapped. Its purpose is to reduce heat and swelling in the limbs.

Thoroughbreds in a Kentucky Derby post parade.
© STEVEN D. PRICE

Power and Speed

A show-jumping class in which the horse's ability to jump high and then fast are tested. A horse that faultlessly jumps the higher and wider fences of the first part of the course goes on to slightly lower fences where the time to complete that part of the course becomes a determining factor.

prairie grass

A variety of hay grass.

Preakness Stakes

The second race of the Triple

P

Crown, held the third Saturday in May at Pimlico Racetrack in Baltimore, Maryland. The race is held at a distance of a mile and three-eighths, shorter than both the Kentucky Derby and the Belmont Stakes.

prebiotic
A nutrient that nourishes the beneficial bacteria in a horse's digestive system. Feeding such a nutrient helps maintain healthy digestive function.

preference list
In racing, a system in which horses with the longest time since their last race or chance to race are given greater consideration to be accepted for the next race for which they qualify.

preliminary
The combined training level between training and intermediate. Often abbreviated as "Prelim," this level is intended to prepare horses and riders for international One Star events. The dressage test may include medium paces at the trot and canter, leg yielding, shoulder-in, rein back, and changes of lead through the trot. The cross-country phase includes lines, corners, simple bounces, slopes, and combinations involving water or narrow fences. The cross-country course will incorporate 28 to 32 obstacles over a distance of 2,200 to 2,800 meters, to be ridden at 520 meters per minute. Fences may be up to 3 feet 7 inches in height, with spreads of up to 4 feet 7 inches and drops of up to 5 feet 3 inches. The show-jumping course includes 11 to 13 obstacles with heights up to 3 feet 7 inches and spreads of up to 4 feet 3 inches.

See also beginner novice; novice; training; intermediate; advanced.

premarin
A hormone-replacement drug for women, made from the estrogen-rich urine of pregnant mares.

See also PMU foal.

premolar
Twelve teeth that are behind the bars and in front of the molars on both the upper and lower jaws.

prepotency
The ability of a stallion to pass on desirable characteristics to his offspring.

pre-purchase exam
An assessment by a veterinarian prior to the sale of a horse, usually conducted by the vet chosen by the prospective buyer. The sale is usually contingent upon the exam.

presentation
In driving, a phase of a combined driving event or a separate event in which entries are judged on the appearance of the horse(s), vehicle, driver, and (if any) grooms.

pressure sore
A wound caused by pressure on a certain point over a sustained period

of time, such as under a bandage or on a horse that spends too much time lying down due to illness.

Prince of Wales spur
The English-style spur that has a thin, curved knob end. Named after the future King Edward VII of Great Britain.

Prix Caprilli
A dressage test that includes one or more jumps.

Prix St. Georges (PSG)
In dressage, the first of the FEI levels. Test movements include canter half pass.

prize list
A booklet that lists the classes, rules, and other pertinent information for a horse show.

probiotic
The beneficial bacteria in a horse's digestive system, available in live cultures as a feed supplement.

produce
The offspring of a mare. The offspring of a stallion is known as his *get*.

program
A publication that lists entries and other information about the event's participants and competitions. Racing programs may also list the morning line odds.

propping
Seeming to push back with the front legs in what appears to be a momentary hesitation. It is usually caused by being startled or a reluctance to continue moving forward.

protest
In racing, a written complaint against any horse that has started in a race, to be made to the stewards within 48 hours after the race was run. An example of a protest may involve the discovery that a certain horse was ineligible for the race in which it ran.

proud cut
To geld a stallion incompletely, leaving behind some of the testosterone-producing tissues. Historically, this was sometimes done deliberately, to produce a nonbreeding animal that retained desirable stallion-like qualities. Due to changes in horsekeeping as well as advances in medical techniques, "proud cutting" no longer occurs. However, a cryptorchid stallion is sometimes inaccurately referred to as "proud cut."

Przewalski's horse.
CREDIT: PHOTOS.COM

proud flesh
Excessive granulation tissue that becomes raised above the level of the surrounding skin and delays healing.

Przewalski's horse
(sh-VALL-sky's horse)
An Asian subspecies of equine (*Equus ferus przewalskii* or *Equus caballus przewalskii,* classification is debated) that is considered the only living truly wild horse.

P

(American mustangs, for example, are descendants of domestic horses and thus are technically feral, not wild.) There are around 1,500 remaining Przewalski's horses living in zoos around the world.

psyllium

A supplement made of the seed husks of the psyllium plant, given to horses who are fed on sandy soil to flush sand out of the intestines, preventing sand colic.

public trainer

In racing, a trainer whose services are available to horse owners in general and who trains the horses of more than one owner. The opposite is a private trainer, who works for only one racing stable.

puissance

A high-jumping contest in which one jump is raised higher in each round. As horses knock down the jump, they are eliminated. The winner is the horse that jumps the highest.

pull

To shorten a mane or tail by yanking out the longest hairs until the mane or tail reaches the desired length. Pulling manes and tails gives them a more natural look than trimming the ends of the hair.

🐾 *Compare to* bobtail; hog; roach, definition 2.

pulley rein

An emergency-brake stopping technique in which the rider

Pulley rein.
CREDIT: JAMES C. WOFFORD

braces one hand against the horse's withers while pulling the other rein back and up with the other hand. The method gives the rider the greatest leverage, which is useful when trying to deal with a horse that has bolted.

pull leather

In saddle bronc riding, to hold onto the saddle; grounds for disqualification.

puppy

In foxhunting, a young hound that has not been entered into the pack.

purchase

The parts of a Western bit above the mouthpiece.

🐾 *See also* shank.

purebred

A horse whose sire and dam are of the same breed.

purple

The color of the prize ribbon awarded for seventh place.

purse

The prize monies offered in a competition. In racing, purses generally consist of nomination, sustaining or entry fees, and any added money such as a sponsor's contribution.

put down

A euphemism for euthanize.

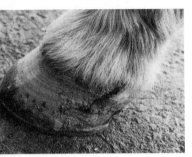

Quarter crack.
© RICHARD KLIMESH

quadrille

A dressage exhibition in which horses and riders execute haute école movements choreographed into dancelike routines and performed to musical accompaniment. Although the word suggests that four horses take part, which was indeed the original concept, quadrilles now consist of four, eight, or twelve. Popular at European courts during the 16th to the 18th centuries, quadrilles are now most frequently seen as part of performances by the Spanish Riding School and the Cadre Noire.

qualify

To become eligible for further competition, such as end-of-year horse show events, by winning a certain number of points or events.

quarantine

A voluntary or mandatory isolation of one horse or a group of horses to prevent the spread of a contagious disease.

quarry

In foxhunting, the fox or coyote that is being hunted.

quarter crack

A crack in the quarter section of the hoof (the portion between the heel and the toe) extending downward from the coronet toward the sole. The most common cause is dryness of the hoof. A bar shoe will stabilize a small crack, which will then be allowed to heal by growing out. Otherwise, the crack must be filled in with a synthetic substance before the bar shoe is attached.

🔵 *Compare to* sand crack.

Quarter Horse

🔵 *See* American Quarter Horse.

Quarter Horse bars

A sizing designation that refers to the gullet width of Western saddles. Although not standardized among manufacturers, approximate gullet widths are as follows: regular Quarter Horse bars, 5-3/4 inches; semi-Quarter Horse bars, 6 inches; full Quarter Horse bars, 6-1/4 to 6-1/2 inches.

quarter marks

A somewhat old-fashioned decorative technique of brushing the

hair on the horse's haunches
into a pattern, usually a check-
erboard shape, using a stencil.
Formerly seen among
racehorses and eventers.

Quarter Pony
A Quarter Horse that matures at
less than 14.2 hands.

quarter sheet
A wool or synthetic fleece sheet
made to cover the horse's back and
hindquarters, for riding in cold
weather.

question
In show jumping and eventing, a
complicated jump or a tricky line
of two or more jumps is sometimes referred to as a "question"
being asked of the horse by the
course designer. The way that the
horse chooses to negotiate the obstacle is called the "answer."

quick
1 *adj.* Having a tendency to approach jumps at a faster than ideal
pace. 2 *n.* The familiar term for
the laminae, or the "live" part of
the hoof, that feels pain and may
bleed if accidentally cut by the
farrier.

quick-release stirrup
An English-style stirrup having
its tread held in place by a strong
rubber band. The rubber band
releases if and when the rider falls
to prevent the rider's foot from becoming caught in the stirrup (and
the rider being dragged). Also

known as a peacock stirrup or a
safety stirrup.

quid
A ball of partially chewed feed,
such as hay or grass, that has been
spit out by the horse. This behavior, known as quidding, is often
the result of a dental problem.

quiet
Term used to describe a horse that
is gentle, not excitable or spooky,
and easy to handle.

quirt
A short, thick leather whip.

quit
In cutting, to stop working a cow,
done when, in the rider's estimation, further working would not
gain any more points. If time permits, the rider may then ask the
horse to cut and work another cow.

quittor
A hoof abscess that works its way
up through the hoof, bursting out
and seeping pus at the coronet
band.

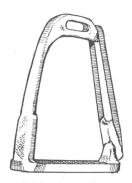

Quick-release stirrup.

R

rabbit

In racing, a horse that is sent to the lead to establish a fast pace. The strategy is for the "rabbit" to tire out other horses so that another horse that is linked with the rabbit in the betting pool can come from behind and win.

rabicano

A coat color in which a few, scattered white hairs appear amid a darker-colored background, usually on the hindquarters and dock.

rabies

A neurological disease transmitted by the bite of an infected animal. A rabid horse may initially be lethargic, but as the disease progresses the horse becomes disoriented and violent. A common symptom is head pressing, in which the horse presses the front of its head against a wall. In the final stages, the horse becomes paralyzed. Rabies is always fatal, and there is no cure.

racing commission

A government-appointed body in charge of regulating and supervising the conduct of racing in a state or province. Often known as a racing board.

racing secretary

In racing, the track official who is responsible for establishing the conditions of races and other general administrative duties.

rack

A rapid lateral gait in which the horse's feet hit the ground individually, ideally in a circular pattern (viz., left hind, left fore, right fore, right hind). The ability to rack is natural to American Saddlebreds, which, when shown at the rack and slow gait in addition to the walk, trot, and canter, are known as five-gaited horses. Other breeds that perform the rack, which is identical to the Paso's gait, include the Racking Horse and Rocky Mountain Horse.

🖤 *See also* slow gait.

radiograph

🖤 *See* X-ray.

rail

1 The inner barrier around a

racetrack. **2** In jumping, a horizontal wooden pole of which many fences are constructed.

rain rot

A fungal skin condition caused by persistent damp weather in which the horse's skin stays wet for a period of time. Usually occurring on the back and haunches, rain rot is characterized by bumpy, scabby skin and hair loss. It is treated with antifungal cleaners and by keeping the horse dry and clean.

ramp

A tooth abnormality in which the surface of the tooth is at an angle. Can be corrected by floating.

rangy (range-y)

A slang term for having an easy and loose movement at all gaits.

rank

Term used for a horse that is difficult to control.

rasp

A large filing tool used by a farrier to shape the edges of the hoof.

ratcatcher

1 In foxhunting, informal clothes (compared to formal hunting attire), such as brown boots and tweed coats, worn during the cubbing season. The word refers to the kind of clothes worn by 19th-century British men whose job was to trap rodents. **2** A woman's collarless riding shirt. Worn with a detachable choker collar (often monogrammed), ratcatcher shirts are appropriate for hunter/jumper horse showing.

rate

1 In working cow horse and roping classes, a horse's ability to maintain relative speed and position on a cow by speeding up or slowing down as necessary, as in "that horse rated his cow just right." **2** In racing, to encourage a horse to settle down and run in a relaxed fashion.

rated show

In hunter/jumper showing, a horse show that is recognized by the USEF and is rated AA, A, B, or C. The rating determines the number of points awarded for placings in each class.

rating

In polo, the number of goals that a player would theoretically score in a game. Ratings are determined by the U.S. Polo Association. In all but the most informal matches, the ratings for all players on a team are totaled, and, to ensure fairness, the lower-rated team begins the match with a score equal to the difference between the two totals. Also known as handicap.

ration balancer

A pelleted feed for horses that contains vitamins and minerals to complement a diet of hay or grass. It is not a grain and is fed in much smaller amounts than grain is usually fed, so it will not cause a horse to become overweight or hot.

reach

Term used when a jumping horse must extend the forelegs farther than normal in order to clear the fence, usually the result of having left the ground too far away from the obstacle.

rearing

A horse's very dangerous habit of standing up on its hind legs in hand or under saddle, as a resistance to going forward. Rearing is a very difficult habit to break and is sometimes considered to be the most dangerous habit a horse can have. In hand, the handler may be struck on the head or face by the horse's front hooves. Under saddle, the rider may fall, or worse, the horse may lose its balance and fall backward, crushing the rider beneath him.

recognized show

A horse show that is sanctioned by and run under the rules of a national horse show organization, with points counting toward year-end awards or championships.

🐎 *See also* schooling show; unrecognized show.

recurrent uveitis

🐎 *See* moon blindness.

red

The color of the prize ribbon awarded for second place.

red dun

A form of dun with a yellowish or tan-colored body color and a mane and tail that are red or reddish, flaxen, white, or mixed. The horse also has a red or reddish dorsal stripe and, usually, red or reddish zebra stripes on legs and a transverse stripe over the withers.

red roan

A bay coat with white hairs that give the coat a reddish tinge. A red roan can have a red, black, or flaxen mane and/or tail.

reed canary grass

A hay grass.

reef

v. To spur a horse harshly, such as to make a bronc buck harder in a rodeo.

referee

In polo, the official who sits in the stands and adjudicates any matter over which the two mounted umpires disagree. Known familiarly as the "third man."

refusal

Describes a horse's failure to attempt a jump. In show jumping and in eventing's stadium-jumping phase, a first refusal is scored as four faults, and a second results in elimination. In eventing, a refusal at a cross-country obstacle is scored 20 faults for the first refusal, 40 for a second refusal at the same obstacle, and elimination for a third refusal at the same obstacle. Commonly known as a "stop."

R

registration certificate

A document issued by a registry that certifies a horse is duly enrolled with a breed organization. The document includes the birthdate and all identification markings of the animal, registration number, owner, and breeder.

Regumate

A hormone-replacement drug for mares that helps regulate the heat cycle, minimizing hormone-related behavioral changes.

rein-back

A movement in which the horse backs up while under saddle. The horse's legs move in diagonal pairs, as in the trot, as opposed to individually, as in the walk.

reining

A Western event or horse show class in which horses are judged on their ability to execute a prearranged pattern of such maneuvers as rundowns, sliding stops, rollbacks, circles, and spins. Scoring is done on the basis of 70 as an average ride, with full or half points added or deducted for the way in which the horse performs each movement.

reins

The straps connecting the bridle to the rider's hands. Although most reins are made of leather, other materials include canvas and cotton rope. Braided leather or rubber covering helps prevent

American Quarter Horse executing a reining pattern.
© D. R. STOECKLEIN/
AMERICAN QUARTER HORSE ASSOCIATION

slipping through the rider's fingers in wet weather.

⬥ *See also* mecate; romal.

Reinsmanship

A driving class in which entries are judged primarily on the knowledge, ability, and skill of the driver and the communication between driver and horse.

related distance

In jumping, fences of which the measurements between them are counted in terms of a set number of horses' strides. Although there is no hard-and-fast rule about when related distances end, the widely accepted limit is beyond eight or ten strides.

release

In jumping, the position of the rider's hands carried or placed so they do not restrict the horse's head and neck from takeoff to landing.

⬥ *See also* crest release; out-of-hand release.

remount

An obsolete term for any horse used for military purposes. The word is based on the cavalry's need for a great many horses to serve as fresh mounts.

remuda (ruh-MYOOD-uh)

A Western term for a herd from which horses that will be used for the day's work are drawn; from the Spanish for "change [of horses]."

renvers (RON-vair)

In dressage, a two-track oblique movement in which the horse's forelegs follow an inner track and his hind legs an outer track.

🌀 *See also* travers.

reserve

1 Second place in the championship award standings. The horse or rider is known as the reserve champion and wins a tricolor ribbon of yellow, red, and white.
2 An honorary or courtesy placing behind a class's ribbon-winners, usually awarded to a rider whose efforts impressed the judge (but not enough to win a ribbon).

resistance

1 Any form of disobedience by a horse that opposes the rider's or handler's request. **2** A body's ability to withstand infection or disease.

resistance-free training

The technique of getting a horse to accept being handled, tacked, and ridden that emphasizes patience and an understanding of the equine mind instead of relying on force.

🌀 *See also* natural horsemanship; horse gentler.

resistant strain

A form of a virus, bacteria, intestinal parasite, or other organism that has evolved to be able to withstand common treatments. Over-use of antibiotics and dewormers can lead to resistant strains and should be avoided.

restricted stakes

In racing, a stakes race limited to horses that meet certain criteria, such as having been bred in a particular state or purchased through or consigned to a particular sale.

return

A clause in a breeding contract that provides that a mare that does not become pregnant may be bred again at no cost.

Rhinelander

A German warmblood breed that was developed in the Rhineland, Westphalia, and Saxony regions. Like other central European warmbloods, Rhinelanders stand approximately 16.2 hands, have good bone and muscle, and are used in dressage and show jumping.

rhinopneumonitis

A contagious upper-respiratory condition with symptoms that include weakness, fever, dry cough, and a nasal discharge. Serious neurological complications may also develop. The virus also causes abortion in pregnant mares. A vaccine offers short-term immunity. Otherwise, administering antibiotics and fluids is the treatment.

ribbon

The traditional rosette prize awarded in horse shows. The ribbon's color designates the order of finish: blue for first place, red for second, yellow for third, white for fourth, pink for fifth, green for sixth, purple for seventh, and

R

brown for eighth. In addition, the tricolor ribbon awarded to the high-point champion of a division is a combination of blue, red, and yellow; the ribbon for reserve champion is red, yellow, and white.

ridden out
In racing, to finish the race under mild urging, usually with a limited use of the whip.

ride and tie
A competition in which teams composed of two humans and one horse cover a distance of between 25 and 40 miles. One person rides the horse as far as he or she thinks the other person can most effectively run, then dismounts and ties the horse to a tree or another object and continues along the course on foot. The second person reaches the horse and rides past the first person. This leapfrog continues until both the rider and the runner cross the finish line. The team that completes the course in the fastest time is the winner.

ride-off
 See test, definition 2.

ridgeling; rig
 See cryptorchid.

riding off
In polo, a defensive maneuver in which a player positions his pony's shoulder against an opposing pony's shoulder so his pony can push the opponent away from being able to stroke the ball or from the line of the ball.

rimfire
A term for a Western saddle's double rigging.

ring
Term for a riding arena.

ring bit
A bit that is in the shape of a circle. Part of the ring goes through the horse's mouth.
 See also Chifney bit.

ringbone
Arthritis of the joints caused by new bone growth around the pastern joint (high ringbone) or around the coffin joint (low ringbone). The growth is precipitated by sudden or constant strain to the foot. Symptoms include heat, swelling, and eventual lameness. If and when corrective shoeing and anti-inflammatory medication can no longer help, surgery may be indicated.

ringmaster
The horse show official who announces the start of each class, customarily by sounding a coach horn. Dressed in a coachman's scarlet coat, the ringmaster also helps with award presentation.

ringworm
A contagious fungus that affects the hair and outer layers of skin. Symptoms include round scaly or crusty patches. Ringworm is treated by topical medication.

riot

In foxhunting, hounds that are chasing an incorrect quarry, such as deer, are said to run riot.

rising

Approaching in age. A horse that is "rising eight" is almost eight years old.

rising trot

The posting trot.

RNPA

In polo, a mallet head having a rounded midsection and tapered flat ends. The initials stand for Royal Navy Polo Association.

roach

1 Curved or rounded, as a roached back of a horse or rider. **2** To trim a mane so short that the hairs stand up, done for appearance, ease of care, and to keep the mane out of the way of the rider.

road gait

In pleasure driving, an extended trot that is faster than the park gait.

roads and tracks

Phases A and C of the speed-and-endurance portion of eventing, roads and tracks serves as a warm-up and cool-down for phase B, the steeplechase, and consists of several miles of slow- to medium-paced trotting or cantering. In the short format of eventing, roads and tracks has been eliminated or shortened considerably.

Roadster Pony

A horse show class in which Hackney ponies pull road wagons or sulky bikes and are judged on their animated walk and trot.

road wagon

A light, four-wheeled vehicle used in Roadster Pony classes.

roaring

A deep, throaty noise made during exercise. It is caused by a partial paralysis of the larynx that surgery is often able to correct.

Rocinante

Don Quixote's elderly and painfully thin horse. The name roughly means "formerly a hack."

rockgrinder

A Western spur with 18 tines on its rowel.

Rocky Mountain Horse

The American breed descended from horses brought to America by Spanish explorers and colonists and characterized by a natural four-beat ambling gait in which all four feet are heard striking the ground individually. Standing 14.2 to 16 hands, with a solid coat (most often a light chocolate brown) and flaxen mane and tail, the Rocky Mountain Horse breed is traced back to Old Tobe, a prepotent stallion owned by Sam Tuttle of Kentucky. Rocky Mountain Horses are used as pleasure mounts and in competitive trail and endurance riding.

Don Quixote and Rocinante.
CREDIT: PHOTOS.COM

Bit with rollers.
© MILLER HARNESS COMPANY LLC

Romal.
© CHERRY HILL

rodeo

A Western competition composed of such events as calf roping, bareback and saddle bronc riding, bull riding, steer wrestling, and barrel racing. The sport developed from informal competitions in which cowboys vied to see who was the best rider or owned the best ranch horse, with wagering backing up their claims. The 1800s saw the first formal rodeos, with entry fees and admission charges making up the prize money. There are now thousands of rodeos in the United States and Canada, together with considerable TV coverage, especially the Professional Rodeo Cowboys Association's year-end National Finals Rodeo in Las Vegas, Nevada.

rogue

Used to describe a horse that is willfully bad-tempered; also, roguey; rogueish.

Rolex Kentucky

The only four-star international three-day event in the United States, ranking alongside Britain's Badminton and Burleigh, as well as the Olympics.

rollback

1 In reining, a movement in which the horse halts, turns 180 degrees by pivoting on the inside hind leg, and then lopes off. **2** In jumping, a series of two jumps, in which the horse jumps the first jump and then immediately reverses direction to jump the second jump in the opposite direction.

roller

1 *See* surcingle.
2 *See* anticast roller.

rollers

Small rotating devices on the mouthpiece of a bit that encourage a horse to salivate. That in turn makes the bit more palatable and the horse more responsive to the bit.

Rollkur

See hyperflexion.

romal (ro-MAHL)

1 A type of rein in which the straps coming from the bit join into one rein at the point where the rider holds them. **2** The Western style of riding in which the rider uses such a rein.

roman nose

Term used for a horse with convex, or bulging, profile.

root

To forcefully extend the head and neck down and forward in an attempt to pull the reins out of the rider's hands.

rope halter

A hand-tied halter made of nylon or cotton rope without hardware. Specially placed knots on the noseband are intended to improve the handler's control of the horse.

roping

See tie-down roping; calf roping; team roping.

R

rose gray

The body color composed of a mixture of chestnut and white hairs.

rosette

1 Decorative, circular leather pieces on a Western saddle, to which saddle strings are often attached. **2** A champion or reserve champion ribbon.

rosinback

The slang term for a draft horse that is used as a vaulting horse in the circus. Dusting a horse's back with rosin reduces the chance of the vaulter's feet slipping.

rough board

An arrangement in which the horse is provided with accommodations, such as a paddock or pasture and a stall or shed. All of the care, such as feeding, watering, stall cleaning, grooming, and exercise, are the responsibility of the horse's owner. The term is sometimes used to refer to pasture board.

🐎 *Compare to* full board.

round

Describes a horse that is ridden on the bit with its back lifted and hind legs stepping well under its body. The graceful arc made by the horse's topline from poll to tail has a "round" appearance.

round and down

In dressage, a way of riding the horse to warm up and stretch, in a round carriage but with the head and neck much lower than would normally be desirable. Ideally, the horse's head should not come behind the vertical during this stretch.

round bale

A large bale of hay weighing up to 1,500 pounds, made by rolling the hay into a cylindrical shape and wrapping it with twine, netting, or plastic. Round bales require special equipment to move, but they are useful for feeding groups of horses outdoors.

Round bales.
CREDIT: PHOTOS.COM

round pen

A large (typically 60-foot-wide), circular enclosure in which horses are trained.

roundup

Gathering pastured cattle or horses into a large group preparatory to moving the herd to another location.

rowel

The pointed wheel of a spur. A roweled spur is a traditional Western accessory. Some dressage spurs have tiny rowels. The length, shape (especially whether the end is sharp or blunt), and number of rowels determine the spur's severity.

Rowels on a Western spur.
CREDIT: PHOTOS.COM

rub

In jumping, contact by a horse's foot or leg against the top of a fence that is not hard enough to knock the fence down; also called a touch or tick.

rub on

To groom, as in "I've rubbed on that horse for a year now."

rug
An old British term for a horse blanket.

Rugged Lark
The first American Quarter Horse to earn the AQHA's Superhorse title twice, in 1985 and 1987. A consistent ribbon-winner in reining, hunter events, Western riding, trail, Western pleasure, and pleasure driving, he was also a successful sire: he became the first Superhorse to sire a Superhorse when his son Look Whos Larkin won that title.

Once retired, Rugged Lark served as AQHA ambassador, with appearances at the 1996 Olympic Games in Atlanta and the 1999 Special Olympics World Games in Raleigh, North Carolina.

Run-in shed.
CREDIT: PHOTOS.COM

run
1 In foxhunting, the entire length of a chase. **2** In Western terminology, to gallop.

run-down
1 In reining, a pattern movement in which the horse lopes or gallops from one end of the arena to the other. The movement begins with rapid acceleration and usually ends with a sliding stop. **2** Excessive flexion of the fetlock joints during fast work, such as racing, causing the backs of the fetlocks to contact the ground. **3** A type of protective bandage worn to protect the ankles against abrasions.

run-in shed
A three-sided, roofed structure in a pasture or paddock that horses may use for protection from the elements.

running martingale
A martingale with two forks that are attached to the reins by means of metal rings, through which the reins slide. Used most often in show jumping and eventing.

running W
A cruel and outdated training device that is used to pull a horse's front legs out from under it.

running walk
A smooth half-walk/half-trot gait natural to Tennessee Walking Horses and certain other gaited breeds.

run out
In jumping, a refusal in the form of evading the fence by swerving off to one side.

rye
A cereal used as feed.

rye grass
A hay grass also used as straw.

The Western saddle.

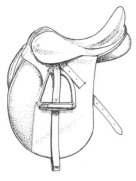

The Eastern saddle.

sack out

To desensitize a horse to various stimuli, such as saddle pads, ropes, whips, plastic bags, and other items, by touching and rubbing them on the horse's body. To some, the term has an unsavory connotation, since the old-fashioned form of sacking out essentially consisted of beating the horse with a wet sack until it gave up resisting. Nowadays, however, this type of sacking out is generally not practiced.

sacroiliac subluxation

Displacement of the sacroiliac joint, resulting in a visible bump at the top of the hip, which is called a hunter's bump or jumper's bump.

saddle

1 The piece of tack in which a rider sits. The two major classifications are the Western, or stock saddle, with its high pommel and cantle designed for comfort and function while doing ranch work, and the English saddle, flatter and thinner to allow greater contact between the rider's seat and legs and the horse. Within the Western category are saddles designed for such activities as roping, reining, and barrel racing, along with ones with ornate silver ornamentation for parade use. English saddles include the forward-seat variety for jumping, an even flatter dressage and gaited-horse type, and others for distance riding, racing, sidesaddle riding, and polo. **2** In driving, the piece of harness on the back of the horse to which the terrets are attached.

saddle bags

A pair of storage sacks carried over the cantle or pommel of a saddle.

saddle blanket

A woven wool blanket used as a saddle pad under a Western saddle.

Saddlebred

 See American Saddlebred.

saddle fitter

A professional who assesses the fit of a saddle on a horse and makes needed adjustments by shifting or restuffing the flocking in the panels.

saddle horse

A horse that is used for riding, as

opposed to a driving horse or a pack horse, for example.

saddle mark
1 A scar in the form of a patch of white hair on the withers caused by pressure from a poorly fitting saddle. **2** A natural marking of white hairs in the area of the back where the saddle would go.

saddle pad
A cloth pad, either square or saddle-shaped, that is placed under the saddle both to cushion the horse's back and to protect the saddle from dirt and sweat.

saddleseat equitation
The English-style technique used to ride American Saddlebreds, Tennessee Walking Horses, and other gaited horses. The rider's position is characterized by straight legs held away from the horse's sides and hands held relatively high.

saddle soap
A glycerin-based soap used to clean and condition leather.

saddle sore
A raw sore on the back or withers caused by the rubbing of a badly fitted saddle or saddle blanket or pad. Treatment includes cleaning and dressing the wound (and draining any trapped pus or blood), followed by rest until the wound has healed.

saddle strings
Thin strips of leather attached to a Western saddle. Originally used to tie items such as ropes to the saddle, they are now largely decorative.

safety
In polo, a penalty resulting from a player stroking the ball over his team's backline.

safety stirrup
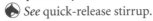 *See* quick-release stirrup.

saline solution
A mild mixture of salt and water used to flush debris from eyes, mouth, or wounds.

salt block
A hard brick of salt, often combined with essential trace minerals, provided to a horse to lick and chew.

sand colic
Colic that results from a buildup of sand in the intestine, such as when a horse's feed is placed on sandy ground or when the animal develops the bad habit of eating sand.

sand crack
A vertical crack in the hoof extending upward from the ground toward the coronet band.
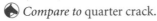 *Compare to* quarter crack.

sandwich box
In foxhunting and in horse show appointments classes, the leather case strapped to the saddle in which sandwiches are carried. The sandwiches they contain are traditionally ham or another

S

plain meat between crustless bread (on the theory that crusts might cause the rider/eater to choke on them).

Santini, Piero
A 20th-century Italian horseman and author, as well as an early advocate of Federico Caprilli's forward-seat riding theories.

savage
Term used when a horse attacks another horse or another living creature (including a human).

sawbuck
A wooden support structure used to attach packs to a pack horse.

sawdust
Fine wood filings used as bedding. Often available in bulk from sawmills, sawdust is soft, absorbent, and inexpensive in lumber-producing regions, but can be dusty.

scalp
To strike and injure the coronet band of the hind foot with the toe of the forefoot.

scarlet
In foxhunting, the proper term for a red coat.
🐎 *See also* Pink.

scenting
In foxhunting, the ability of hounds to follow a fox's trail.

school
v. To train a horse.

schooling ring
The warm-up area at a horse show. Known in other countries as the collecting ring.

schooling show
An unrecognized horse show that is intended to be a young horse's or novice rider's initial exposure to competition.

school movements (or figures)
Exercises and movements to improve balance, rhythm, and timing of horse and rider associated with classical horsemanship, such as the shoulder-in, renvers, passage, and piaffe; also known as manège movements.

Schwung
From the German word for "momentum," this dressage term describes the transmission of an energetic impulse created by the horse's hind legs into the horse's forward movement. An elastically swinging back is essential.

sclera
The white outer membrane of the eyeball, best known among horsemen as the human-eye feature of the Appaloosa. When a horse is alarmed, the sclera may also become visible.

scope
1 A horse's ability to jump high height and width.
🐎 2 *See* endoscope.

scopy
Describes a horse that jumps in

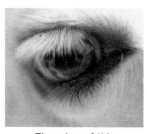
The sclera of this horse's eye is visible.
CREDIT: PHOTOS.COM

good form, revealing a potential ability to jump much higher if needed.

Scotch

Of a calf-roping horse, to halt before being given the cue to do so; also called *set up*.

Scotch spire

In driving, the tall decorative projection on the harness collar. Chiefly worn on the show or exhibition harness of draft horses.

Scout

The pinto ridden by Tonto, the faithful companion of the Lone Ranger, in the *Lone Ranger* movies and television series.

scratch

To withdraw an entered horse from a race or horse show class. In racing, scratch time is generally 24 hours before race day, although for stakes races, horses can be scratched up to 15 minutes before post time. In most instances, horse show entries can be scratched the day of the competition only with a veterinarian's approval.

scratches

A fungal infection of the lower legs associated with muddy conditions. Symptoms include scaly bumps and scabs on the backs of the pasterns and fetlocks, hair loss, and swelling of the lower legs in severe cases.

screw

Antiquated term for a worthless or worn-out horse.

scrim

A lightweight stable sheet made of a net fabric used in hot weather to keep a horse cool and to keep flies off.

scurf (or scarf)

A dermatological condition marked by scaly or encrusted skin. Shampooing with tar-based or other types of medicated soap is the treatment.

seat

1 The portion of a saddle that accommodates the rider's buttocks. **2** A secure position in the saddle, as in the expression "She has a good seat." **3** A specific style of riding, such as Western stock seat and English hunt seat or saddleseat.

seat of corn

On the sole of the hoof, the point at which the corner of the frog meets the edge of the bars.

sebum

The waxy secretion of the horse's skin, which protects the skin against cold and precipitation, as well as giving a shine to a regularly groomed coat.

second-year green

A show hunter in its second year of competition at a recognized horse show. Fences in this division are set at 3 feet 6 inches. Following a horse's second-year green year, it completes in the Open division.

S

see a distance
 See distance.

seedy toe
A separation of the wall of the hoof from the laminae.

segunda
A snaffle bit with a raised horse-shoe-shaped center that acts in the manner of a port.

selenium
A trace element available in grass forage in some areas. In other areas, selenium must be fed to the horse as a supplement. Caution must be taken not to overfeed selenium, since it is toxic in high amounts.

self-carriage
The ability of a horse to move in a light and balanced fashion without the assistance or support of the rider's reins.

Selle Français
The sport horse of France, first bred in Normandy in the 19th century by crossing Thorough-breds with native warmblood stock. The result was a horse that resembles the Thoroughbred in size and quality, with an athleticism that lends itself to show jumping in particular. The formal name, *le cheval de selle français,* translates as "French saddle horse."

senior
1 A horse above the age of five.
2 A person 18 years or older.

Below 18, a rider, driver, or handler is a junior.

senior feed
A concentrated feed specially formulated to meet the nutritional needs of an older horse.

serpentine
A movement called for in several dressage and other riding tests that is composed of a series of linked S-shaped changes of direction across an arena.

serviceably sound
The condition of a horse that is not completely free from physical infirmities, but is healthy enough to perform its job.

sesamoid (SES-a-moid)
One of two small bones above and at the back of the fetlock joint. Sesamoiditis is an inflammation of these bones that comes from a strain of the ligaments that hold the bones in place. The treatment is support bandages or a cast, anti-inflammation medication, and rest.

set
In jumping, to design or build a course of obstacles, as in the sentence "The course designer set a challenging course for the Grand Prix."

set back
Of a tied horse, to pull back hard against the tie rope in an attempt to break free. Setting back is a very

difficult, in some cases impossible, habit to break.

set down

In racing, to suspend or to be suspended from riding or training, typically after a jockey has been found guilty of committing a foul, or a trainer for an infraction of the rules of racing.

settle

1 To allow a horse to relax at the halt. **2** To allow a herd of cattle to become accustomed to the arena. **3** To impregnate a mare.

set up

 See Scotch.

sex allowance

The practice of allowing fillies and mares to carry less weight when racing against male horses.

shadbelly

A formal riding coat with a waist-length front and long tails. Worn over a lighter-colored vest and shirt, a shadbelly is traditional in upper-level dressage tests and im-portant hunter classes. (The word was inspired by the pale stomach of the shad fish.)

shadow roll

In racing, a piece of sheepskin placed across a horse's nose to block the sight of distracting shad-ows on the ground.

shakeytail

Slang for a Saddlebred horse.

shank

1 The long, leverlike pieces of a curb or pelham bit to which the reins are attached. The longer the shank, the greater the bit's leverage action. **2** Any part of a Western bit below the mouthpiece. **3** The rope or strap by which a haltered horse is led. Many shanks have a section of chain above a leather strap; the chain can be placed across the horse's muzzle for greater control. Also known as the lead shank. **4** *v.* To harshly discipline a horse by jerking on the lead rope, espe-cially if the horse has a chain over its nose.

shape

In cutting, to move the herd at the beginning of the round so that the most cuttable cows stay to the front and the least desirable ones rejoin the main herd at the back fence. Shaping is the job of the turnback riders.

shavings

Small, thin strips of wood used as stall bedding. In many parts of the country, shavings are more acces-sible and less expensive than straw bedding.

sheath

The tube of skin that surrounds the penis. For sanitary reasons, the sheath must be periodically cleaned.

shed

1 To lose a seasonal hair coat as an-other coat grows in. Horses shed

Dressage rider wearing a formal riding coat, or shadbelly.
© ED CAMELLI

American Quarter Horse wearing a shadow roll and blinkers.
© AMERICAN QUARTER HORSE ASSOCIATION

Shetland pony.
© ED CAMELLI

twice a year in response to the changing length of the daylight hours. In the fall, they shed their short summer coat as the heavy winter coat grows in, and in spring they shed the winter coat as the summer coat grows in. **2** To give off a contagious virus or bacteria.

shedding blade
A grooming tool with an oval, serrated metal blade, used to remove loose hair and dirt.

shed row
1 In racing, the backstretch area of stables that have outside walkways below an overhanging roof. **2** A stable that consists of a row of stalls, the doors of which open directly to the outdoors, as opposed to having a covered aisle.

sheet
1 A light blanket, usually made of canvas, cotton, or nylon, worn by horses when a wool or quilted blanket would be too warm. **2** A cooler.

shelly
Brittle or crumbly hooves.

Shetland
A breed of pony native to the Shetland Islands of northern Scotland. Its origins are uncertain, although speculations include Spanish horses and Icelandic ponies that grew small because of the region's sparse vegetation. Shetlands are tiny, measuring 10 to 12 hands, with shaggy coats and short legs.

Shipping boots.
CREDIT: J. SHIERS

Remarkably strong for their diminutive size, they are used for riding and for pulling wagons.

shipping boots
Protective padded coverings for the lower legs, worn during van or trailer trips.

Shire
The largest of the draft breeds, originating in the north of England. Because of its size—it can reach 18 hands and weigh more than a ton—the breed is thought to have the closest connection to the Flemish War Horse. Shires have prominent eyes, a broad forehead, a relatively long neck, and muscular shoulders and hindquarters. Like other draft breeds, they are used for hauling and other transportation work.

shivers
A disorder most common among draft breeds, in which the horse holds the affected hind leg up and out, while the muscles quiver. An episode can be brought on by backing, turning, stepping over an obstacle, or during farrier work. Between episodes, the horse appears normal. The cause of shivers is not fully understood, but recent research indicates a possible link to EPSM.

shoe boil
Capped elbow. Caused by a horse habitually lying down on his own front shoe, resulting in bursitis of the elbow. Can be prevented by

S

the use of a shoe boil boot,
or "donut," that is worn around
the fetlock and prevents the shoe
from contacting the elbow.

shooting brake
In driving, a four-wheeled vehicle
with one or more rows of seats
that can be folded or removed to
make room for luggage, especially
for sporting gear.

short format
In eventing, a revised and somewhat controversial format in which
phases A, B, and C (roads and
tracks and steeplechase) have been
eliminated, leaving only phase C,
the cross-country. Some competitors feel that this move will result in
less well-conditioned horses, since
the endurance day is less grueling.
Others support the change, both
because it is expensive to maintain
the large amount of property needed
for a long-format event and because
it allows non-Thoroughbred horses
(who tend to have less natural endurance) to be competitive at the
top level of the sport.
Compare to long format.

short shod
Shod with shoes that are too small
for the horse's feet.

short stirrup
In hunter/jumper competition, a
hunter or equitation division for
young child riders, typically with
jumps up to 2 feet in height. The
age limit depends on the particular show, but often the maximum

age for short stirrup is 12 or 14.
See also long stirrup.

shoulder
The portion of the horse's body
between the neck and barrel, to
which the forelegs attach.

shoulder-in
A three-track school movement in
which the horse travels forward
with its forequarters directed toward the inside of the arena. When
done properly, the inside hind foot
and the outside forefoot travel on
the same track.

Shoulders, Jim
Jim Shoulders won more PRCA
(Professional Rodeo Cowboys
Association) titles than any other
cowboy, including five World All-
Around Rodeo Champion Cowboy
titles (1949 and 1956–1959),
seven Bull Rider championships
(1951 and 1954–1959), and four
Bareback Rider awards (1950 and
1956–1958). He was the first competitor to win three events at the
world championships: Bareback,
Bull Riding, and All Around, in
1956.

Shire.
© AMERICAN SHIRE HORSE ASSOCIATION

show
In racing, to finish in third place.

show hunter
A horse or pony that is shown in
hunter classes, as distinguished
from a field hunter.

show jumping
A horse show division in which

Sickle hock.
© CHRISTINA BERUBE

Side reins.
© RICHARD KLIMESH

Nineteenth-century illustration of a sidesaddle rider.

horses and riders compete over fences. Judging is objective and is based entirely on speed and ability to leave the jumps up.

showmanship
A Western horse show class for youth and amateur exhibitors in which how well the exhibitors present their halter horses is judged. The quality of the animals is not taken into consideration.

shy
To suddenly swerve around an object perceived as frightening; to spook.

sickle-hocked
A conformation fault in which the hocks and lower hind legs curve under the body.

sideboards
In polo, low fencing around the playing field that helps keep the ball in play.

sidebone
A hardening of the cartilage, occurring most usually in the forefeet. Although sidebone will not of itself cause lameness, it can lead to corns and cracked heels. Thinning the hoof to relieve pressure across the heels, together with corrective shoeing, will help a horse with sidebones.

sidepass
A lateral maneuver in which the horse moves to the side, with no forward or backward motion.

sidepull
A type of bitless bridle often used by Western riders on young horses. The reins attach to the sides of the noseband and put pressure on the opposite side of the horse's face, literally pulling the horse's head to make a turn.

side reins
A training device most often used in longeing, consisting of a pair of reins that run from either side of the saddle or surcingle to the bit rings or the cavesson. Side reins influence a horse's balance and head carriage, especially with regard to flexion.

sidesaddle
A style of horsemanship for women in which the rider sits with both legs on (usually) the left side of the saddle. The style originated during the 14th century, before which women rode astride. A 19th-century invention, the leaping head is a curved, armlike projection over which the rider drapes her right leg for security, especially while jumping. Sidesaddle hunter classes, in which riders wear formal riding habits, are a feature of some hunter/jumper and Arabian horse shows.

silks
In racing, the distinctive shirt and cap worn by jockeys or drivers to identify the horse's owner, or, sometimes, the entry's post position. Silks are registered with the appropriate governing body, such

as the Jockey Club for Thorough-bred racing and the U.S. Harness Racing Association for Standard-breds. The word refers to the garments originally having been made of silk, although they are now nylon.

Silver
The white horse of the crime-fighting Lone Ranger in the Western movies and television series.

simple change of lead
The change of lead at the canter or lope through the trot. The horse makes the transition down to one or more trotting steps before striking off on the other lead, as distinguished from a flying change of lead.

See also lead.

single foot
Another term for slow gait.

singles
In driving, a competition for vehicles pulled by one horse.

Compare to pair; four-in-hand.

sire
A horse's father.

Sir Wrangler
This Appaloosa, the 1977 grand-son of Hall of Famer Prince Plaudit, earned a Canadian National Championship as a weanling, then went on to win the Western pleasure championship in the Grand National Show at the Cow Palace and became the Pacific Northwest's first ApHC Club champion. The stallion sired 219 halter and performance competitors who earned 14 bronze, one silver, and one gold medallion, in addition to three bronze superior achievement certificates.

sitting trot
A trot to which the rider does not post.

skene
In polo, a mallet head that has a flat bottom and both ends tapered at the same angle; it was designed by Bob Skene, a noted polo player.

skewbald
The coat of a pinto that consists of patches of white and any color other than black.

Compare to piebald.

skid boots
Protective devices worn on hind-leg pasterns and fetlocks. They are also known as sliding boots because of their protection against the abrasion of sliding stops in reining, roping, and other Western events.

skirt
1 On a Western saddle, the portion of a saddle under the cantle. **2** On an English saddle, the flap over the stirrup bars; its purpose is to protect the rider's leg from rubbing against the girth buckle and the stirrup bar.

A horse's skull.
CREDIT: PHOTOS.COM

Sleigh.
CREDIT: PHOTOS.COM

A sliding stop.
© LESLI KRAUSE GROVES

skull
The system of bones that makes up the head.

skull cap
 See caliente.

slab-sided
A conformational type in which the sides of the barrel (rib cage) are somewhat flat rather than rounded.

slant-load trailer
A trailer in which the horses stand at an angle, with their heads toward the front left corner of the trailer and their haunches toward the right rear corner, and are separated from each other with divider panels. With this configuration, it is possible to fit more horses into a shorter length of trailer, but since the width of the trailer is limited to the road's width (usually 8 feet), very large horses may not be able to fit.

sleigh
A horsedrawn vehicle with runners instead of wheels, to be used in snowy conditions.

sliding stop
See stop.

slip
To lengthen the reins by letting them slide through the fingers.

slobber straps
On a Western bridle, short leather straps that connect a snaffle bit to mecate reins.

sloppy
In racing, a track surface marked by abundant surface water.
Compare to muddy.

slow
In racing, a track surface having damp and clinging footing.

slow gait
A lateral gait in which the horse's feet hit the ground individually, natural to American Saddlebreds and other breeds. It is similar to, but slower than, the rack. Also known as single foot.

slow-legged
The natural athletic ability of a horse to move its legs slowly and with self-carriage at the walk, trot, and, especially, the lope. Desirable in Western pleasure horses.

Smoky The Cow Horse
A classic children's novel by Will James, the book traces the life of a Western horse from foal to ranch work. Told from the horse's point of view, the story offers a realistic picture of ranch life in the early 20th century.

smooch
In racing, the kissing "chirp" sound made by jockeys to encourage horses to run faster.

snaffle
A bit with a straight or jointed mouthpiece, without a port; the reins connect directly to the rings of the bit. The snaffle is one of the

two major categories of bits (the curb is the other). Working primarily on the corners of the horse's mouth, a snaffle exerts more direct pressure than a curb's leverlike action does. This direct pressure is useful for turning as well as stopping the horse. In general, the snaffle is a milder bit than a curb.

🔵 *See also* elevator bit; gag snaffle; Kimberwicke; pelham.

snip
A white marking near the nostrils.

Snowman
One of the best-known show jumpers of the 1950s and '60s, the "Cinderella horse" Snowman had been rescued from the slaughter house by Harry deLeyer. Under deLeyer, the gray ex-plowhorse won important classes at Madison Square Garden's National Horse Show in 1958 and 1959. He was the American Horse Show's Association Horse of the Year in 1958 and 1959, and he won the Professional Horsemen's Association Championship both years as well. So well-mannered that a child could ride him, he once won a lead-line class and an open jumper championship on the same day.

snow pads
Pads for horseshoes that prevent snow and ice from balling up under the hoof during freezing weather. The pads may be flat or may have a convex section that "pops" the snow out of the hoof with each step.

snub
To tie a horse with a very short tie rope.

sobreandando
🔵 *see* Peruvian Paso.

sock
A white marking on the cannon, from the coronet halfway to the knee on a foreleg or halfway to the hock on a hind leg.

sodium pentobarbital
A lethal drug used for euthanasia.

soft
1 In racing, a turf surface of deep to heavy footing with substantial moisture. **2** Of a rider's hands, sensitive to the horse's mouth. **3** Of a horse's mouth, sensitive to the bit and the rider's hands.

🔵 *Compare to* hard mouth.

sole
The bottom or undersection of the foot, surrounded by the hoof wall.

sophomore
1 A three-year-old racehorse. **2** A horse in its second season of competition.

soring
The illegal practice of applying chemical irritants to the lower legs or soles of gaited show horses in order to produce a high-stepping action.

sorrel
A reddish or copper-red body

A sloppy track.
CREDIT: PHOTOS.COM

Snaffle bit (full-cheek type).
© CHERRY HILL 2000

A horse with white socks.
CREDIT: PHOTOS.COM

color; the mane and tail are usually the same color as the body, but they may be flaxen. Although often considered a Western term for chestnut, sorrel is a somewhat lighter reddish-brown than chestnut.

sound

In healthy condition. The word usually refers to an absence of lameness.

sour

1 Describes a horse that is unhappy and resistant in his work, generally due to overuse or poor riding. **2** Of cutting cattle, unresponsive to the horse. Overuse in the cutting arena is the main cause.

soybeans

A legume plant used as feed.

spade bit

A curb bit having a narrow port with a square top (the spade). Two pieces of wire called "keepers" are attached to the bottom of the spade piece and each cheekpiece. The mouthpiece is joined to the cheekpieces either by a hinge (making the bit a loose-jaw or soft spade) or by welding (a solid-jaw or hard spade). Although the potential for extreme pressure against the roof of the mouth has given the spade bit the reputation of being severe, in the hands of an experienced rider it is no more harsh than any other curb bit.

Spanish Riding School

The establishment in Vienna, Austria,

dedicated to the preservation of classical horsemanship. Founded in the 17th century with horses imported from Spain (hence the name), the school moved to its present baroque headquarters in the Hofburg Palace in 1735, where performances are open to the public during spring, winter, and fall months. The Lipizzaner horses are trained and exhibited by riders in Napoleonic-era uniforms to the highest standard of haute école horsemanship.

See Lipizzaner.

Spanish walk

A classical dressage movement distinguished by well-elevated forelegs. Its supposed origin was to prevent horses from trampling young plants in Spanish vineyards.

spavin

An enlargement of the hock.

See also bog spavin; bone spavin.

spay

To surgically remove the ovaries of a female horse. Spaying is far less common than gelding male horses, and is usually done only if a mare has ovarian tumors or has extreme or violent reactions to her heat cycles.

speaking

In foxhunting, the baying or barking of a hound during a chase. Also called giving tongue.

speculum

A device used to hold open a

Spade bit.
© CHERRY HILL 2000

Spanish Riding School.
CREDIT: STEVEN D. PRICE

horse's mouth for dental work or veterinary examination.

speed and endurance

The second day of a three-day event, comprised of the roads and tracks, steeplechase, and cross-country phases. Usually referred to just as the cross-country.

 See short format.

speed class

In show jumping, the familiar term for a one-round class in which the fastest time determines the winner, with penalty seconds added to the actual time for any knockdowns.

spin

1 In reining, a maneuver in which the horse makes one or more 360-degree turns while pivoting around an inside hind foot.
2 To eliminate from a competition, such as a three-day event, due to unsoundness detected by a veterinarian during a mandatory inspection.

splay-footed

A conformation fault in which the toes point out and away from each other.

splint

An inflammation of the ligament that attaches the splint bone to the cannon bone of a front leg. They most often happen following a kick or another blow to the area, or from stress due to exertion or faulty conformation. Swelling and heat are the symptoms, as

well as an obvious lameness. The treatment includes ice, anti-inflammatory medication, and, if a bony growth develops on the splint bone, surgical removal of the growth if needed. In many cases, the bony growth is just a cosmetic blemish that does not cause lameness.

splint boots

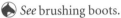 *See* brushing boots.

splinter-belly

A slang term for a horse whose jumping style is to skim across the top of a fence without rounding its body into a noticeable arc.

split reins

Reins with ends that are not joined, characteristic of Western tack.

spook

To suddenly startle at a real or imagined event or object, such as rustling tree branches. Upon spooking, an undisciplined horse may buck, spin, or bolt. A trained horse should have been taught to "spook in place"—that is, to jump slightly as a natural reflex, but then remain standing, awaiting the rider's aids. A horse that is prone to spooking is called a spooky horse.

sport boots

Horse boots made of neoprene, which wrap completely around the cannons and fetlocks, including a strap to support the suspensory ligament.

Speed-and-endurance segment of three-day event.
© CHERRY HILL

Spinning.
© CHERRY HILL

S

English spur.

sport horse
A type of horse with conformation and movement suitable for the English performance disciplines (dressage, eventing, jumping).

spread
Any jump that has width, including oxers, water jumps, banks, and ditches.

sprint
A race under one mile in length.

spurs
Metal devices strapped to the heels of boots to emphasize the rider's leg aids. Western spurs customarily have rowels. Among types of English spurs are the medium-long-necked Prince of Wales, the short-necked Tom Thumb, and the blunt hammerhead.

spur stop
On a horse that is trained to respond to it, to halt a horse by exerting steady pressure with both spurs. The spur stop is used only in the Western disciplines, particularly Western pleasure, to enable the rider to slow or stop the horse without using the reins.

Square bales.
CREDIT: PHOTOS.COM

square
1 At the halt, standing with straight legs and with the four hooves at each corner of an imaginary rectangle—that is, without any feet forward or back. 2 In gaited horses, this refers to a clean, four-beat tempo in the gait.

square bale
A rectangular bale of hay, weighing 30 to 100 pounds, comprised of several flakes and bound together with two strands of twine.

stable
A structure in which horses live; familiarly called a barn.

stable vice
An unwelcome habit such as stall-walking or cribbing, often caused by boredom.

stacked
A Western style of jeans legs with several accordion-like folds between the knees and cuffs when the wearer is standing. The folds straighten to cover the entire length of the wearer's legs when the person is on horseback.

stadium jumping
Another name for the show-jumping phase of eventing.

stakes
1 In racing, a race for higher-caliber horses in which the owners of entered horses post a nominating and starting fee, which is added to the purse. 2 The class in a horse show division with the largest amount of prize money.

stakes placed
Finishing second or third in a stakes race.

stakes producer
In racing, a mare that has produced

at least one foal that finished first, second, or third in a stakes race.

stakes winner
A horse that has won a stakes race.

stall
A compartment of a stable in which a horse lives.

🐎 *See also* box stall; straight stall.

stall guard
A restraint made of canvas or another fabric that keeps a horse inside a stall when the door has been opened or removed.

stallion
An ungelded male horse of three years or older.

stall rest
A period of confinement prescribed for a horse with an illness or injury, during which the horse must not be turned out or exercised.

stall walking
A stable vice in which a horse constantly walks back and forth inside its stall. The habit comes from being bored due to inactivity.

stamp his get
Of a stallion, to produce offspring that closely resemble their sire.

stand
To offer a stallion for breeding.

standard
The wooden post that holds the cups in which the rails of a jump rest.

Standardbred
The breed most closely associated with harness racing. Although the nominal foundation sire was Messenger, a Thoroughbred imported to the U.S. in the late 18th century, the most influential stallion was Hambletonian. Foaled in 1849, he sired more than 1,300 foals, and most Standardbreds can trace their ancestry back to him. The "standard" in the breed's name comes from the requirement in 1879 that horses had to trot or pace one mile in 1 minute 20 seconds or less in order to be eligible for the American Trotting Registry. Standardbred harness racing has been a popular U.S. pastime at county fairs since after the Civil War, as well as at harness raceways throughout the world. Horses race as either trotters or pacers (the proclivity for pacing is hereditary and is enhanced through training). Drivers sit in bike-wheeled sulkies, and races begin with the assistance of a mobile starting gate. Most races are at a distance of one mile, which the better horses cover in under 2 minutes; pacers tend to be somewhat faster than trotters. The most famous race for Standardbreds is the Hambletonian, for three-year-old trotters, held in August at The Meadowlands in New Jersey. Pacing's classic race, also for three-year-olds, is The Little Brown Jug held in September at the Delaware, Ohio, Fairgrounds.

Standardbred.
© KENTUCKY HORSE PARK

S

Applying standing bandages.

Starting gate.
CREDIT: PHOTOS.COM

Steeplechase race.

standing bandages
Thick cotton wraps used to prevent swelling and injury during shipping or while the horse is in its stall.

standing martingale
A type of martingale with one strap that runs from the girth between the horse's front legs, through a neck strap, and to the cavesson noseband. The noseband automatically restrains a horse if he tries to raise his head too high, without any action from the rider.

star
A white marking on the forehead.

stargazer
The term for a horse that carries its head in the air.

start
1 To train a horse to accept the saddle, bridle, and rider for the first time. The term "started under saddle" generally refers to a horse that has been walked and trotted with a rider. 2 The beginning of a race. 3 Used to identify the number of times a horse has raced, such as "The horse had five starts and three wins."

starter
In racing, the official in charge of overseeing the beginning of a race, especially with regard to making sure the field gets off to a fair start.

starter race
In racing, an allowance or handicap restricted to horses that have run for a specific claiming price.

starting gate
In racing, the multistall apparatus (or in harness racing, the vehicle) from which horses begin a race.
🏇 *See also* mobile starting gate.

state-bred
In racing, a horse bred and/or foaled in one of the United States and which meets the criteria to be eligible to compete in special races or purse supplements.

steady
To slow a horse's speed and stride, to improve its balance, or to prevent it from reaching a jump too soon.

steel gray
The body color composed of a mixture of black and white hairs.

steeplechase
1 A race in which horses jump a course of brush or wooden fences. The name comes from impromptu 17th-century races where foxhunters raced across country toward a church steeple, the most visible landmark in the area, and jumping whatever obstacles stood in their way.
🏇 *See also* hurdle race; point-to-point.
2 The portion of the speed-and-endurance part of a three-day event that involves a jumping course of hedge obstacles at high speed.

S

Steinkraus, William

William Steinkraus rode for the United States Equestrian Team's show-jumping squad for 22 years, during which time he was captain for 17 years. He rode in five Olympic Games, with his most notable win the Individual gold medal aboard Snowbound at the 1968 Mexico City Olympic Games, when he became the first American ever to win an individual equestrian gold medal. Steinkraus later served as USET president and board chairman.

step oxer

An oxer whose three or more elements are set progressively higher.

stern

In foxhunting, a fox hound's hind-quarters.

steward

1 A horse show official who adjudicates alleged rule violations. **2** In racing, one of the officials who rule on foul claims, institute inquiries, and enforce other regulations.

stick

1 In jumping, describes a horse that hesitates before leaving the ground. **2** A term for a whip or crop. **3** The familiar term for the measuring device, usually an oversized ruler with a sliding crossbar, with which a horse or pony's height is measured, as in the phrase "Put a stick to that horse."

4 In polo, a familiar term for mallet. The term "stick-and-ball" refers to personal practice time.

stifle

The joint between the thigh and the gaskin, the equivalent of the human knee joint.

stifley

Describes a horse that has weak stifles or suffers from upward fixation of the patella.

stillborn

A foal that is born dead.

stirrup

One of the two metal or wood attachments to the saddle that support the rider's feet. Among the Western varieties are the oxbow and Visalia; the most popular English type is the Fillis.

stirrup bar

The metal device on a saddle that holds the stirrup leathers. A hinge that opens when pressure is applied is intended to let the stirrup leather slip out so a fallen rider cannot be dragged.

stirrup cup

In foxhunting, a drink given to mounted hunters before the start of a meet.

stirrup leathers

The straps that attach to the saddle and from which stirrups are suspended.

William Steinkraus on Snowbound.
COURTESY OF THE U.S. EQUESTRIAN TEAM

Step oxer.
© ED CAMELLI

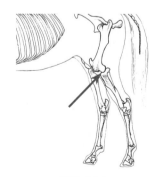

Stifle joint.
© CHRISTINE BERUBE

S

stock

 See stock tie.

stocked up

Lower legs that are slightly swollen so that the tendons are filled in with a soft swelling, generally not resulting in lameness. The horse's lymphatic system requires movement to flush fluids from the lower legs, so horses that are stalled for long periods of time may have a tendency to stock up. Exercise is the best remedy.

stock horse

A horse belonging to any of the breeds traditionally used for Western ranch work—American Quarter Horses, Paints, and Appaloosas—or a grade horse of Quarter Horse type. Stock horses are characterized by a stocky build, athleticism, and above all a quiet and workmanlike attitude.

stocking

A white marking extending from fetlock to knee or hock.

stockman

Australian term for rancher or cattleman.

stock seat

Describes Western-style riding. The word *stock* originally applied to a supply of cattle, and by extension, a ranchman.

stock tie

A knotted white neck cloth worn during the formal foxhunting

Stock tie.
© ED CAMELLI

A reining horse's dramatic sliding stop.
© AMERICAN QUARTER HORSE ASSOCIATION

season and by some upper-level dressage and combined training riders. The ends are pinned to the rider's shirt to keep them from flapping. The garment can serve as an impromptu sling in the event the rider's arm is damaged in a fall.

stock trailer

A type of trailer with semi-open sides and no interior divider panels. Typically used to transport livestock such as cattle, a stock trailer may be used to transport horses if it is large enough.

stone

In racing, a unit of British weight equaling 14 pounds, used in racing as the measure of weight that a horse must carry in a race.

stone bruise

An injury to the sole or frog caused by a pebble or stone. Removing the offending object is the usual remedy, along with rest.

stop

1 In reining and working cow horse classes, a halt from the gallop in which the horse shifts its weight to its haunches and slides to a complete stop, its hindquarters seeming to "melt" into the ground. Also known as sliding stop. **2** In jumping, the informal term for a refusal.

straight

In riding, *straight* does not simply mean moving in a straight line. It also refers to moving "straight" on

S

a circle or bend—that is, the hind legs follow in the tracks of the front legs, and neither the fore-hand nor the haunches swing in or out from the ideal track.

straight-load trailer

A horse trailer in which the horses face straight forward, side by side, separated by divider panels.

See also slant-load trailer; stock trailer.

straight stall

A rectangular compartment in a stable in which a horse lives, usu-ally not wide enough for the horse to turn around; tie stall.

Compare to box stall.

strangles

A contagious abscess of the lymph nodes of the neck or jaw. Symptoms are loss of appetite, nasal discharge, and coughing, in addition to swelling of the lymph nodes. Treatment involves draining the nodes and adminis-tering antibiotics. Also known as distemper.

strap goods

Tack and other items made of thin strips of leather, such as bridles, harnesses, halters, reins, and so on.

straw

The stems of oat or wheat plants, dried and used as bedding in stalls.

strawberry roan

A nickname for a red roan.

stretch

In racing, the straight portion of the track leading to the finish line; also called the home stretch.

stretchy circle

The familiar term for the move-ment in Training and First Level dressage tests in which the horse is encouraged to stretch its head down and forward while trotting on a 20-meter circle.

stride

The full length of one cycle of steps at any of the gaits. The size of a stride can be adjusted by col-lection and extension.

See also add a stride; leave out a stride.

strike

To aggressively thrust a front hoof forward in an attempt to hit or threaten a person or another horse.

string

A group of horses owned by an individual that are available for his use, such as a string of polo ponies.

stringhalt

A muscle condition revealed by the exaggerated involuntary flexing of the hock joint while the horse is moving. Sometimes the hind leg is lifted so high that the animal kicks itself in the belly. Of unknown cause, stringhalt can often be corrected with muscle relaxants or the removal of a section of the affected leg muscle.

A string of polo ponies waiting to play.
CREDIT: PHOTOS.COM

A strip, or conformation class.
CREDIT: S. D. PRICE

Suckling.
CREDIT: PHOTOS.COM

Standardbred and sulky.

strip
1 A narrow marking extending vertically between the forehead and nostrils. **2** A familiar name for a horse show conformation class (the horse is shown stripped of its saddle).

strongyles (STRONG-jiles)
A parasitic disease transmitted by bloodworms that causes anemia and intestinal tissue damage. A deworming program is both the best prevention and cure.

stud
1 A stallion used for breeding. **2** Removable horseshoe caulks used for extra traction in slippery conditions.

stud book
A record of the pedigrees of the members of a breed.

stud chain
A short shank of chain attached to the end of a lead rope or longe line. The chain is passed through the rings of the halter and over the horse's nose to provide greater control for the handler.
🐎 *See also* lip chain; war bridle.

subcutaneous
An injection given between the skin and the muscle. Sometimes abbreviated as SQ.

substance
A complimentary word describing good bone and muscles.

suck back
To resist the rider's forward aids by slowing down or shortening stride, often accompanied by dropping behind the bit.

suckling
A foal that receives its nourishment from its mother's milk. A foal that begins to take nourishment on its own is then known as a weanling.

sudden death
In polo, an extra period when the score is tied at the end of regulation play. The first team to score wins the match.

Suffolk Punch
A breed of draft horse originating in the English county of Suffolk. The foundation sire was Crisp's Horse of Ufford, foaled in 1760. Compact in size and chestnut in color, the Punch stands about 16 hands and weighs close to one ton when full-grown. It is used for agricultural work and for pulling wagons.

sulky
The two-wheel cart used in harness racing. Bicycle or disc wheels support the lightweight metal frame and the driver, who sits with extended legs right behind the horse. Light sulkies called bikes are used in some Roadster Pony horse show classes, in which the drivers wear harness racing silks. The name comes from an old English word having the same root as "sulk" or "brood," suggest-

ing that someone who is pouting would prefer to be alone in a one-person vehicle. Also known as bike.

supplement
A medicinal, herbal, or nutritional product fed to horses to fulfill a certain need. Supplements may support joint health, help a horse gain weight, supply missing vitamins and minerals, or help grow stronger hooves and hair, among other things.

surcingle
1 A strap that fastens around the horse's girth to hold a blanket in place or to attach training devices such as side reins. **2** A strap that fastens around the horse's girth to provide extra security for a racing saddle; also known as an overgirth.

surrogate mare
A mare that takes the place of a foal's dam. In the case of embryo transfer, the surrogate carries the embryo to term and cares for it after birth. In the case of foal rejection or the death of the dam, the surrogate "adopts" the foal after birth.

suspension
A horse's ability to appear to "float" above the ground while in motion.
 See also moment of suspension.

suspensory
The ligament behind the knee or the top of the hind-leg cannon bone. Attached to the sesamoid bones, it supports the fetlocks.

swagger tabs
The short strips of leather or cloth sewn into the back of a riding boot and used to pull the boot on; bootstraps.

swamp fever
 See equine infectious anemia.

swan neck
An undesirable neck conformation in which the neck is too long and thin and tends to curve like the neck of a swan.

swap ends
To turn around very quickly, usually in midair while bucking.

swap leads
Familiar term for doing a flying change of lead.

swayback
A distinctly concave backbone, especially behind the withers. A swayback is often, but not always, a sign of age.

sweat
A bandage or wrap applied to a horse's leg, often accompanied by a poultice, to allow heat and moisture to build up under the wrap and reduce swelling. In halter horses, a neoprene sweat may be applied to a horse's neck and throatlatch to reduce their thickness.

sweat scraper

A grooming tool, either in the form of a long, hard plastic strip or a curved rubber squeegee with a handle, used to scrape excess water from a horse's coat after bathing.

Swedish oxer

In jumping, a fence composed of two sets of rails that slope in opposite directions to look like an X when viewed from the front or rear.

Swedish oxer.
© ED CAMELLI

Swedish Warmblood

A breed native to Sweden, developed as a military mount by crossing Thoroughbreds, Trakehners, and Hanoverians with native horses. Strong, compact, and with kind dispositions, Swedish Warmbloods have proven to be outstanding dressage horses.

sweeny

An atrophy of the shoulder muscles caused by damage to the nerves of that area. If anti-inflammatory medication proves inadequate, surgery to repair the muscles is usually indicated.

sweet feed

Grain mixed with molasses or another sweetener. The addition of the sugary ingredient binds the loose grain together and makes the mixture more palatable, so even the most finicky eater will be more likely to consume its entire ration. However, the high sugar content makes it a poor choice for high-strung or obese horses, or those with Cushings disease.

sweet iron

A metal used to make bit mouth-pieces. The taste of the metal is supposed to encourage the horse to salivate and accept the bit more readily.

sweet itch

An allergy to biting insects that occurs seasonally in affected horses. Common symptoms are severe itching, hair loss, and weeping sores.

swells

The raised area at the pommel of a Western saddle, under the horn. The swells help to hold the rider in place.

Swift, Sally

See Centered Riding.

synovial fluid

The thick, honey-colored fluid that lubricates the joints.

synthetic saddle

A saddle made of durable fabric. Lightweight and relatively low cost, it is popularly used in competitive trail riding.

table

1 A cross-country jump that the horse must jump up onto and then jump off the other side.
2 In show jumping, the various classifications in the rule book.

tack

A collective term for saddles, bridles, harness, and other items that horses wear.

tack trunk

A large container in which saddlery and other items for horse and rider are kept; also known as a tack box.

tack up

To prepare a horse to be ridden by grooming, saddling, bridling, and applying any other needed tack or boots.

tail bag

A cloth container in which the tail is wrapped to be kept clean.

tail blocking

The deadening of a horse's tail by cutting the nerves or by injecting chemicals in order to prevent the horse from expressing displeasure in the show ring by swishing or wringing its tail.

tail female line

The female (bottom) side of a horse's pedigree. Sometimes referred to as simply the "tail line."

tail male line

The male (top) side of a horse's pedigree.

tail shot

In polo, a stroke in which the player's mallet makes contact with the ball behind the pony's hindquarters.

take

The portion of money wagered that the state and racing commission deduct before the pari-mutuel payoff is computed.

take up

In racing, to restrain a horse sharply to avoid causing or becoming involved in an accident.

tally-ho!

1 In foxhunting, a shout of encouragement to the hounds when a fox is first sighted. [From Old French, a huntsman's cry, perhaps related to *allez,* meaning "go!"]. **2** *[Without the exclamation point]* A mail coach or four-in-hand driving vehicle.

tanbark
Chips of the bark of certain trees once used for tanning leather and then as footing for riding arenas. The word now metaphorically refers to the horse show ring.

tandem
In driving, a two-horse hitch with one horse in front of the other.
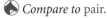 *Compare to* pair.

tapadero
A leather cuplike device over the front of some Western stirrups, to protect the rider's feet against thorns and other sharp objects. May be abbreviated as taps.

tap root
The oldest identifiable ancestor of a horse on the female side.

tarpan
A prehistoric wild horse type that ranged from Southern France and Spain eastward to central Russia. The original wild tarpan died out during the late 19th century when the horses' natural forest and steppe habitat was destroyed to make room for more people.

   The modern tarpan is a genetic re-creation of the original wild breed based on genetic material from several European pony breeds, including the Icelandic pony, that had descended from the prehistoric tarpan. Mares from these breeds were then mated to Przewalski's horse stallions during the 1930s. Standing about 13 hands high, the modern tarpan is dun in color, with a thick, thatched mane. The head is large, with massive jaws and thick neck. The hooves are dark and very tough, never requiring shoes.

tattoo
An identification marking of letters and/or numerals placed under a horse's upper lip. Combinations and sequences of letters and numbers can indicate the year the animal was foaled, as well as other data. Racetrack officials examine tattoos before the horses leave the barn area for their race to ensure the proper horses will compete on that day.

team
Two or more horses who are trained to work together in harness.

team penning
A Western event in which teams of three riders remove three specified cows from a herd, then drive them in an enclosure (the pen) at the opposite end of the arena. Riders coordinate their efforts, especially with regard to making sure the cows don't slip back to the herd, by shouts and hand signals. The team that pens the three cows in the fastest time wins.

An ornate tapadero.
© CHERRY HILL

T

Team roping.
© LESLIE KRAUSE GROVES

team roping

A Western event in which two ropers, the header and the heeler, constitute a team that attempts to rope a calf or steer in the shortest amount of time. As soon as the header has roped the calf's head, the heeler tosses a loop around one of the animal's hind legs. Time is taken when the calf is stretched out. The activity is based on the ranch chore of immobilizing a calf or steer for medical attention.

See also tie-down roping.

teaser

As used in the breeding process, a male horse that provokes the mare to be bred. Once the mare demonstrates her receptiveness, the teaser is replaced by the breeding stallion.

teats

A mare's udder.

Technical Delegate (TD)

The official at a dressage, driving, or combined training competition who is responsible for interpreting and enforcing the rules of that sport's governing body.

telescoping intestine

A type of colic in which the intestine folds in on itself like a telescope.

Tellington-Jones, Linda

An animal behaviorist whose "TTouch" method employs a variety of techniques of touch, movement, and body language, including circular movements of the fingers and hands all over an animal's body. The technique is intended to expedite the healing of ailments and injuries as well as to change undesirable habits or behavior.

tempi changes

In dressage, several flying changes of lead in sequence. One-tempi changes occur every stride, while two-tempi changes occur every other stride.

tempo

Italian for "time."
The speed of footfalls at a gait.

tendon boots

Leather covering worn on the backs of the ankles of the forelegs to protect against hind feet striking the forefeet.

tendonitis

Inflammation of a tendon.

ten-minute box

In eventing, a mandatory rest stop on endurance day between phase C and phase D, in which a veterinarian checks the horse's vital signs before allowing the pair to continue.

Tennessee Walking Horse

The American breed of saddle horse noted for its smooth running walk and rocking-chair canter. Developed before the Civil War as a comfortable mount on which plantation owners could inspect their vast holdings, the Tennessee Walker combined

Tennessee Walking Horse.
© STUART VESTY/TENNESSEE WALKING
HORSE BREEDERS' & EXHIBITORS'
ASSOCIATION

T

strains of Thoroughbred, Saddlebred, Standardbred, and Morgan.
The horse stands approximately
16 hands high, with an arched
neck, deep chest, and short back.
The breed is now used as a pleasure and show horse.

tenosynovitis

Inflammation of the sheath surrounding a tendon.

tent pegging

A game in which contestants try
at the gallop to spear one or more
small wooden stakes embedded in
the ground. Tent pegging began as
an exercise among British cavalry
units stationed in India in the 19th
century.

terret

On a harness, a loop or ring on
the saddle through which the
reins pass.

test

1 In dressage, a stipulated sequence
of movements and transitions,
which vary among the dressage
levels, on which horses and riders
are judged. **2** In horse showing,
an additional round of competition in horsemanship and other
classes to give the judge further
information on which to base his
placements. Depending on the
class, tests can include further
work along the rail or over fences,
executing certain patterns, and
even answering oral questions
posed by the judge. Also known
as a ride-off.

tetanus

A severe, often fatal, bacterial
infection marked by rigidity of
muscles, especially of the head
and face, a "sawhorse" stance,
and convulsions. Also called
lockjaw, tetanus most often is
the result of a puncture wound
that allows the bacteria to enter
the body. Treatment includes
tetanus antitoxin, sedatives,
muscle relaxants, and intravenous
fluids.

Tevis Cup Endurance Ride

The most famous 100-mile
endurance ride in the United
States, named for Lloyd Tevis
(1824–1899) by his grandson
Will Tevis, an early benefactor of
the Ride. The trophy is awarded
to the first rider to complete the
100 miles whose mount is "fit to
continue." The ride takes place
from Lake Tahoe to Auburn,
California. Winning times over
the past decade have been under
16 hours.

**Thoroughbred being exercised
during a morning workout.**

therapeutic riding

See hippotherapy.

third eyelid

See nictitating membrane.

Thoroughbred

The breed closely associated
with flat and steeplechase racing
because of its superlative speed
at distances over a quarter mile.
All Thoroughbreds can trace their
ancestries back to one or more
of the three foundation sires:

T

the Byerly Turk, Darley Arabian, and Godolphin Barb, that were bred to native English mares in the 17th and 18th centuries.

Standing at approximately 16 hands, the lithe and long-legged Thoroughbred is powerful and graceful. In addition to its use as a racehorse, the breed has achieved great success as a show hunter and jumper, foxhunter, and dressage mount, and by its contributions to the heritage of such breeds as the Standardbred, American Quarter Horse, Saddlebred, and the European warmbloods.

thoroughpin
A swelling of the tendon sheath above the hock joint. Although the cause remains unknown, it may come from conformation problems. The treatment is anti-inflammatory medication.

Thrush.
© CHERRY HILL

three-day event
In eventing, a full event including all phases, with dressage on the first day, speed and endurance on the second day, and stadium jumping on the third day. Shorter events may be one- or two-day events or horse trials.

three-gaited
Describes American Saddlebreds that move at the walk, trot, and canter.
🔹 *Compare to* five-gaited.

three-point contact
In hunter-seat equitation, the rider's position in which the legs and

seat are in contact with the horse. Also known as full seat.
🔹 *Compare to* half seat.

throatlatch
1 The portion of the body between the neck and the lower jawbone. **2** The bridle strap that buckles under a horse's throat. Its purpose is to prevent the bridle from slipping over the animal's head.

throttle
Term for the throat, gullet, or windpipe.

through
In dressage, the quality of a horse that is relaxed, free of tension, supple, and obedient, responding to the rider's aids—particularly the half halt—through its whole body, from the hindquarters through the back and into the bridle.

throw-in
In polo, the "face-off" in which the referee tosses the ball onto the ground in front of the gathered players. A throw-in begins play at the start of each chukkar and resumes play after some penalties.

thrush
An infection of the frog of the foot. Easily identified by the foul odor of the dark fluid discharge, thrush often results when a horse inhabits a dirty or damp stall or pasture. Treatment includes trimming the affected tissue, cleaning the foot, and better stable management.

thruster
In foxhunting, a thoughtless and potentially dangerous rider who races past others.

thumps
A spasmodic breathing condition also known as synchronized diaphragmatic flutters. Occurring after strenuous exercise, it is characterized by convulsive twitching of the flanks. Treatment includes rest, administration of electrolytes and water, and grazing (grass contains essential minerals to replace those lost in exercise).

Tibbs, Casey
From 1949 to 1959, superstar rodeo cowboy Casey won nine world championships in the Rodeo Cowboys Association (now the Professional Rodeo Cowboys Association, or PRCA), including six Saddle Bronc victories, one Bareback Bronc championship, and two all-around titles. His record remains unbroken.

tick
1 A parasitic, blood-sucking insect that can transmit diseases such as Lyme disease and erlichia.
 2 *See* rub.

tie-back surgery
A surgical procedure to treat roaring; laryngoplasty.

tied at the knee
A conformation defect marked by visibly constricted tissue behind and below the knee. The condition restricts a horse's action.

tie-down
The Western term for a standing martingale.

tie-down roping
In rodeo, an event in which the cowboy who ropes, dismounts, and ties three of the calf's legs in the fastest time is the winner. Formerly known as calf roping.

tie stall
A largely obsolete type of horse stall in which the horse stands tied to its manger. The rectangular stall is not wide enough to allow the horse to lie down or turn around. Also called a straight stall.

tie up
To suffer severe muscle cramps, usually after unaccustomed exercise.
 See azoturia.

tight
In jumping, a takeoff distance that is uncomfortably close to the fence; also known as *deep*.
 Compare to long.

timed event
Any competition, such as barrel racing, calf roping, or pole bending, in which the time to complete the course or otherwise finish the exercise will determine the order of finish.

time fault
In a timed event, especially show

Tie-down roping.
© LESLI KRAUSE GROVES

Timothy.
CREDIT: PHOTOS.COM

Tobiano.
© CHERRY HILL

Totalizator board.
CREDIT: PHOTOS.COM

jumping or cross-country, a penalty assessed for exceeding the time limit. In the case of cross-country, there is also a minimum time, and time penalties may be assessed for completing the horse too quickly.

timothy
A type of grass used as hay.

titer
A measure of the level of specific antibodies in a blood sample. An elevated titer is indicative of illness or infection.

tobiano (tow-be-AN-o)
A Paint or pinto coat of primarily white with overlaid patches of color.
 See also overo.

Todd, Mark
This outstanding New Zealand three-day eventer won Olympic Individual gold medals in 1984 and 1988 on his horse Charisma (he also competed in show jumping in the 1988 and 1992 Games). He won Team gold medals in the 1990 and 1998 World Championships. The FEI named Todd Horseman of the Century.

toe
The front portion of the foot.

toed-in
 See pigeon-toed.

toed-out
 See splay-footed.

tolt
The comfortable running walk of the Icelandic Horse.

Tom Thumb
1 A Weymouth bit with a low port, straight mouthpiece, and short cheekpieces. Only slightly more severe than a snaffle, the Tom Thumb, like other Weymouths and pelhams, is often used by people who think the look sets off a horse's head in an attractive way. **2** A spur having a short neck.

tongue tie
In racing, a strap or tape bandage with which the horse's tongue is tied down, to prevent the animal from swallowing the tongue and choking.

topline
1 The contour of a horse's back from withers to tail. **2** The upper portion of a family tree that indicates the horse's paternal breeding.
 Compare to bottom line.

Topsail Whiz
The only stallion to produce a champion in every division of the National Reining Horse Futurity, Topsail Whiz became in 2006 only the second NRHA $4,000,000 sire (Hollywood Dun It was the first). His son The Great Whiz presently holds the record as the highest money-earning three-year-old in NRHA history.

totalizator board (tote board)
In racing, the electronic display

that gives up-to-the-minute odds and the amounts of money bet on the various wagering pools.

touch

🐎 *See* rub.

tout (rhymes with "shout")
A racetrack figure who claims to have advance information on a race and is eager to share it—for a price. (From a Middle English word meaning "peek," as if spying to learn inside information about a horse's condition, training, etc.)

toxin
A poison produced by a living thing, such as a plant, bacteria, insect, or snake.

trace
In driving, one of the straps by which a horse is harnessed to a vehicle.

trace clip
A clipping pattern in which tracks along the belly, girth, and chest are trimmed. The horse is clipped where harness traces would come into contact with the animal, hence the name.

trace minerals
Minerals that are needed by the body in very small amounts.

trachea
The canal that allows passage of air from the nostrils to the lungs and vice versa.

🐎 *Compare to* esophagus.

track
1 *n.* The path taken by the horse's feet, either individually or in pairs of the left or the right feet. **2** The path around a riding arena. **3** Describes a race course. **4** *v.* To move around a ring or arena. The phrase "track to the left" indicates moving in a counterclockwise direction.

🐎 *See also* two-track.

track up
At the walk or trot, to reach so far forward with the hind legs that the hind hoofprint lands inside the front hoofprint. Desirable in a dressage horse.

trailers
Extensions on the back of a horseshoe used to change the breakover point.

trail horse
1 A Western horse show class in which horses are judged on their ability to deal with the varieties of obstacles found on an actual trail ride. Obstacles along the course might include a bridge to be crossed, rails laid out to form a T or L through which the horse will move at the walk or rein-back, and a mailbox that the rider will open while the horse stands quietly. **2** A horse that is trained and used for riding on trails, rather than in an arena.

trainer
The person who conditions and prepares horses for racing or showing or who educates a horse.

A shoe with trailers.
CREDIT: PHOTOS.COM

A trail horse class.
© WYATT MCSPADDEN/AMERICAN
QUARTER HORSE ASSOCIATION

T

training

The eventing level between novice and preliminary. The dressage test may include lengthening at the trot and canter, 10-meter trot circles, and 15-meter canter circles. The cross-country phase includes obstacles formed of two or three elements involving banks, drops, and ditches, as well as jumps into and out of water and narrow fences. The cross-country course incorporates 20 to 24 obstacles over a distance of 2,000 to 2,400 meters, to be ridden at 420 to 470 meters per minute. Fences may be up to 3 feet 3 inches in height, with spreads of up to 3 feet 11 inches and drops of up to 4 feet 7 inches. The show-jumping course includes 11 to 13 obstacles with heights up to 3 feet 3 inches and spreads of up to 3 feet 9 inches.

🦢 *See also* beginner novice; novice; preliminary; intermediate; advanced.

training scale

The classical dressage concept in which each of six levels of training is based upon earlier building blocks. The steps of the training scale (with their original German equivalents) are: 1. relaxation (*Losgelassenheit*); 2. rhythm (*Takt*); 3. contact (*Anlehnung*); 4. impulsion (*Schwung*); 5. straightness (*Geraderichtung*); 6. collection (*Versammlung*).

Trakehner (tra-KAIN-er)

1 A warmblood breed that originated during the early 18th century in an area that has been (according to the prevailing geographical boundary) eastern Germany or western Poland. Infusions of Arabian and Thoroughbred blood contributed to the Trakehner's deep chest and strong back and legs. They are used primarily for show jumping and dressage. **2** A cross-country obstacle used in eventing, composed of a post-and-rail fence set in a dry ditch.

transition

A change between two gaits, such as from trot to walk, or within a gait, such as from working trot to extended trot.

trap

In driving, a light two-wheeled carriage.

Traveller

General Robert E. Lee's mount for much of the Civil War. A gray, Traveller was described by Lee as having "fine proportions, muscular figure, deep chest, short back, strong haunches, flat legs, small head, broad forehead, delicate ears, quick eye, small feet, and black mane and tail."

travers (tra-VAIR)

In dressage, a two-track oblique movement in which the horse's forelegs follow a single outer track and his hind legs a single inner track.

🦢 *See also* renvers.

tree

The frame of a saddle. A spring tree,

Trakehner.
© PAT GOODMAN/AMERICAN TRAKEHNER ASSOCIATION

A Western saddle tree.
© CHERRY HILL

usually found on jumping saddles, has metal strips that allow some flexibility, while rigid trees, such as those on dressage and Western saddles, are relatively inflexible.

trial

1 In racing, an event in which eligible horses compete to determine the finalists in a nomination race. **2** A combined training competition that takes place over one or two days; also called a horse trial. **3** A dressage competition.

tricolor

1 The familiar name for the three-colored prize ribbons awarded to a horse show division champion (blue, red, and yellow) or reserve champion (red, yellow, and white). **2** A pinto horse that is bay with white spots and black points.

trifecta

In racing, a type of wager in which the bettor must select the first three finishers in exact order; also known as a "triple."

Trigger

The palomino ridden by the cowboy movie and television star Roy Rogers.

trim

To shorten, balance, and shape the hooves with nippers and a rasp. Horses need to have their hooves trimmed by a farrier every four to eight weeks, even if they are barefoot.

trip

Familiarly, a round in an over-fences horse show class.

triple

A series of three show-jumping obstacles in a line with related distances, usually between one and three strides apart.

Triple Crown

Collectively, the Kentucky Derby, Preakness Stakes, and Belmont Stakes races. Since the "youngest" of the races, the Kentucky Derby, was inaugurated in 1875, eleven Triple Crown winners have swept all three: Sir Barton (1919), Gallant Fox (1930), Omaha (1935), War Admiral (1937), Whirlaway (1941), Count Fleet (1943), Assault (1946), Citation (1948), Secretariat (1973), Seattle Slew (1977), and Affirmed (1978).

troika

In driving, the traditional Russian carriage or sled pulled by three horses harnessed three abreast and controlled by four separate reins in the driver's hands, two for the center horse and one for each of the outside horses. The center horse trots, while the outer horses gallop; from the Russian word for "three."

Trojan horse

In Greek legend, the huge wooden horse built by the Greeks and left outside the walls of Troy during the Trojan War. When the curious

A replica of the Trojan horse.
CREDIT: PHOTOS.COM

T

The trot.
© CHERRY HILL

Greeks hauled the horse inside the city, Greek soldiers who had been hiding inside the horse came out and opened the city's gates to allow other soldiers to enter. In the battle that followed, Troy lost the war.

trot
The two-beat gait in which the horse's feet move in diagonal pairs. The sequence of footfalls is left hind and right fore, then right hind and left fore.

See also jig; jog; long trot; post.

trotter
A horse that trots. Specifically, a Standardbred that races at the trot rather than the pace.

trotty
In gaited horses, tending to trot rather than gait correctly.

tryptophan
A naturally occurring enzyme believed to have a calming effect, available as a feed supplement for excitable horses.

TTouch
See Tellington-Jones, Linda.

tube
To insert a tube through a horse's nostril into its stomach to deliver medication; or, to hydrate the horse, water.

tucked up
Standing with the abdomen tight-ened, loin rounded, and hind legs slightly under the body, with an overall tense appearance; indicative of colic or other painful condition.

turf horse
A Thoroughbred racehorse that races well on a grass (turf) track as opposed to a dirt track.

turnback
In cutting competitions, one of the riders who keep the herd together so that those cattle do not interfere with one being worked.

turn on the forehand
A change of direction in which the horse halts, then circles his hindquarters around his forelegs.

turn on the haunches
A change of direction in which the horse circles his forequarters around his pivoting hind legs.

turn out
v. To put a horse outside into its pasture or paddock.

turnout
1 *n.* A pen or pasture that a horse is put into for free exercise or grazing. **2** *n.* A horse's physical appearance at a show, including body condition, grooming, braiding, and condition and appropriate-ness of tack. **3** *adj.* Describes a blanket or sheet that is durable and waterproof enough to be used on a horse that is turned out.

T

tush
The canine tooth of the horse. In mares this tooth is very small and usually does not break through the gums, but in males it is large and somewhat pointed.

twist
The portion of the saddle between the rider's thighs.

twisted intestine
🔹 *See* gastric torsion.

twisted-wire snaffle
A snaffle bit with a corkscrew-shaped mouthpiece. The wider the corkscrew's spiral, the milder the bit's effect.

twitch
A device that puts pressure on the horse's lip, used during a medical examination or treatment to distract the animal's attention from another part of its body.

two-phase
An eventing competition that combines any two of the three phases of an event, usually dressage and show jumping. Unrecognized and for schooling purposes.

two-point
🔹 *See* half seat.

two-track
Any of the lateral movements in which the horse moves forward and sideways simultaneously, the animal's feet moving in separate but parallel paths.
🔹 *See also* half pass; renvers; travers.

tying up
🔹 *See* azoturia.

typey
A slang term for a horse that conforms to the conformation standards of its breed and thus is the correct "type."

Using a twitch.

ulcer

An irritated sore in the stomach or intestines caused by stress or a diet with too much concentrate and not enough roughage. Can be diagnosed via endoscope and treated by adjusting the horse's routine and diet or adding a magnesium supplement.

ultrasound

A veterinary procedure in which pulses of high-frequency sound waves are directed into the body. Ultrasound can be either diagnostic or therapeutic. Diagnostic ultrasound produces an image on a screen, which the veterinarian can examine for evidence of soft tissue injury or, in the case of a reproductive exam, pregnancy. Therapeutic ultrasound is used to stimulate blood flow, promote healing of tendons and ligaments, and break up abnormal soft tissue, such as adhesions or scarring.

umpire

In polo, the mounted official who throws in the ball and calls fouls. Outdoor polo uses two umpires, one on each side of the field; arena polo uses only one.

undefended penalty shot

In polo, a penalty shot that the opposing team may not try to block, thus giving player taking the shot a clear chance at the goal. *Compare to* defended penalty shot.

underrun heels

Abnormal hoof shape in which the heels are low and are at a lower angle than the front of the hoof. Can be caused by poor conformation or poor trimming and shoeing.

undershot

A conformation defect in which the lower jaw extends beyond the upper jaw; also known as monkey-mouthed.

ungulate

A mammal that has hooves.

unhandled

A horse that has not had any training at all, including halter training. Such a horse may be fearful or distrustful of humans.

unicorn

In driving, a three-horse hitch

U

with one leader and two wheelers.

United States Equestrian Federation (USEF)
The national federation and regulatory body of horse sports in the United States, headquartered in Lexington, Kentucky.

United States Equestrian Team (USET)
The USET Foundation's role is to help provide funding for the High Performance competition, training, coaching, travel, and educational needs of America's elite and developing athletes in partnership with the U.S. Equestrian Federation.

The phrase "High Performance" refers to upper-level international competition.

United States Polo Association (USPA)
Polo's governing body in this country.

United States Trotting Association (USTA)
The governing body of Standardbred racing, located in Columbus, Ohio.

unrecognized show
A horse show that is not sanctioned by a national horse show organization, and therefore does not count toward year-end awards. Such a show is often less expensive and less formal than a recognized show.
⬤ *See also* schooling show.

unseat
To jostle a rider out of balance.

unsoundness
An imperfection or physical condition, such as lameness, that restricts a horse's usefulness.

up
1 The direction away from the gate of a ring or arena. To jump up a particular line of fences is to start by jumping the fence closest to the gate and then head away from the gate.
⬤ *Compare to* down.
2 Spirited and energetic.
3 Carrying the head, neck, and forehand in an elevated frame.

up-down lesson
A lesson for beginning riders, so called because of the "up-down, up-down" instructions given for the basics of posting to the trot.

uphill
1 A conformational type that makes it easier for a horse to shift its weight to its hindquarters while being ridden. A high-set neck, withers higher than the croup, and elbow level with or higher than the stifle are some characteristics of a horse that has an uphill build. **2** A way of going in which the horse's forehand is lightened and its hindquarters are lowered, allowing more powerful impulsion and freer use of the forehand.

upward fixation of the patella
(UFP)

A condition in which the stifle joint becomes "locked" or fixed in the extended position, either for an instant or for a longer period of time. Under saddle, it may feel as if the horse's hind leg is buckling as the stifle locks briefly and then releases; it has been described as feeling as if the horse is "stepping in a hole." UFP can result from either poor conformation (an excessively straight stifle), weakness in the stifle, stall confinement, or a combination of factors. Treatment includes strengthening the stifle by using hill work, transitions, and ground poles; estrogen therapy; internal blistering of the stifle; or in extreme cases, surgical severing or perforation of the patellar ligament.

urticaria

An allergic skin condition triggered by histamine.

 See also hives.

use

In showing, to place a competitor. A judge is said to "use" the competitors who place in the ribbons.

using horse

In Western parlance, a horse that is used on a working ranch, as opposed to a show or pleasure horse.

uveitis

 See moon blindness.

vaccination

The injection of a dead or weakened form of a virus or bacteria to encourage the body's production of antibodies, thereby rendering the body immune to that particular disease; immunization. Horses must be vaccinated against specific ailments once or twice a year. Veterinarians should be consulted to determine the appropriate vaccines based on geographic region and the horse's level of exposure to other horses.

valet

In racing, the attendant who takes care of a jockey's equipment.

vaquero (va-CARE-oh)

The Spanish word for cowboy.
⬤ *See also* buckaroo.

vault

To mount a moving horse by leaping onto its back from the ground.

vaulting

A sport in which participants leap on and off a moving bareback horse and perform gymnastic maneuvers while standing, kneeling, or lying on the horse's back.

vehicle

The umbrella term for a wagon, cart, or coach pulled by one or more driving horses.

Venezuelan Equine Encephalomyelitis (VEE)

A highly contagious viral disease affecting the central nervous system. Occurring in warm climates but only very rarely in the United States, its symptoms include fever, loose bowels, and severe disorientation. It is invariably fatal.

ventral

A directional indicator that refers to the lower, or belly, side.
⬤ *Compare to* dorsal.

vertebra

One of the bones of the spine.

vertical

Any type of jump composed of a single element of width.
⬤ *Compare to* oxer.

Vertical fence.

vet check
1 Any of the mandatory physical examinations during a distance ride or a combined training event. Medical professionals assess the horse's condition with regard to its ability to continue in the competition.
◓ *See also* CPR.
2 Prepurchase exam.

veterinarian
A licensed doctor who treats animals.

Vetrap
A type of elastic bandage used for medical treatment and to wrap legs for support.

vice
Any of several specific bad habits of the horse, including cribbing, wind-sucking, weaving, wood-chewing, stall kicking, stall-walking, and pacing. Stable vices are usually caused by boredom, confinement, isolation, or lack of sufficient forage.

view
In foxhunting, to spot a fox emerging from a covert.

view halloo!
In foxhunting, the attention-getting shout uttered by the first person to view the fox.

Visalia (vis-SAIL-ya)
A Western bell-shaped stirrup favored by calf ropers for its ease in dismounting.

vixen
In foxhunting, a female fox.

voice
One of the rider's aids used to urge or soothe the horse. A cluck of the tongue or a kissing sound (jockeys call it "smooching") is the traditional signal to ask a horse to move forward or to encourage a moving horse to move faster. "Whoa" is the vocal signal to halt.

volte
In dressage, a circle measuring six meters in diameter.

voluntary withdrawal
The decision by a rider not to continue in a competition. The reason may be an injury or a substandard performance.
◓ *Compare to* elimination.

V

W

wagonette

In driving, a four-wheeled vehicle with one seat facing forward and, behind it, two benchlike seats set lengthwise and facing each other.

walk

The slowest of the natural gaits. It is a four-beat gait, with the following sequence of footfalls: 1. left hind foot, 2. left fore 3. right hind, and 4. right fore.

walk on!

A direction to a horse to begin to walk. Of British origin, it is routinely used in driving and less often in other English disciplines.

walkover

In racing, a race in which only one horse takes part. The horse must complete the course, sometimes done at a walk, in order to be entitled to the purse.

walk-trot class

A horse show class in which competitors are required only to walk and trot, not to canter or lope.

walk-trot horse

A three-gaited American Saddlebred (as distinguished from the five-gaited variety).

wall

1 The hard supportive structure of the hoof. 2 In show jumping, an obstacle that is visually solid. The wall may be made of wood and painted to look like bricks or stones.

walleye

A blueish eye surrounded by white. Although widely considered to be unattractive, it is not considered a conformation defect.

war bridle

A halter with a rope, chain, or cord that passes through the horse's mouth over the upper gums. Pressure on the lead rope causes the gum line to tighten, causing severe pain. A war bridle is used to force a horse to stand still, generally for veterinary care. Variations are known as a gum line or lip chain.

'Ware! (short for "beware")

In foxhunting, a warning of some sort of danger. For example,

W

"'Ware hole!" alerts riders to a hole in the ground.

warmblood
A type of sport horse that originated in Europe through the selective breeding of Thoroughbreds or Arabians (the so-called hot breeds) and draft horses (the cold bloods). The result produced such breeds as the Selle Français, Trakehener, Oldenburg, Hanoverian, and Swedish and Dutch Warmbloods. Originally bred as cavalry horses, warmbloods are now prized for dressage and show jumping.

warm-up
1 In racing, a pre-race slow gallop or canter to the starting gate. **2** Any exercise intended to loosen up a horse for any further physical activity. **3** A relatively easy class entered at a horse show for the purpose of letting the horse see the arena and the jumps before a more important class.

washy
In racing, broken out in a nervous sweat in the paddock or on the way to the starting gate.

Waterford bit
A snaffle bit with many small links in the mouthpiece. The flexibility of the bit discourages horses from leaning or pulling on the reins.

water jump
In eventing, a cross-country jump in which the horse must jump down into a pool of water. In show jumping, a jump in which the horse must jump over a pool of water without touching it.

wave mouth
A tooth abnormality in which the shape of the teeth along the jaw forms a wave pattern. Can be corrected by floating the teeth.

way of going
Another term for action.

wean
v. to separate a foal from its mother, thus breaking their dependence on each other. Foals are typically weaned between four and six months of age.
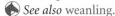 *See also* weanling.

weanling
A foal that is no longer dependent on its mother's milk for nourishment. Once the weanling reaches 12 months, it is called a yearling.

weaving
A stable vice in which the horse rocks or swings its head from side to side, often the result of boredom or isolation.

web
The width of one branch of a horseshoe.

web reins
Reins made of heavy cotton or nylon cloth.

wedge pad
1 A plastic or rubber pad inserted

Water jump.
CREDIT: S. PRICE

between the hoof and the shoe that is thicker in the rear than in the front, thus raising the heels slightly. Also called a degree pad. **2** A special saddle pad that is thicker in the cantle area than in the pommel area. Used to adjust an ill-fitting saddle.

A Western riding class.
© WYATT MCSPADDEN/AMERICAN QUARTER HORSE ASSOCIATION

weedy
A thin body with little flesh, as if as thin as a weed.

weigh-in
In racing, the post-race procedure where the clerk of scales makes certain that each jockey carried the correct assigned weight.

weigh-out
In racing, the pre-race procedure where the clerk of scales makes certain that each jockey will carry the correct assigned weight.

weight-for-age
In racing, a fixed scale of weights to be carried by horses according to age, sex, distance of race, and season of year.

weight pad
In racing, the pad worn under the saddle that holds, if necessary, lead bars that make up the difference between the jockey's actual weight and the weight the horse has been assigned to carry.

Welch, Buster
Five-time National Cutting Horse Association futurity champion and four-time open world champion, Welch as been elected to the NCHA Hall of Fame, NCHA Riders Hall of Fame, American Quarter Horse Association Hall of Fame, and the Texas Cowboy Hall of Fame.

Wellington boots
Knee-high rubber work boots, traditionally in an olive green color; sometimes called Wellies.

well let-down
Having short hind cannon bones, considered an indication of strong hindquarters.

well-mounted
Riding a horse that is suitable for the rider's size and purposes.

well sprung
A rib cage that is large and rounded, implying plenty of room for a large heart and lungs. Sometimes used as a euphemism for "fat."

Welsh
A native British pony now prevalent in the United States. The Welsh is sturdy under saddle or in harness and a talented children's show hunter pony. Welsh ponies are divided into four sections according to size and type: section A, formerly known as the Welsh mountain pony, under 12 hands; section B, the Welsh pony of riding type, a fine-boned pony up to 13.2 hands in Great Britain or up to 14.2 hands in the United States; section C, the Welsh pony of cob type, a heavier pony up

to 13.2 hands; and section D, the Welsh cob, a heavier pony of 13.2 hands and up, traditionally used for driving.

Western Horsemanship
A horse show class in which the rider's stock-seat form and control are judged. Riders first individually ride a prescribed pattern that may include straight lines, curves, and circles, then work as a group at the walk, jog, and lope.

Western Pleasure
A horse show class in which the horse's performance as an enjoyable mount is judged. Riders must hold the reins in one hand (and not switch hands during the class), nor can they touch their horses or tack with the free hand.

Western Riding
A horse show class in which the horse is judged on the quality of gaits and especially on prompt and accurate lead changes. Riders perform one of two preselected patterns that involve riding over or around a log and pylons.

West Nile virus
A viral disease first recorded in the Western Hemisphere in 1999, West Nile virus is now found throughout the continental United States. It is carried by birds and transmitted to humans and horses by mosquito bites. Symptoms in horses may include loss of appetite, depression, fever, weakness or paralysis of the hind limbs, impaired vision, and ataxia. It is frequently fatal and may cause long-term neurological damage in surviving horses. A vaccine is available, but there is no cure once a horse has contracted the virus.

Westphalian
Some authorities consider the Westphalian warmblood as a strain of Hanoverian horses that were bred in the German state of Westphalia. However, others consider Westphalians to be a distinct breed. In any event, the horses are used in dressage and show jumping.

Weymouth
The curb bit of an English double bridle.

wheat
A cereal of which the stalks are used as straw.

wheat bran
The ground husks of the wheat plant, traditionally used to make bran mash for horses. Bran is high in phosphorus, so it can upset the calcium-phosphorus ratio if not balanced with another feed.

wheel
In racing, a bet in which one horse is combined in an exacta or trifecta with all other horses in the race, with that horse bet to win. That horse's winning means an assured payoff on the exacta or trifecta bet. A part wheel involves one horse with selected other

Wheat.
CREDIT: PHOTOS.COM

horses; a back wheel involves choosing the horse that will finish second with multiple combinations with all the other horses bet to win.

wheeler(s)
In driving, the horse(s) hitched next to the vehicle.
 See also leader(s).

whinny
One of the vocalizations of the horse, similar to a neigh but generally softer.

whip
1 A thin stick carried by the rider or driver and used to urge or correct a horse. **2** The driver of a vehicle, so called for the whip he or she carries. **3** In foxhunting, a colloquial term for whipper-in.

whipper-in
In foxhunting, a hunt staff member who keeps the hounds together as a pack; also known as whip.

white
1 The color of an albino horse, having pink skin; all other "white" horses, no matter how colorless their coats appear to be, are properly described as gray and have dark skin. **2** The color of the prize ribbon awarded for fourth place.

white line
The junction of the sole and the wall of the hoof. Horses that have foundered have a widened white line.

Windrows.
CREDIT: PHOTOS.COM

whoa
The traditional vocal request to ask a horse to halt. Pronounced "hoe" or "woe."

whorl
A distinctive swirl of hair in a horse's coat. Most horses have one or more whorls on their foreheads; some horses have whorls in other locations, such as on the neck or flank.

Wiescamp, Hank
This noted livestock auctioneer founded a line of Old Fred–bred Quarter Horses that became known simply as "Wiescamp Horses." He began an Appaloosa breeding program in the late 1950s with Peavy Bimbo, a notable sire of broodmares who, when bred to Wiescamp's Appaloosa sire, Red Plaudit, produced outstanding performers, including Hall of Fame inductee Prince Plaudit.

wild
Not domesticated.

Wilkinson, Dale
Wilkinson is the only person to have won both National Reining Horse Association and National Cutting Horse Association Futurity championships. The American Quarter Horse Association designated Wilkinson as Horseman of the Century.

Williams, Jimmy
Using imaginative and innovative training techniques, the California-

based Williams became a leader in developing riding styles during the middle part of the 20th century. Best known as a trainer of show-jumping riders, Williams also appeared in numerous films as a stuntman.

Wimpy

As the 1941 Fort Worth Exposition and Fat Stock Show grand champion stallion, Wimpy was the first horse to be registered in the new American Quarter Horse Association stud book. He sired 170 registered foals, one AQHA champion, and innumerable halter and performance winners.

wind puffs

Swellings on the side of the tendon just above the fetlock. Caused by excessive stress on the joint, confinement after exercise, or faulty shoeing, wind puffs are treated by applications of ice, supportive bandages, and rest. Also known as wind galls.

windrows

Cut hay that has been raked into long mounds to dry before being baled.

wind-sucking

1 The stable vice of sucking air into the lungs while biting onto a solid object such as a window ledge or feed bin. Often caused by boredom, this bad habit can be discouraged by a cribbing strap that is buckled snugly around the horse's neck and restricts the amount of air the horse can take in.

 See also cribbing.

2 Of a female racehorse, drawing air into the vulva, which can result in vaginal infection. Corrected or prevented with a Caslick's operation.

winging in

An undesirable movement, caused by poor conformation, in which the horse's legs swing inward and interfere with each other; also known as pigeon-toed toeing in.

winging out

 See paddling.

wings

Gatelike barriers on the sides of a jump that discourage horses from running out at the obstacle. Most commonly seen in steeplechase and hurdle races.

wink

In a mare, to repeatedly open and close the vulva, indicating receptivity to breeding.

winner's circle

In racing, the enclosure where winning horses are brought and where trophy ceremonies are held.

wither relief pad

A saddle pad with a cutout in the withers area to alleviate pressure from the saddle.

withers

The highest part of the back, where it meets the base of the neck. A horse's height is measured from the withers to the ground.

 See also hand.

Withers.

W

with the motion

🐎 *See* motion.

wobbler syndrome

The common name for cervical vertebral malformation, wobbler syndrome is a neurologic condition caused by a developmental malformation of the vertebrae in the neck that impinges on the spinal cord, producing muscle weakness and impaired coordination. It usually appears in fast-growing or large male horses before the age of four and, in some cases, may be treated surgically.

wolf tooth

A premolar that is unnecessary for chewing and likely to interfere with the bit; the tooth is therefore routinely extracted before the horse begins its training.

Working hunter class.
© WYATT MCSPADDEN/AQHA

wood-chewing

A stable vice in which the horse bites, chews, and sometimes ingests wood, such as stall walls or fences. Caused by boredom, confinement, or insufficient long-stem forage in the diet.

working

In dressage, the basic gaits, in which strides are not as big as in the medium or extended gaits.

Working Cow Horse

A Western horse show class composed of two phases. In the first, the "dry work," the horse and rider execute a reining pattern. The horse then works a cow by first holding it at the end of the arena, then drives the cow along the arena fence in both directions and finally moves the cow into the middle of the arena and turns it in both directions.

Working Hunter

A horse show class or division in which the horse's jumping style over fences is judged. The term *working*, in the sense of performing, distinguishes these horses from conformation hunters. "Working" is also the division that follows Second-Year Green. Fences range in height from 3 feet 6 inches to 4 feet.

World Cup

Dressage and show-jumping competitions under the aegis of the FEI and held at important horse shows throughout the fall and winter months. Competitions are divided into 14 leagues worldwide. Ribbon winners in each event receive points toward qualifying for the World Cup finals held each spring.

World Equestrian Games
(WEG)

Quadrennial international competitions held by the FEI in dressage, combined driving, endurance, show jumping, reining, three-day eventing, vaulting, and, beginning in 2010, para-equestrian dressage. As with the World Cup, locations of these events vary.

wormer

Oral medication that rids the

W

horse of internal parasites. The medication can be administered in the form of paste or liquid. The word is used interchangeably with dewormer.

wrangler

The Western term for a ranch hand whose chores range from schooling horses to escorting dude ranch guests.

wrap

A general term for a lower-leg bandage worn for support and/or protection.

Wright, Gordon

An influential hunter/jumper trainer and commentator of pre–World War II America, Wright virtually invented and then popularized the clinic form of instruction. His revision of the U.S. Cavalry School Manual is largely responsible for the spread of hunter-seat horsemanship. In addition, Wright coached a generation of riders that included George Morris and William Steinkraus.

wrong lead

The incorrect lead at the canter, such as the left lead when circling clockwise. When done intentionally as a suppling and balancing exercise, it is called the countercanter.

wry neck

A fetus or newborn foal whose head and neck are bent backwards.

W

Xenophon (430 BC–355 BC)
Greek author of the first ex-
tant treatises on horsemanship.
His *On Horsemanship* and *On
Cavalry* suggested that trainers
accomplish their goals through
an understanding of the horse's
mentality instead of using brute
force.

X-ray
A veterinary diagnostic prodecure
in which X-ray radiation is sent
through the body and projected
onto a radiographic plate. X-rays
reveal bones, and so are used to
detect fractures, arthritis, and
other bone injuries or disease.

xx
In the pedigree of a warmblood or
other crossbred horse, "xx" next to
a horse's name indicates that the
horse is a purebred Thoroughbred.
🌀 *See also* ox.

X

Yabusame (ya-boo-SAH-me)
Classical Japanese horsemanship
that includes shooting a bow and
arrow at the gallop.

yahoo
Derogatory term for a person
who rides or handles horses in a
reckless or thoughtless manner.

yearling
A horse between the ages of 12 and
24 months.

yellow
The color of the prize ribbon for
third place.

yielding
In racing, a turf surface having
deep footing but without the presence of moisture.
   ● *See also* soft.

yoiks! (pronounced "hoi"
and shouted in a high-pitched
voice)
In foxhunting, a cry of encouragement by the huntsman to the
hounds. The word is thought to
have come via Old French from
the Latin word meaning "there!"

yoke grill
A metal grill that is inserted into
a stall door. The shape of the grill
allows the horse to put his head
out, but prevents him from reaching other horses or items hung on
the stall front.

young entry
In foxhunting, young hounds that
are not yet ready, whether by age
or training, to join the hunt's pack.
Also, hounds and young riders
hunting for the first time.

young rider
In dressage competition, a rider
who is less than 21 years old.

youth
In Western showing, a rider who
is less than 18 years old.

Yoke grill.
CREDIT: CAROLINE DOWD

Y

zebra

The striped wild equine native to Africa. Some, but not many, zebras have been domesticated to the point of accepting a rider. There are several species of zebra, including Grevy's zebra *(Equus grevyi)*, mountain zebra *(Equus zebra)*, and plains zebra *(Equus quagga)*.

zebra dun

A dun with black stripes on its forearms.

zigzag

In dressage, a movement ridden at the trot or canter, consisting of a series of half passes across the arena, alternating from left to right. In canter, the horse must perform a flying change when changing direction.

zony

A hybrid between a zebra and a pony.

zoonose

An infectious disease that is transmittable from animals to humans, such as West Nile virus, which can be transmitted from birds to humans by way of mosquitoes.

zorse

A hybrid between a zebra and a horse.

Grevy's zebra.
CREDIT: PHOTOS.COM

Z

Akhal-Teke Association of North America
295 Anderson School Lane
Staunton, VA 24401
TEL (540) 886-1870
FAX (540) 885-1451
www.akhaltekes.org

American Quarter Horse Association
P.O. Box 200
Amarillo, TX 79168-0001
TEL (806) 376-4811
FAX (806) 349-6401
www.aqha.com

American Saddlebred Horse Association
4083 Iron Works Parkway
Lexington, KY 40511-8434
TEL (859) 259-2742
FAX (859) 259-1628
www.saddlebred.com

International Andalusian and Lusitano Horse Association
101 Carnoustie North, Box 200
Birmingham, AL 35242
TEL (205) 995-8900
FAX (205) 995-8966
www.ialha.org

Appaloosa Horse Club, Inc.
P.O. Box 8403
2720 West Pullman Road
Moscow, ID 83843-0903
TEL (208) 882-5578
FAX (208) 882-8150
www.appaloosa.com

International Colored Appaloosa Association, Inc.
P.O. Box 99
Shipshewana, IN 46565
TEL (574) 825-3331
FAX (574) 825-3331
www.icaainc.com

Arabian Horse Association
10805 East Bethany Drive
Aurora, CO 80014-2605
TEL (303) 696-4500
FAX (303) 696-4599
www.arabianhorses.org

Cleveland Bay Horse Society of North America
P.O. Box 483
Goshen, NH 03752
TEL (860) 774-5433
www.clevelandbay.org

Clydesdale Breeders of the U.S.A.
17346 Kelley Road
Pecatonica, IL 61063
TEL (815) 247-8780
FAX (815) 247-8337
www.clydesusa.com

American Connemara Pony Society
P.O. Box 100
Middlebrook, VA 24459
www.acps.org

American Cream Draft Horse Association
193 Crossover Road
Bennington, VT 05201
TEL (802) 447-7612
FAX (802) 447-0711
www.acdha.org

**American Dartmoor
Pony Association**
203 Kendall Oaks Drive
Boerne, TX 78006
TEL (830) 249-8103
FAX (830) 249-7322
E-MAIL ADPAsec@aol.com

**Dartmoor Pony Society
of America**
145 Upper Ridgeview Road
Columbus, NC 28722
TEL (704) 894-5672

**Dutch Warmblood
Studbook In North America,
KWPN/NA**
P.O. Box 0
Sutherlin, OR 97479
TEL (541) 459-3232
FAX (541) 459-2967
www.nawpn.org

**Norwegian Fjord
Horse Registry**
1203 Appian Drive
Webster, NY 14580-9129
TEL (585) 872-4114
FAX (585) 787-0497
www.nfhr.com

**Friesian Horse Association
of North America**
4037 Iron Works Parkway,
   Suite160
Lexington, KY 40511-8483
TEL (859) 455-7430
FAX (859) 455-7457
www.fhana.com

**Galiceno Horse Breeders
Association**
Box 219
Godley, TX 76044-0219
TEL (817) 389-3547

**American Hackney Horse
Society**
4059 Iron Works Parkway, A-3
Lexington, KY 40511-8462
TEL (859) 255-8694
FAX (859) 255-0177
www.hackneysociety.com

American Haflinger Registry
1686 East Waterloo Road
Akron, OH 44306-4103
TEL (330) 784-0000
FAX (330) 784-9843
www.haflingerhorse.com

**American Hanoverian
Society, Inc.**
4067 Iron Works Parkway, Suite 1
Lexington, KY 40511-8483
TEL (859) 255-4141
FAX (859) 255-8467
www.hanoverian.org

**American Holsteiner
Horse Association**
222 East Main Street, Suite 1
Georgetown, KY 40324-1712
TEL (502) 863-4239
FAX (502) 868-0722
www.holsteiner.com

**United States Icelandic
Horse Congress**
6800 East 99th Avenue
Anchorage, AK 99507
TEL (907) 346-2223
FAX (907) 346-2223
www.icelandics.org

The Jockey Club
(Thoroughbred)
821 Corporate Drive
Lexington, KY 40503-2794
TEL (859) 224-2700
FAX (859) 224-2710
www.jockeyclub.com

**Lipizzan Association
of North America**
P.O. Box 1133
Anderson, IN 46015
FAX (765) 641-1208
www.lipizzan.org

**American Miniature Horse
Association, Inc.**
5601 South Interstate 35W
Alvarado, TX 76009
TEL (817) 783-5600
FAX (817) 783-6403
www.amha.org

**American Miniature
Horse Registry**
(*see* American Shetland
Pony Club)

**Missouri Fox Trotting Horse
Breed Association, Inc.**
P.O. Box 1027
Ava, MO 65608-1027
TEL (417) 683-2468
FAX (417) 683-6144
www.mfthba.com

**International Morab Breeders
Association and Registry**
732 S. Miller Court
Decatur, IL 62521-1618
TEL (217) 428-5245
FAX (217) 428-5245
www.morab.com

**American Morgan Horse
Association, Inc.**
122 Bostwick Road
Shelburne, VT 05482-4417
TEL (802) 985-4944
FAX (802) 985-8897
www.morganhorse.com

National Show Horse Registry
10368 Bluegrass Parkway
Louisville, KY 40299
TEL (502) 266-5100
FAX (502) 266-5806
www.nshregistry.org

Nez Perce Horse Registry
P.O. Box 365
Lapwai, ID 83540
TEL (208) 843-7392
www.nezpercehorseregistry.com

**Oldenburg Registry North
America & International
Sporthorse Registry**
517 DeKalb Avenue
Sycamore, IL 60178
TEL (815) 899-7803
FAX (815) 899-7823
www.isroldenburg.org

**American Paint Horse
Association**
P.O. Box 961023
Fort Worth, TX 76161-0023
TEL (817) 834-2742
FAX (817) 834-3152
www.apha.com

**Palomino Horse Breeders
of America**
15253 East Skelly Drive
Tulsa, OK 74116-2637
TEL (918) 438-1234
FAX (918) 438-1232
www.palominohba.com

**Paso Fino Horse
Association, Inc.**
101 North Collins Street
Plant City, FL 33566-3311
TEL (813) 719-7777
FAX (813) 719-7872
www.pfha.org

Percheron Horse Association of America

P.O. Box 141
Fredericktown, OH 43019-0141
TEL (740) 694-3602
FAX (740) 694-3604
www.percheronhorse.org

North American Peruvian Horse Association

(Peruvian Paso)
3095 Burleson Retta Road, Suite B
Burleson, TX 76028
TEL (817) 447-7574
FAX (817) 447-2450
www.napha.net

Pinto Horse Association of America

7330 NW 23rd Street
Bethany, OK 73008
TEL (405) 491-0111
FAX (405) 787-0773
www.pinto.org

Rocky Mountain Horse Association

P.O. Box 129
Mt. Olivet, KY 41064
TEL (606) 724-2354
FAX (606) 724-2153
www.rmhorse.com

American Shetland Pony Club

(*encompasses* The Classic
American Shetland Pony, The
Modern American Shetland
Pony, The American Miniature
Horse Registry, *and* The
American Show Pony Registry)
81B Queenwood Road
Morton, IL 61550
TEL (309) 263-4044
FAX (309) 263-5113
www.shetlandminiature.com

American Shire Horse Association

1211 Hill Harrell Road
Effingham, SC 29541
TEL (843) 629-0072
www.shirehorse.org

Swedish Warmblood Association of North America

P.O. Box 788
Socorro, NM 87801
TEL (505) 835-1318
FAX (505) 835-1321
www.swanaoffice.org

Tennessee Walking Horse Breeders' and Exhibitors' Association

P.O. Box 286
Lewisburg, TN 37091-0286
TEL (931) 359-1574
FAX (931) 359-2539
www.twhbea.com

American Trakehner Association, Inc.

1536 West Church Street
Newark, OH 43055
TEL (740) 344-1111
FAX (740) 344-3225
www.americantrakehner.com

American Warmblood Registry, Inc.

P.O. Box 197
Carter, MT 59420
TEL (406) 734-5499
FAX (775) 667-0516
www.americanwarmblood.com

American Warmblood Society
2 Buffalo Run Road
Center Ridge, AR 72027
TEL (501) 893-2777
FAX (501) 893-2779
www.americanwarmblood.org

**Welsh Pony and Cob Society
of America, Inc.**
720 Green Street
Stephens City, VA 22655
TEL (540) 868-PONY (7669) or
(540) 868-7669
www.welshpony.org

APPENDIX
EQUESTRIAN ORGANIZATIONS

American Association for Horsemanship Safety

4125 Fish Creek Road
Estes Park, CO 80517
TEL (866) 485-6800
FAX (512) 488-2319
www.horsemanshipsafety.com
Information on horsemanship safety and legal liability, provided by a not-for-profit corporation dedicated to education on safety and training riding instructors in safe practices.

American Driving Society

1837 Ludden Drive, Suite 120
P.O. Box 278
Cross Plains, WI 53528
TEL (608) 237-7382
FAX (608) 237-6468
www.americandrivingsociety.org
Organization promoting the sport of competitive and pleasure driving.

American Endurance Ride Conference

P.O. Box 6027
Auburn, CA 95604
TEL (530) 823-2260
TOLL-FREE (866) 271-AERC
FAX (530) 823-7805
www.aerc.org
National governing body for long-distance riding.

American Horse Protection Association

1000 29th Street, N.W.
Suite #T-100
Washington, D.C. 20007-3820
TEL (202) 965-0500
FAX (202) 965-9621
Organization concerned with the welfare of wild and domestic horses.

American Horse Publications

49 Spinnaker Circle
South Daytona, FL 32119
TEL (386) 760-7743
FAX (386) 760-7728
www.americanhorsepubs.org
A nonprofit association established to promote better understanding and communications within the equine publishing industry. Members include equine-related publications, writers, editors, students, organizations, and businesses.

American Riding Instructors Association

28801 Trenton Court
Bonita Springs, FL 34134
TEL (239) 948-3232
FAX (239) 948-5053
www.riding-instructor.com
Provides listings of instructors certified by the organization.

American Vaulting Association

8205 Santa Monica Boulevard,
#1-288
West Hollywood, CA 90046
TEL (323) 654-0800
FAX (323) 654-4306
www.americanvaulting.org
Promotes vaulting in the United States. Web site has results, rules, photos, and membership information.

Fédération Equestre Internationale (FEI)

Avenue Mon Repos 24
1005 Lausanne
Switzerland
TEL 41 21 310 47 47
FAX 41 21 310 47 60
www.horsesport.org
The international governing body of horse sports. Web site lists results and other news about international jumping, dressage, eventing, reining, driving, vaulting, and para-equestrian competition.

Intercollegiate Horse Show Association

IHSA National Secretary
2019 Stillwell Beckett Road
Hamilton, OH 45013
TEL (513) 529-2352
www.ihsa.com
The IHSA now consists of more than 300 colleges and universities across the United States. IHSA shows provide the horses on which riders compete as individuals and teams in English, Western, and dressage classes to earn points toward qualifying for regional and national finals.

International Side Saddle Organization

P.O. Box 161
Stevensville, MD 21666-0161
TEL (410) 643-1497
FAX (410) 643-1497
www.sidesaddle.com
Devoted to the promotion and preservation of sidesaddle riding.

Masters of Foxhounds Association of North America

P.O. Box 363
Millwood, VA 22646
TEL (540) 955-5680
FAX (540) 955-5682
www.mfha.com
The governing body of organized fox, coyote, and drag hunting in the United States and Canada.

National Barrel Horse Association

725 Broad Street
Augusta, GA 30901-1050
TEL (706) 722-7223
FAX (706) 828-3909
www.nbha.com
Promotes and oversees the sport of barrel racing.

National Cutting Horse Association

260 Bailey Avenue
Forth Worth, TX 76107
TEL (817) 244-6188
FAX (817) 244-2015
www.nchacutting.com
Promotes and regulates the showing of cutting horses. Sanctions most of the cutting events held in the United States and abroad.

National Intercollegiate Rodeo Association

2316 Eastgate North, Suite 160
Walla Walla, WA 99362
TEL (509) 529-4402
www.collegerodeo.com
Governing body of intercollegiate rodeoing at 100 college rodeos a year, over 3,500 student members annually, and 137 member schools and universities.

National Reining Horse Association

3000 NW 10th Street
Oklahoma City, OK 73107
TEL (405) 946-7400
FAX (405) 946-8425
www.nrha.com
The national governing body of the sport of reining.

North American Riding for the Handicapped Association

P.O. Box 33150
Denver, CO 80233
TEL (800) 369-7433
FAX (303) 252-4610
www.narha.org
Promotes and supports therapeutic riding for people with disabilities.

Professional Rodeo Cowboys Association

101 Pro Rodeo Drive
Colorado Springs, CO 80919-2301
TEL (719) 593-8840
FAX (719) 548-4876
www.prorodeo.org
Sanctions and promotes professional rodeoing. Web site lists events, tours, and standings.

United States Dressage Federation

4051 Iron Works Parkway
Lexington, KY 40511
TEL (859) 971-2277
FAX (859) 971-7722
www.usdf.org
Dedicated to the promotion of dressage. Web site includes events calendar and links.

United States Equestrian Federation

4047 Iron Works Parkway
Lexington, KY 40511
TEL (859) 258-2472
FAX (859) 231-6662
www.usef.org
The national equestrian federation of the U.S., acting as the regulatory body for the Olympic and World Championship equestrian sports, as well as many breeds and disciplines of competition. Web site lists rules of competition, competitor points and standings, and membership information.

United States Equestrian Team Foundation

1040 Pottersville Road
Gladstone, NJ 07934
TEL (908) 234-1251
FAX (908) 234-0670
www.uset.org
Selects, trains, equips, and promotes equestrians to represent the United States in the Olympics and other major international competitions.

United States Eventing Association

525 Old Waterford Road, NW
Leesburg, VA 20176
TEL (703) 779-0440
FAX (703) 779-0550
www.useventing.com
National organization of three-day eventing and combined training horse trials. Web site indicates competition schedules for events at all levels.

United States Polo Association

4037 Iron Works Parkway,
  Suite 110
Lexington, KY 40511
TEL (859) 219-1000
TOLL-FREE (800) 232-USPA
FAX (859) 219-0520
www.uspolo.org
*Promotes the sport and coordinates
and supervises national and inter-
national polo games.*

APPENDIX
HORSE-RELATED WEB SITES